THE WILLOW

Mervyn Linford was born in 1946. He left Timberlog County Secondary Modern School in Basildon at the age of fifteen and has lost count at over two hundred jobs, including: transport, construction, sales, and the army. He has always had a love of poetry and started to write seriously when he was twenty-seven years old. He has been widely published in magazines, anthologies, and newspapers and has won and been highly commended in a number of poetry competitions such as: first prize in both The John Clare Cup and The Hastings Open. His work has been broadcast on national and local radio and he has had four collections of his poetry published: 'Two Essex Poets' with the late Frederic Vanson, and 'Talking to the Bees' both by The Brentham Press of St Albans; and 'Autumn Manuscript' and 'The Beatitudes of Silence' by The Littoral Press of Southend on Sea. 'The Willow Pond' is his first prose work to be published. The sequel: 'Bullshit and Bootlace-Ties' is finished and ready for print and he has two other works waiting for publication: a lyric novel 'The Weather Man' and a novella, 'The Rise and Fall of Snowy Garden'. He now lives in Southend on Sea where apart from writing both prose and poetry he concerns himself with love, nature, and spiritual matters.

Comments on the author's work:

Two Essex Poets (with Frederic Vanson)
    Brentham Press.
'Linford is a man with a notebook out in the landscape of
Essex..... I thoroughly enjoyed all of his poems and look
forward to his next collection. Two Essex Poets is definitely a
book to treasure.'
    Angela Topping – ORE.

Talking to the Bees – Brentham press.
'I think it rather remarkable that, given the quality of the
work, you have not yet found a publisher. I should imagine
that one of the other smaller presses or indeed one of the
larger commercial houses will, in the near future, succumb to
your work. I certainly hope so.'
    Michael Schmidt – Carcanet: 1992.

Autumn Manuscript – The Littoral Press.
'Linford is a craftsman of the finest sort. He carves meaning
and metaphor, observation and emotion, into dynamic shapes
– leaving no unpolished images.'
    Hilary Mellon – SOL.

The Beatitudes of Silence – The Littoral Press.
'There are some lovely and fully achieved poems here.'
    Harry Chambers – Peterloo Poets.

THE WILLOW POND

MERVYN LINFORD

THE LITTORAL PRESS

First Published in 2004

The Littoral Press
38 Barringtons, 10 Sutton Road,
Southend on Sea, Essex. SS2. 5NA.
United Kingdom

British Library Cataloguing-in-Publication Data
A catalogue record of this book is available from
the British Library

ISBN 0-9541844-2-4

Printed by 4Edge Ltd, Hockley, Essex.

For Clare

CONTENTS

AUTHOR'S NOTE

Memory and perception are fallible. If you asked anybody mentioned in this memoir just how they remembered the time, places, people, and events recorded, it is almost certain that their interpretations would be somewhat different to mine. There are bound to be differences as well as commonalities - this is only natural. All I've tried to do is to be as honest as possible about the way I personally remembered and perceived some of the main events in my childhood. Whilst writing the book I came to realise just what a problem child I must have been, and although at the time I thought that my parents were unnecessarily strict I can now see that they were faced with a prepubescent dilemma of immense proportions, one that they could only deal with in the best way they knew how. I never went short of anything as a child and the older I get the more love and respect I feel for my long-departed mother and father. My brother is five years older than me and as a consequence of that fact we were never very close as children, but since my parents have passed away we've become closer than we've ever been, and I am proud to call this lovely man my friend.

Mervyn Linford
Southend on Sea
Essex. 2004.

Chapter 1. Loose ends - New Horizons.

It was one of those August days. One of those bygone, half-forgotten, 'there were summers in those days,' sort of days. At the back of the Rathbone Street Market, between the bombsites and the glassworks, the results of another, 'war to end all wars,' could be seen in the guise of prefabricated buildings. Those regimented lines of post-war asbestos, angled at the essence of utility. It was eggs on the pavement, frying, sort of weather. Pigeons in rickety lofts, crooned and bubbled in the heat. Chickens in the rat-infested yards, scratched at the tufted ground, hungry for the thinnest pickings. On that spit-roasted, dog dozy, fly buzzing doldrums of a day, my life was about to change forever. The powers that be, in deference to the principals of liberal minded beneficence, had offered the residents of this somewhat un-des residential quarter the option of a new start. Not just a new start, but a new start in a New Town. Like a rash of incurable philanthropy building-sites were breaking out all over the Home Counties and beyond. Basildon, as yet a figment of my 'Swallows and Amazons,' 'Wind in the Willows,' childlike imagination, was soon to become my formative landscape. But as yet it was London. A London of the trolley bus and the last trams, of horses and carts and the technological wonder of the first electric milk floats.

It was there on that hot August day early in the decade of hope and ration books that the removal van drew up outside. From that point onwards imagination and adventure were to be constantly allied. Young as I was I was fired with the pioneering spirit. For me at least the removal van could have been a part of any of the legendary wagon trains opening up the West. The porters in their aprons and cloth-caps could just as easily have been cowboys in chaps and leather waistcoats. "What d'you want shifted furst missus," they harmonized, and slowly we decamped. Sticks of furniture, moth-eaten rugs and a 14-inch state of the art, black and white Fergusson television-set joined the trickle of possessions deemed indispensable to our new lives. I was impatient for the off. Not for me the interminable goodbyes to weepy neighbours. Not the kisses and the handshakes or the promises to keep in touch. A new life beckoned. There was territory to be claimed. Land to be staked. As a special treat I was allowed to travel in the back of the van. I stood up with my arms across the tailboard and waited for my past to recede.

At six years of age you may think that the past was in rather short supply; but past there was in plenty. I was born in Hampshire, but that as well as just about everything else that had happened in my life thus far was due entirely to the war. According to family tradition I could have been born in any number of places. I was an integral part of a pregnancy at various locations throughout London. Was on the verge of birth in Folkstone and finally came up, or down, for air in Westover Road, Fleet, near Aldershot. My memories of Hampshire stretch little further than the umbilical cord itself. I remember a bridge, a river, what I've subsequently found out to be watercress and inconceivably to me a vision of goldfish. This set of somewhat disjointed psychological memorabilia have since been explained to me in terms of separate events in a logical sequence of time, but for me they're inextricably linked and form part of my unique mythic development. To put it another way, I'd like to be able to claim rustic origin - to explain my life as it now is as the inevitable consequence of my earliest experiences. Unfortunately, truth is, that apart from those few rather vague bucolic reminiscences, my real foundations are those of the city. The Thames is in my blood. Every slick polluted corpuscle slopping against the grey wharves of my brain. My mind is bricked-in and stacked-up layer upon layer into the grim smoke-confusing skies of E16. Pie and mash was my gestation and sarsaparilla the baptism.

My recollections take me by the hand and I find myself in my grandmother's house at Leicester Avenue. I was there for a street party. Festival of Britain or Empire day, I couldn't tell you. All I know is that it was a party, that I was being dressed

2

up as Little Boy Blue in reams of crepe paper, and that I didn't like it. Mind you, at least I won a prize. It could have been worse, my brother was entered as a Red Indian and it took a week to scrub him free of boot-polish. As is the case with most people of note, I had an Irish grandmother. It seems almost obligatory. There's something deeply unsettling about a purely Anglo-Saxon heritage - a truly atavistic sense of tribal guilt. Claims of Celtic ancestry abound; we seem to need them somehow. Rumour has it that Katy Kerns, nee Barnet, wasn't really Irish at all, but that her mother was. Kinsale and Cork are somewhere there in the background, with my lapsed catholicism to the fore. Whatever the reality, priests are more familiar to me than vicars and words like shenanigan come easily to the lips. In my own way I idolized that woman - that grey-haired diminutive goddess with a red-faced devilish temperament. What she lacked in physical stature she more than made up for by an abundance of spirit. Always dressed for work, her day-clothes protected by a floral pinafore with a large pouch in the front of it, she sat there in her chair by the pot-black stove for all the world like some sort of monarch of misrule; legs dangling like a naughty child. Her pinafore was better than a Jamboree-Bag. A lucky dip of the first order. "You in me pinny agin boy, what yer afta?" she'd say. Well, there were things in there to activate the sparkle in the eyes of innocence. The commonplace took on an inordinate mystery: plasters and boiled-sweets, sticky with their different reasons, pennies and bits of string, a bottle-opener for her Guiness. I especially remember the packets of Woodbines with their orange and green art-nouveau design, resonant of exotic places, like an archetypal jungle of the mind, sibilant with coiling snakes and raucous with macaws and parakeets.

My grandfather was a different proposition altogether. He lived deep in the mists of Apocrypha. Did he play for Aston Villa in the days when footballers turned up for the match in top hats and tails? Was he really once a professional boxer? I know he fought in the First World War but where he fought I couldn't tell you. I think he worked for the local council, and yet spent most of the Depression unemployed. Taciturn would be an understatement. He sat in the chair opposite my grandmother, mostly obscured by the Daily Herald. Plumes of smoke billowed out from behind the headlines and the sport's page. An occasional hand thrust out a spill into the stove, and then drew back a flickering flame into his private world of newsprint and Nutbrown. "Don't listen to im," my grandmother used to say. Which was ironic to say the least. At Christmas though there was a metamorphosis. In the topsy-turvy world of Saturnalian Cockneydom, silence was broken. He would dress up as a woman displaying all the garishness of a pantomime-dame. He would mince about the house singing and dancing as terrified children scattered in his wake. At tree-picking time he was transformed again into a somewhat taller, thinner than usual Father Christmas. I don't think that I was ever really fooled, but it didn't matter, the willing suspension of disbelief came easily in those days.

Uncles and aunts were legion. My mother had six sisters and two brothers. The house seemed always to be full. At Christmas dinner there were two sittings, one for the children and then another for the adults. Poor as they were the season of peace and goodwill was celebrated in a manner fit for royalty. They saved all year for this annual blow out and no expense was spared. The kitchen was a veritable slaughterhouse. Ovens were spitting and sizzling with their loads of turkey, goose, rabbit, pork and chicken. The pantry was hung with all kinds of cooked meats, which were gamey enough to have been the envy of any country mansion. Barrels of beer were set up on trestles in the backyard and wooden crates with their quart-bottled cargoes of stout and brown-ale were stacked to the ceiling on the back porch. We children weren't forgotten either. There were those drinks that memories are made of: ginger-beer, cream-soda, dandelion and burdock, and of course the ever popular Tizer, fizzing up your nose and making your eyes water. In that Aladdin's-Cave of a front room, decked out for the festivities, we feasted like

4

we'd never done before. There were crackers and party hats, screams of laughter, sleeves dipped in gravy and jelly and cream on the tips of indelicate noses. Nobody cared, nothing mattered; we were free, licence had been given. Great wedges of Christmas pudding buckled the table. There was treasure in every piece. Silver-joeys, wrapped in greaseproof paper, had been carefully inserted so as nobody went without. It was a three-day party. 'Knees-up-muvver-Brown', Jimmy Shand, granny on the piano thumping away with one hand and picking out a tune with the other. Uncles and aunts were tipsy and giggling. Caterwauling through the old songs, sharp and flat and discordant; setting the teeth on edge. Adults never went to bed. They stayed up for three nights. Sleeping in chairs, playing cards, drinking themselves sober. Beds were reserved for the children - three at one end and three at the other. Too excited to sleep, rooms were awash with whispers. Moonlight filtered through chinks in the curtains. It was a silent-movie world of silhouettes and shimmering silver. Stories of ghosts and rattling skeletons, goose-pimpled the flesh and lifted the hairs on the back of the neck. But sleep would come at last, as inevitable as the end of Christmas itself. Light was engulfed. Laughter extinguished.

My first school was St Teresa's Roman Catholic Primary School in Canning-Town. My memories of it are somewhat shadowy. That first morning, hand in hand with my mother, walking beneath the trees at the edge of the Hermit Road Recreation Ground still fills my mind with terror. There it was that another small birth took place. Had I been dangled by the feet and slapped bodily into the shock of existence, my screams and tears could not have been more authentic. There it was that the seeds of recalcitrance were sown. Being dragged away by a nun off into the unknown, never again - as I thought at the time - to see my kith and kin, was a jolt to the system that I've never fully recovered from. There it was that my first groping intellectualisms grasped at the meanings of distrust. My propensity towards the solitary life had its roots - in what I saw then - as that early betrayal. Much of my earliest school experience was clouded by that event. The rest is rather vague. Beanbags are a more prominent feature than I think they should be, though the symbolism eludes me. School dinners made their queasy mark: fish in white sauce, cabbage, boiled beyond the bounds of credibility and reeking of some antediluvian drainage duct, and of course, tapioca, that slippery excuse for frog's-spawn, forced down the throats of the innocent in the name of: "You're lucky you're not starving and living in Africa."

After measles and sundry other infantile infections I settled into a somewhat uneasy truce with my warders and my surroundings. Strangely, when I think of present day realities, I was allowed to make my own way to and from school. It was then that my imagination began to expand in ways not conceived of by your average dour educationalist. The Church of the Holy Trinity, or as we knew it, Trinity Church - a black towering edifice that somehow managed to survive the worst excesses of The Blitz - was encompassed by houses in various states of bomb-damaged dereliction. One of those houses - a large three-storied dwelling - stood on its own amongst the piles of rubble. Some of its walls were missing. It could be peered into as you might look into an open doll's-house. In one room a bent and buckled bedstead was perched precariously on the edge of oblivion. In another, where the blast echoing cupboard doors hung broken and askew, striations of incoming light filtered through the loose and missing slates to animate a dance of glittering dust. There, it was rumoured, a doctor had committed suicide; hung himself at the top of the stairs in a fit of morbid depression. That was our house of do-and-dare and there it was that we tested ourselves. Discovered the limits of our bravery. The staircase was built into a brick extension on the outside of the house. A series of steps and level planes zig-zagged their way up to the topmost landing. There, there swung a noose. Whether it was a memento mori from the rumoured suicide or just put there for a jape by one of the local wags, nobody knew. Suffice it to say that for us children it was real enough. Only once did I make the nerve-racking ascent. I can still smell the brick-dust and the damp. Can hear the creaking of the stairs and the beating of my tiny heart, trapped like a mouse behind the wainscot. When I got to the top - more breathless with anxiety than exertion - I saw the noose highlighted in the shadows by the slant of incoming sunlight. My fear was almost palpable. I was close to paralysis. Then someone behind me screamed and a flock of escaping pigeons exploded on thunderous wings. Never was an exit more undignified. Discretion being the better part of a rout, the residue of whatever bravery I had, remains there in that house; a ghost in search of another ghost; that haunts me still.

From the back of the removal van London started to contract. My frame of reference had begun to alter. Perspectives were shifting. What was once in the foreground of my life had now moved from the middle-distance to become nothing more than a diminishing speck on the receding horizon. Between my future and me lay the industrial wasteland of the city's outskirts. Terraces of Victorian and Edwardian houses were being replaced by tracts of derelict land, factory chimneys and slag heaps. A concrete bridge carried us over a tidal creek, where wooden wharves, derricks, and a tumbledown paintworks clung to the edges of the polluted waterway. Precarious stacks of rusty oil-drums towered over waste-lots. In all directions everything seemed to be in a state of ruin or decay. Industrial buildings of every conceivable shape and size were to be seen in various stages of dilapidation. Asbestos, tin and corrugated iron; these were the things of Empire. The materials, 'the sun never set on.' Here and there, the half-hearted attempts at cultivation - the dig-for-victory plots of hungry Londoners - had reverted to scrub and brambles. Occasionally, where the more persistent amongst them had stuck to the task, oases of prelapsarian greenery repaid their efforts with a meagre crop of homegrown vegetables. Eventually, beyond the motor-works, the rows of Lombardy-poplars and the brick-built, sports-fielded suburbs, we found ourselves on the edge of the Essex marshes.

Romance had entered into my life. By no stretch of the imagination could that country have been called beautiful in any conventional sense of the word. But for me the wide marshland fields, counterpointed by elms and crisscrossed by dykes and ditches flashing in the sunlight, were the start of a love affair that enthralls me still. Sheep were still an integral part of the marshland economy in those days and for me, a child of the city, they were the first and enduring symbols of my changing fortune.

By the time we were approaching our destination it was early afternoon. Whether or not summers were hotter in those days, I wouldn't like to say, but hot it certainly was. An outcrop of low hills skirted the Thames marshes. Tortuous creeks curved and coiled through the sweeping delta. Their silver scales glinting in the hazy heat. We passed an inn called The Barge. It stood at the top of Wharf Lane. An elm-lined shadowy descent to the level crossing on The London Tilbury and Southend Railway, and beyond that to a timber-yard and Vange Wharf itself. Unbeknown to me at the time, tens years hence would see some of my earliest work experience gained in that very timber-yard. But for now it was a by-road to the sea Somewhere to launch my imaginary ships, to set sail for adventure with the sun's radiant doubloon hanging in the rigging. About half a mile further on we went under a railway bridge and then turned left into Sandon Road. This was one of the few metalled roads in the area. It was bordered on both sides by a rare assortment of single-storey dwellings. Some were solid enough, brick-built with tiled roofs and having the luxury of flagstone paths and patios. Most however, were not so well constructed. Wood, tin, asbestos and corrugated iron were as much in evidence there as they were on the journey through the outskirts of London. There was a difference though. Here there was a pride in the materials. These shacks - originally summer homes only, but now occupied all year because of their proximity to a bombed-out city - were really well looked after. Paint and pebble-dash, orchard trees, shrubs and cottage flowers had marked each of those unassuming houses with the stamp of individuality. There was something about them of the home and castle mentality so much associated with the English mind.

Where the old metalled surface ended, a newer, wider, concrete road began. On one side of the road ran the Fenchurch-Street railway line and on the other there was a hawthorn thicket and a stand of two large elms. As yet there were no pavements. We passed a few more bungalows set back in their own fields and orchards, and then drew up outside our new home. The area that I was moving into was officially known as Barstable, but to most of the residents and me it was to become known as the Luncies Road Estate, a name derived from one of the larger local farms. At that time - other than in the eyes of planners - Basildon as we know it today, scarcely existed. Apart from Barstable the only other estate - a mile or two across the fields to the northwest - was called Whitmore Way. The change could not have been more complete. As modern as our new homes were, three-bedrooms, two inside toilets, one upstairs and one down - luxury indeed! - we were nevertheless islanded on all sides by much older and more bucolic patterns of existence. From west, through north to east, we were surrounded by a patchwork of farms, smallholdings, unmade-roads, woodlands and thorn thickets. To the south the ancient flood plains of the Thames stretched out from Fobbing to Benfleet and beyond. All this - appropriately enough for the Essex creeks and marshes - was to be my oyster. Whether the pearls thus formed are to be considered as those of wisdom, is not for me to say. But pearls they were, cultured or otherwise.

The tailboard of the removal van was lowered and out I leapt like a diminutive lion into my new domain. There, in the heat - the freshly smelt, sea-breezed and country heat - my wide-eyed, tree climbing self, was about to be born. There, through a pride of days. Through a sun-scratch, grass in the teeth twiddle of a rock-hard, clay-chasmed, August, life was to begin in earnest. Neighbourliness began at once. East End

9

hospitality had been transposed. The next-door house in our particular terrace was already occupied. No sooner had the removal van drawn up, than we were invited in for tea and the welcoming committee. For my part I was given the option of either joining them or making my first tentative explorations of the area. Having at that age something of an aversion to tea and adult company, I chose the latter. Opposite our house there was a large field. A field burnt straw-coloured by the long, dry summer. Scattered pell-mell across it were sundry clumps of hawthorn and bramble and at the edge nearest our house there was a small depression. Rumour had it that this was a bomb-crater, the result of an enemy bomber dropping the last of its load while being chased by RAF fighters after a raid on London. If that's true, then it lends credence to the maxim that if you look hard enough you can find some good in just about anything. Bone-dry in summer, this somewhat unremarkable concavity would fill to the brim in winter and spring and become my own private pond, replete with newts and tadpoles. Fate was definitely on my side. Apart from the pond, at no more than stepping distance from the end of our terrace a large billowy oak marked the spot where a cross-country footpath straddled the road. I say footpath but that would be to underestimate both its lineage and its mystery. Locals called it the alley, the back-path, and most deliciously to me, the bridle path. What connotations. What glorious visions of highwaymen and musketeers, of moonlit, midnight dashes, of steamy-nostrilled, foam-flanked, owl hooting escapades. Absolutely nothing before or since has made as much of an impression on my mind as that sinuous thoroughfare through the wilderness. On that first day I dared not venture very far. My erstwhile lion-hearted self was back with the hanged man. The noose at the top of the stairs in far-off London swung here as well, in the guise of a child's swing dangling from a bough of the billowy oak.

Back at the house things were being put in order. The removal had been achieved, albeit mostly in the form of yet to be unpacked wooden-crates and cardboard-boxes. You may at

10

this point be wondering, why thus far, I've said so little about my father and mother. To say nothing of my brother who's five years older than myself. The truth is that I don't think any of us given the option would have chosen each other as soul mates. We were as different as dreams and daylight. All three of them had what I considered to be strong, logical personalities. Being the youngest member of the tribe I felt that my place in the pecking order left a lot to be desired. No doubt they would have a very different view of the situation. But as a unique human being in my own right, what else can I do but assess it from the admitted bias of my prepubescent vantage? My parents were good - if somewhat strict - dutiful, God-fearing on the one hand, and fearing nothing on the other, sort of folk. My brother, by virtue of the five- year's difference in our ages, seemed more an adjunct of parental control than someone to share my new-found excitements. All in all they appeared to my underdeveloped and highly suspicious - not to say superstitious - mind, like rational demons haunting the periphery of an otherwise totally irrational, spontaneous and idyllic existence. No doubt all three of them will be mentioned again periodically: my mother as the major influence in the development of my neurotic personality, my father as the personification of fear itself, and my brother as the role-model for fishing and affairs of the heart. But for now I must slip back into solipsistic mode and interpret the universe from the only place I can know for certain. My own demented mind!

Having been allotted a bedroom I was anxious to discover the view from the window. The garden - still more reminiscent of a builder's-yard than anything approaching the council-house equivalent of suburbia - stopped at the edge of a small field. On the other side of the field were two more rows of terraced houses. In front of one of those was a group of hawthorn bushes. In front of the other stood a tall solitary oak, home to the massed accumulated tangle of a magpie's nest. To the left - no more than fifty foot-itching yards away, was the soon to be explored, all-enticing bridle path. By the side of the path was one of the plotlander's shacks. A ramshackle building, cobbled together with wood and tin. In its garden there were apple, plum and pear trees. Old rickety sheds, stacks of kindling and a well, stood witness to the rigours of self-sufficiency. In that shack there lived a hymn singing, hard working, old time evangelist known locally by the acronym ELIM - Lil. Being accustomed to rats - due to my Canning-Town upbringing - I was neither surprised nor mortified to see them there in abundance. The place was alive with them. Not just at ground level either. More than once I saw them in broad daylight sauntering along the veranda roof, as bold as you like. How they got up and down from there I never found out, all I knew was that rats in the plotlands were as common as sparrows. Many a time on looking into a well you'd see the bobbing, bloated carcass of a drowned one. "Don't forget to boil the water before drinking it," was one of the more sensible local maxims. Personally, I've never been afraid of rats. I'm not saying that I'd like to fill my trousers up with their wriggling, whiskered weight. It's just for all the undoubted problems they cause, I still have a sort of sneaking regard for them. Their survivability is stupendous. Mankind and rats go together. Wherever humans are, rodents are there to take advantage of anything we care to give them, wittingly or otherwise. I find it strange - diseases aside - that tame, white rats of the children's book variety can be thought of as cute; while their duskier cousins elicit screams of terror, traps, poison and armed-to-the-teeth rustic vigilante groups. Still, it's easy for me to say, I've never kept chickens!

Dawn broke to a new day and a new life. Breakfast was a meal to be endured. I wasn't interested in cornflakes, toast and jam, tea or anything else for that matter. All I wanted was to be free of familial restraints and to reconnoitre the soon to be legendary bridle path. I made my first major sortie down the alley from the side of the road opposite to our house. On entering the cavernous shade, with hawthorn and dog-rose bushes on one side and fully-grown privet hedges on the other, I was immediately assailed by the smell of the place.

Smells and the bridle path went together. Not bad smells either. Whatever the season of the year the air was redolent with some commensurate perfume: sometimes musky, sometimes dank, sweet and fermenting in late summer or early autumn, tangy in mist and fog, or acrid with bonfire smoke. And how to explain the subtle aroma of frost or the rising volatile essence from a mulch of decaying leaves is beyond the skills of this particular writer. On that day however it was musky - hot and musky. Crickets and grasshoppers augmented the heat with their rasping insect equivalent of love-songs. Monotonous through five well rounded syllables the ringdoves tuned-in their recorders. Flies with bottle green and metallic-blue bodies droned through the slanting shafts of sunlight and a common-lizard skittered across the path. What the path itself was made of I'm not certain. It was as hard as concrete but darker in colour and more gravelly in texture. It had been laid in a continuous length but by now - due to wear and tear and the vagaries of climate - it was beginning to crack and break up. There was hardly a level plane of any consequence. Dislodging slabs were arranged at various angles of opposition to each other. To run along this path - or worse still, to cycle at full speed - was to take one's life in one's hands, especially as a deep ditch ran along its entire course. It was a bone-breaker in summer and as unfathomable as Davy Jones' locker after the rains of autumn. As I ventured a little further into the alley I came across a wooden-gate set well into the privet, privet that had grown over as well as around it. Through this sombre archway I could see a small, squat, single-storied house. It was simply a tiny rectangle, pebble-dashed on the outside and roofed in slate. At its front three steps led up to a veranda. On that veranda there were a set of cane chairs, a small table, and a four-feet high wooden balustrade topped by thin horizontal planking. On this were rested flowerpots of various shapes, sizes and colours: earthenware and china, glazed or unglazed, glass and porcelain, patterned or otherwise. From these flourished a display of geraniums that would have lifted the heart of the organizer of the Chelsea Flower Show itself. The subtle and contrasting shades of pink and red were highlighted by the enlightened placement of white-blooming varieties. Was I dreaming? Was this where I had come to Live? I couldn't believe my luck. It was better than a dream. As long as I could stay awake it would be there. None of that, "if only I could remember it," or "if I could just pick it up where I left off." This was for real, and it was mine, all mine! There too was where I encountered my first real plotland orchard. It was a veritable Eden of trees, grass, daisies and dandelions. There would I bite the fruit, yet retain my innocence a little longer. Magic names and scents and flavours hung from that Merlin's Cave of an orchard. Great pendulous William's pears, gleaming like yellow lanterns, Victoria plums - as big as a child's fist - tempting the tongue with their sweet-sharp juices, and apples of every kind bearing names that are memories only: James Grieves, Codlings, Pippins, Bramleys, Worcesters and Blenheims. There too the greengage and the half-forgotten bullace, rounded their succulent flesh, as the cherry-ripe dangle of mimic earrings were sucked to the core of their nectared bones, and then spat from the sweetened lips of my sated childhood.

Chapter 2 - St Josephs.

Summers don't last forever. Even the seemingly longest, hottest and most idyllic of them must - it appears - come to their inevitable soggy end. I come from a family that used to be known - a mite irreverently, I might add - as one of mixed origin. That is to say that one half of the parental duo - ipso facto, my mother - was Catholic, and that the other half - not so ipso facto, guess who? - was Protestant. It seems that my father had tried his best to follow the course of conversion but had failed at the last ecumenical hurdle. Nevertheless, in accordance with Papal-edict, he had agreed that my schooling - both moral and intellectual - should be handed over to the Roman Catholic Church and its allied system of religious education. The first problem to overcome was one of omission. Despite the supposedly omnipotent presence of God, the communion of saints and the apostolic order, there seemed to have been something of a heavenly oversight. Pitsea - land of the heathen that it was - was without a Catholic school to call its own.

Thus it was that on a wet and windy September morning I found myself running along - somewhat unenthusiastically - behind my mother, *en route* to the school-bus pick-up point. Even on the worst of days there is joy to be had by the adventurous of spirit. What kind of joy would this be, you might say, on such a torrential, windswept, school-looming slop of a day? Puddles, I answer, unhesitatingly! Puddles, scourge of the adult, manna to the young and the young at heart! " 'urry up, we're goin' ter miss the bus! Git out o' that warta, I've jus' polished them shoes! What the dickens d'you fink yer up ter?" Ah, joy to the ears it is, even now. What child - one conjectures - has never experienced the pleasures of teeming rain? Not least - one suspects - because of the growing awareness that the very same natural phenomenon is the one most despised by their elders and betters. What adults

15

even, when propelled down the conduits of memory by the flashfloods of recollection, cannot remember - albeit with a sigh - the Pooh-stick escapades of their former lives? There by the raging gutters - oblivious to the screeching of my mother and the imminent inclemency of spilt ink and arithmetic - I followed my lolly-stick canoe down the Zambezi-like water courses of my imagination until it was lost forever over the precipitous edge of a gully-sucking drain. Onward I splashed under the dripping trees. Out into the cats and dogs, lashing at a slant, full pelt of the earlier than expected equinoctial blast. I crossed the main London Road without a care. Was scolded and ear-clipped for my thoughtless trouble and told to shut-up and shelter in the louring doorway of a nearby shop. I wiped the rain off the window and peered inside. That was a real shop. Not in a million years would it have qualified for a hygiene-certificate. There, everything was dusted with flour, and floured with dust. Produce and packaging were in enmity in those days. Barrels and bins were full to overflowing with all kinds of powdery and granular substances. Sugar and flour - webbed and foot-printed by mice and spiders and speckled with unspeakable black excrescences - vied for my attention with the rolled down sacks of split peas and pigeon-mixture. Butter was in slabs, cheese was mouldy, and bacon sliced wafer-thin and salt-cured wispy before one's very eyes. The proprietary brands come flooding back: Brasso, at its knick-knack polishing best, Cherry-Blossom, for boots black or brown and for the smudged unsightly thumbprint on a stiff, studded and detachable collar, Blue-Bags for white washing, and Sunlight Soap for the dreaded duck-bobbing, ear, nose and throat clinical scrubbing on a Friday night. Next door to that shop was the shoe-repairers, known locally as the 'snobs.' There it was that a grey-haired, wizened, little old man, wearing a leather apron and with gold-rimmed spectacles perched on the end of his nose, hammered away at his last. He was then - and still is to my retarded mind - the template for every idea I've ever had about elves beavering away for Father Christmas in the frigid but frolicsome workshops at the North Pole. What a

16

lovely, leathery smell exuded from that place. What a tick, tacks in the mouth, tock of a rhythmical music came from the swing of his arm's precision. Here was the world of William Morris, writ large, the life-enhancing qualities of craftsmanship. Here, and by these methods, the workingman would overcome the tyrannical predations off his capitalist overlords and reform the social system to one of equality and justice for all. Work and workers would become as one. Opposites would be united. The last and all-redeeming higher synthesis would be finally and irrevocably achieved. Thus spake the personifications of hope gathered collectively in the precincts of that pivotal decade. Thus speak they still from the precincts and shopping malls of the nihilistic nineties. Here in this no hope, hole in the pocket, terminal brink of Giro-mania.

The bus drew up and to my dismay another small severance of the umbilical cord was about to take place. Not only was I going to a new school, but this time I was going to a new school on my own. Apart from the driver, we had our minders. A couple of old-time Catholic women well versed in the arts of scruffing the neck and dusting the seat of the pants. The bus was a green, crash-geared, vintage Eastern National double-decker. Inside it was a wondrous mix of wood, leather and metal, and the windows had either windy-handles or pop-up slit-eyed louvres. I believe that the collective noun for a busload of demented children is a riff-raff. Riff-raff we were. On that bus there were more decibels per/cubic inch than would eventually emanate from the ill-fated expansion-chambers of the TR2. Upstairs, our test-bedded feet clattered across the gridded metal floors and beat out an interminable mind-numbing tattoo. Pigtails were pulled and screams were issued in reply. The sounds of slapped legs and insolence drifted from the ever-changing directions of our patrolling warders. Between bouts of tears and giggling, blood-curdling cries and hoots of uncontrollable laughter, I managed to see something of the countryside out of the rain-washed, steamed-up windows of that omnibus from hell.

Early wet September was still more part of summer than it was of the approaching autumn. All was green fields, green hedgerows and green trees. A sopping, many-toned, paradoxical kaleidoscope of greenness was all there was of the world to be seen between Pitsea and that other marshland settlement, Stanford-le-Hope. The Five-Bells, Springfield and the Homesteads, were all places hardly noticed on that particular journey, that have since become the stock-in-trade of my earliest memories. The Five-Bells, an inn at the foot of a line of low hills facing southwards to Fobbing marshes and beyond to the Thames-Haven oil-refineries, was in those days a sleepy little corner of the world meandering around the lazy curve of a slow S bend. There under a group of the once ubiquitous elms, stood the blacksmiths with its forge. It was there that the protean character of metal was first perceived by my inquiring mind. What Prometheus had stolen, the blacksmith tamed, and by Jove he knew it. There it was that I saw the lifted feathery hooves of giant shires and the enormous muscular bulk of the Suffolk-punch. It was there that I heard the resounding, resonant ring of hammer on anvil. Where white-hot metals yielded to the blacksmith's awesome power. Where bellows puffed and wheezed and blasted. Where smoke and sparks and coal-dust erupted from the molten core of the forge, like the fiery-breath of some infernal creature. Where tongues of glimmering iron were thrust into vats of water. Where the scolded air was tempered in a cloud of steam, and the ears' involving labyrinths rang and recoiled from the hiss of imagined serpents.

Springfield, a tiny hamlet straddling the crossroads between the Five-Bells and the Homesteads, was the birthplace of my earliest agricultural experiences, peas and potatoes being the favoured crops in the area. As one who has been gainfully employed in harvesting both of these commonplace comestibles, I would say - pod for pod - that peas are by far the easiest proposition in terms of energy expended. Although, as is the way with all economies - the rural one being no exception - the harder, bent-double, back-breaking work of potato-picking offered the better financial returns. However, my back and the potato harvest never really came to terms with one and other. Radox, White-Horse oil, and bread-poultices were no substitute for the pleasures of a vertical existence. Say what you will. Quote Darwin or Desmond Morris if you must. But as far as I'm concerned walking along at ninety degrees to the perpendicular is not my idea of homo sapiens in their most sophisticated mode. Just the memory of it is enough to start a dull, unremitting ache in the depths of my lumbar region. I gave it my best shot - as they say in more progressive, go-for-it parts of the world. - but I'm afraid that my best shot was nothing less than a blank. Potatoes need a more heroic, how-the-west-was-won, sort of spirit than I could ever muster. No, for me it was peas. Petits pois, mange-tout, marrowfat, or any other variety you'd care to mention. I could sit down on the job with just a pile of sacks and a sunny day to keep me company. What more could you ask? I can't remember just how much I got paid for a sack-full now, pennies, shillings, groats? It's all far too long ago. What I do remember is being bored stiff with the time it took to fill a sack with peas. They were no ordinary sacks. Oh no! They were sacks designed by a committee of niggardly Essex farmers. To fill them up, one of my diminutive stature needed to stand on tiptoe with arms at full stretch. Needless to say, in order to lessen the effort involved a number of nefarious ploys were attempted. Padding out with vines was a favourite. Though most employers were up to that one. Seeing as they weighed the sacks as well, it was quite easy for them to sort out the wheat from the chaff - metaphorically speaking. The more conniving amongst us supplemented the vines with clods of clay or flint nodules. Even then, a good shake and a kick to the bottom of the sack exposed the deception - if somewhat painfully! All in all the farmers were on to most of the wrinkles. If there were other more successful scams, then I didn't know about them. For me it was always the hard slog of honest physical labour. Good for the soul, but lousy for the piggybank!

The Homesteads - next stop Stanford-le-Hope - lived up to its name. This was the bungalow-belt in earnest. Slightly more up-market than the plotlands proper. Although still surrounded by farms and woodland, to my young self it had something of the air of prosperity about it. For a start we had travelled through it on a bus. Which in itself presupposes a road of sorts. Mind you, prosperity had yet to deal a blow to the highway's equivalent of crop-circles - namely potholes. These mysterious entities - if a hole can be rightly called an entity - appeared out of nowhere. It was a Bermuda-Triangle for the local authorities. Council workmen sent out to do battle with these alien invasions had been known to disappear for days on end. Only to be found at last huddled together over black, steaming kettles in sundry sheds half-hidden at the ends of cul-de-sacs. Brave men that they were - despite the perils of the British climate and the far greater evil of the time-and-motion-study man - they kept the arteries of commerce - and in my case, education - open. So, like it or not, Stanford-le-Hope came shuddering into view. The church and the portals of an educational establishment little changed since the relief of Mafeking were about to extend - in the form of priests and nuns - a disciplinarian's welcome to the approaching rabble.

This was the archetypical school of every conceivable scholastic nightmare. It was the epitome of traditional values. Its very structure seemed designed to instill the maximum amount of fear possible. The redbrick, towering Victorian edifice glared back at the sun-shot clearing of the storm, from its monumental high sash- windows. It had all the drama of a biblical epic. A vision of Elijah controlling the tempest at will. I could hear the implications, rain or drought, don't ask the meteorologists just study the biblical texts, its fundamental to your spiritual development. I was on my knees already. I'd seen the light, but the light in conjunction with a star, a lone expending brilliant, powerless in the face of the second law of thermodynamics. Islanded and oppressed by the surrounding aeons of eternal darkness. "Form yourselves into five straight - I said straight! - lines," came the strident command from the oft-times vesper whispering lips of a Whirling Dervish of a nun. It had begun. My infantile version of the Enlightenment, countered by bouts of Torquemada-like inquisition, had moved into its catechismal phase. Question and answer was to be our modus operandi. We were to be told what the questions were then given the appropriate answers to be learnt by rote. This was education in the strictest sense of the word. Seated at our sloping wooden desks - pens at the ready - we would be expected to respond to any doctrinal whim of our peripatetic, desk-slapping mentors. On that particular day, prison itself, the very dungeons of the most dismal of medieval castles, would have seemed preferable to what I was about to endure. My newfound surroundings will no doubt be familiar to many amongst you. The parquet flooring - buffed to a pernicious brilliance - waited like sheet-ice for the unwary speedster. The fifteen-foot high ceilings added greatly to one's sense of inferiority and the blackboard and easel dominated the unfathomable foreground of each unintelligible classroom. The desks - as already noted - were of the wooden sloping variety, and unless my memory deceives me, seats were hard, attached and uncomfortable to live with. Along the top of the desks ran a groove. There we kept our pens and pencils. At the far end of the groove was the inkwell. Into this was inserted a small, cylindrical, porcelain pot, filled at intervals with what I've since come to know as octopus-oil. If you'd seen some of my earliest attempts at writing, the significance of the metaphor would become immediately apparent. Even now, whilst penning longhand this humble little autobiography, my fear of the handwriting class and my continually thwarted efforts to master the art of penmanship, haunt the very margins of the page. Things became so bad, that along with other graphical degenerates, I was relegated to the boiler-room for extra reading and writing lessons. Down there, deep in the bowels of that ship of knowledge, we were coached - not to say terrorized - individually. We sat on hard, slatted, wooden benches ranged either side of a white-scrubbed trestle table.

21

There, with a scratchy overloaded pen and wads of blotting paper that didn't blot, I wrote out the individual letters of the alphabet a million miserable times. There too, the repeat after me, spelling exercises helped to formulate a neurotic lexicographical disposition that plagues me to this very day.

Back upstairs in class on that first day I began to look about me at some of my fellow inmates. There was a plump little red-faced boy with the unusual - seeing as it was a Catholic school – Jewish sounding name of Finglestein. Still, being well and truly in the land of original sin he wouldn't have to bear the full weight of the cross entirely on his own. Hearne, another remembered only by his surname, had white speckles and blotches behind all of his fingernails, which seem to suggest some sort of calcium deficiency. Whatever, the nickname of Mr. Pastry was inevitable. One whose name I can remember in full - can never forget in fact - was Jethro Buckley. He was reputed to have come from one of the large Essex gipsy families. Whether this was so - he certainly had something of a wayward and recalcitrant spirit - I couldn't rightly say. What I do know is, he was about to become a good and loyal friend, although, the word friend could just as easily be translated - accomplice - for all intents and purposes. Most of my early troubles were either influenced or instigated by this devil-may-care apotheosis of a fallen angel. Strangely, I remember next to nothing in the way of girls at that particular time. Girls on the bus I recall, but they could have been destined for elsewhere. Sandals, white-socks and gingham dresses come to mind but the faces are vague and I couldn't put a name to any of them. I was at that stage in my life when girls were considered to be surplus to requirements. Mothers-and -fathers and doctors-and-nurses were pleasures as yet to be refined. For now, apart from my female kith and kin and the unmerciful sisters of infinite wisdom, it was to be a predominantly masculine world.

Boys one instinctively understood. What to other eyes was seen as mischievous, sullen, or even as downright obstreperous, was to the stripling mind as natural as the clash of conkers or the sidelong, vituperative, mumbling of curses. Autumn was our arena. That postage-stamp of a playground appeared to us to be of inordinate dimensions. Running along the edge of the road, around the front of the school and up to the entrance of the church itself, our limits were defined by the spiky green spears of the statutory cast-iron railings. To the south, a low, grey, stonewall separated us from the convent and its thin-lipped and beady-eyed sorority. Between them and us grew temptation in the form of raspberries, gooseberries and blackcurrants. At the sunset end of the playground were sited the 'offices of ablution,' more commonly known as the 'bogs.' There sinks and urinals were open to the elements and even the cubicles themselves - owing to the dilapidated state of their corrugated iron roofs - could be considered more of an *en plein air* experience than other more delicate descriptions could confer. Over and above that high-stench, putrefying cesspit of an excuse for a toilet, spread out the leaves and branches of two tall and partially entwining walnut trees. Once again God had intervened. He, in His high-minded beneficence had decided to create something close to paradise here on earth. Boys and trees are inseparable, although, say that to an operative in the fracture-clinic and the shortest of shrift will become your true and just deserts. However, there in the mellowest of seasons, the green-splitting globes of the crop in question gave us a glimpse of their cerebral centres. Continuing with the mental metaphor, one has to ponder on the origin of the word 'nutty' itself. This - almost literally - cortex of a shell certainly inspired behaviour from both myself and others that could definitely be termed, as my mother might have said, "free pence short of a shillin'." What possible vestige of sanity is to be found in the vision of a group of vociferous louts hurling great knobbly cudgels up into the trees immediately above their young and barely protected craniums? No good could come of it, you might say. And you wouldn't be far wrong. Cudgels and heads not infrequently came into contact with one and other. Lumps the size of eggs at a first holy-communion breakfast sprouted from the skulls of black, blond and ginger-haired urchins with equal vigour. Those more akin to monkeys than to the be-cudgelled Neanderthals below, leapt about in the trees with all the agility of arthritic squirrels. If you've ever seen a wildlife film of monkeys in full swing - or more appropriately heard the sound of them in full cry on the approach of a predator - then you will have some idea of the shrill-throated, high-flung, pandemonium that I'm talking about. Walnuts in great showering cascades tumbled, split, burst out and rolled off in all directions. A veritable Gatling gun of ricocheting shots reverberated off the corrugated-iron roof, to where the resultant downfall of scattering prizes had yet to run the gauntlet of the ear-ripped, legs-bitten, rugby-tackling maniacs of St Joseph's seminary for the mentally insane.

One of the unsolved mysteries of primary school education is that of that excruciating sub-occult phenomenon - the verruca - or more commonly, the wart. From time immemorial the esoteric significance of warts has been paramount. Why else would such a plethora of folklore have been built up around them? Rubbing one's hands under the waning moon is supposed to be effective in their removal. Whether or not it does anything for those growing under the feet is a matter for the clairvoyant amongst you. Tales of touching the dead or their accoutrements as being methods equally efficacious when it comes to the magical removal of these mysterious tumescences - also abound. As a last example - sufficient I feel to satisfy the hermetic temperament of the most supernatural of minds - I shall relate the following: Take a length of string. Tie in it as many knots as you have warts. Touch each wart with each knot, and then throw the whole caboodle over the back of your left hand shoulder into a stagnant pond. As the strings decays your warts will disappear. But of course, you must not tell anybody. Who would! I beg to ask? This brings me to the most painful and embarrassing point of the story thus far. I may have lacked the mental capacity for the full acquisition and weight of religious and secular knowledge, but I certainly didn't lack the physical wherewithal when it came to the accumulation of warts. Warts and I had something of a newly acquired affinity. That school was a wart-mine. The richest seam of warts in Christendom was to be found in those unhallowed catacombs. Everyone had warts. Even the nuns and priests had warts. But they it seemed only had venial warts. Warts of the mortal variety were reserved for us of the prepubescent sinning persuasion. I had them on my feet, knees and hands. Fortunately my blond, blue-eyed, cherubic face was spared the ravages of those pestilent blemishes. Placed - as they were in my case - strategically, the more spiritually adept amongst my contemporaries may have been inclined to think of them not as warts, but as stigmata. But for me alas, they were just warts. Being in the cloistered halls of Catholic learning, recourse to the more superstitious means of eradicating the affliction were of course unthinkable. Even prayer it seemed was not enough. Once again - as so often happened in my life - fate intervened. St Josephs and the clinic were mercifully separated by half a mile of blossoming suburbia. As if of divine providence my suffering was compensated for by the twice-weekly journeys through that oasis of health and freedom. Lessons could be forgotten. Knowledge was to be no more than the white puffs of amorphous clouds as they traversed and dusted the infinite spaces of the sky's blue slate. All was trees and birds and gardens. It was the acme of didacticism. All I wanted to know; all I needed to know was there. The clinic was a different kettle of conundrums. There after booking in and waiting the statutory aeon whilst pretending to read magazines you wouldn't even if you could, you were finally ushered into the surgery. There it was that prodding and poking became a way of life. Why should one be made to strip, cough, poke your tongue out and be weighed, all in the name of a cure for warts, passeth all understanding. But then, such is the innocence of youth. There, warts were regarded at clinical distance with no more than a tong-like nod towards the arts of diagnosis. In the dispensary - the twentieth century's answer to the coven - a ritualistic violet-coloured potion was being concocted on my behalf. This was to become my indelible trademark, more conspicuous even than the cross of ashes thumbed into the forehead at the beginning of Lent. I, the blue-spotted one, would be known henceforth, from afar.

Part of the school - in every sense of the word - the church of St Josephs lifted its bell-ringing, mass-summoning tower into the grey-skied, low church, heaven of that town on the edge of the Essex marshes. It was from there that the full and chastening power of Catholic ritual was to be daily performed for the betterment of my eternal soul. Whether from behind a mesh in a dark and dingy cubicle or kneeling in front of the priest - enthroned in his full regalia - confession and its subsequent absolution were to become my *raison d'etre*. I was undoubtedly a sinner. It was common knowledge. My mother knew it, my father knew it, and the nuns knew it. Even the priest - oblivious to any attempt at mitigation on my part - sided with the rest of them. One soon learnt that the sin of inventing a sin was far easier to live with than trying to explain one's innocence to a disbelieving confessor. "Fergiv' me farver for I 'ave sinned, it's bin seven days since me last confession." "And what have you to confess my son," came the intoned reply.
"I stole a penny from me muvver's purse farver," I lied, "You know that's very wrong of you, don't you," reprimanded the priest. "Yes farver I do," I continued contritely. "I won't do it agin, honest." I knew that this relatively minor infringement of celestial law would be treated as venial only. Both parties would be satisfied. A sin had been admitted and absolution administered. Tacit agreement as to one's place in the hierarchy of goodness was all that was required. Only the penance remained. "Two Hail-Marys and three Our-Fathers, kneeling outside on the gravel," came the theological command. This may seem somewhat harsh to the uninitiated, but for someone who has prostrated himself and prayed fervently at all fourteen guilt-inducing stations of the cross, this was a real - if somewhat knee-cratering - cinch.

On occasions, sins of a more mortal magnitude - such as the obvious sacrilege of wearing a hat in the inner sanctum, or giggling while crossing oneself with holy water - were reported to the Mother Superior. She was superior by name and superior by nature. That red-faced, black-cloaked, banshee of a woman, drilled into the world and its unsuspecting occupants through a pair of all-seeing, all-knowing, laser-focused eyes. The whole terrifying effect enhanced and magnified by horn-rimmed, pebble-glazed spectacles. When summoned to her office, previous threats of purgatory and hellfire were relegated to the rightful significance of their lower order. There she would stand, stiff as a crucifix and far less forgiving. An assortment of canes of varying lengths and diameters were removed slowly, one at a time, from a long leather tube and then tested for curve and swishability. Throughout this unnerving process the rising pitch of verbal chastisement always preceded the inevitable caning. "Hold out your hand! " Thwack! "The other one!" Thwack! The pattern of my religious life had evolved. Flagellation in one form or another was to be the scourge of my tender years. The evidence of the accumulated effect of those beatings exhibited itself in the manner of raised, hard, calloused skin that remained on the palms of my hands until well beyond the demise of puberty.

Chapter 3. Witches and Whizzbangs.

Transgressions were manifold. Despite the threats of eternal damnation, two of the most abhorred dates of the festal year - when looked at from an ecclesiastical point of view - were nevertheless indulged in to the full by the backsliding adepts of our less than sacred community. Halloween and Guy-Fawkes continued to exert their pagan influence in the face of a millennium of crusades against infidel and heretic alike. Having achieved the safe distance of five heathen miles between Pitsea and Stanford-le-Hope, the two great fire and spirit festivals of the northern calendar were to be celebrated regardless.

Not withstanding the derivation of the word Halloween, All-Saints and All-Souls were to be forgotten in favour of witches, wizards, slit-eyed gleaming pumpkins and apple bobbing. Perhaps not the trick-and-treat party-night of a festival that it's become nowadays, it was nevertheless highly regarded by the young and Nordic-hearted. St Michael's church - perched on the top of a hunchback-hill overlooking the marshes and encircled by two or three stands of towering elms - afforded the necessary atmosphere. There at dusk on one grey and misted late October day - looking for all the world like the set of a Hammer-Horror movie - myself and a straggling band of boot-scuffing, shoulder-shrugging oiks, made the ascent towards that squat castellated tower so rightly patronized by one of Christianity's most famous dragon-slayers. There in the owl-hooting twilight of an x-rated, eye-covering feature, we'd come to confront the Devil. Unbeknown to us a couple of local roughnecks, half our age again and secure in the knowledge of that fact, had prefigured our arrival. Bravely - with feet and minds going in opposite directions - we passed under the lych gate and stood defiantly in God's cold acre. The black pall of a funereal darkness fell from the wings of returning rooks. Skeletal shivers ran as fleet-footed as spiders from coccyx to cerebellum. Muscular co-ordination was of the essence. At any moment messages of fight or flight would be communicated throughout our bodies from a million and one as yet unsuspected ductless glands. The stomach would lose its pound of flesh and take on a ton of lead as compensation, and the heart like a manic balloon would expand to the point of bursting in its prison of rattling ribs. By the south-porch a freshly dug grave with its attendant mound of excavated earth waited for that band, of by now, somewhat dispirited ghost-hunters. Secreted within that macabre chamber our unanticipated assailants were prepared. At the prearranged instant they arose wailing in unison from the grave, each with a writhing Medusa-like crown of turf attached to his loutish skull. Nothing I could say now could possibly describe the shock of that chimerical moment. Me and my, for once, struck dumb as well as dumbstruck companions were, in accordance with the myth, petrified. Having neither the courage nor the requisite magical accoutrements, when blood, adrenalin and everything else necessary for the revivification of the frozen metabolism had returned to its rightful place - we legged it into the night.

Even before Halloween, nay, even before the very end of summer itself, Guy-Fawkes was already being planned, prepared for and discussed. September, that sweet and sour, sloe-black, mellowest of months found us after school and at weekends foraging the hedgerows like a tribe of ragamuffin pygmies. It was the land of the blackberry. Of dew-webbed and spidery early morning grasses, where hawthorn and brier, blackthorn and bramble, were crystal diademed and shot through with misted watery sunlight. If asked to chose a favourite month there would of course be twelve near equally praised contenders. But September, that equinoctial, pivotal world between light and darkness, garlanded with flowers, bulging with fruit and illuminated by the kindled fires of autumn leaves, wins by a wisp of gossamer. Nothing burns quite so gently as the pallid candles of the wayside toadflax. No lanterns glimmer with a more pale and feathery light than those of the wild-hop. What diffuse glow of summer in retreat could compare with the smoky heads of a field of scabious? What is more seasonally satisfying than to see on the looping staves - of the as then - high-tech, telegraphic wires, the crotchets and quavers of gathering swallows adding their valedictory music to the year's unsung lament?

Into that dreamy, moist-eyed eclogue of romantic idealism marched Pitsea's answer to the Seven Dwarfs. Hi, Ho, indeed, was the order of the day. Axes, single and double-headed, saws, single and double-sided, ropes and Powerful Pierre mentalities were ready to be swung, drawn and tugged into lumbering action. Into that rustic idyll the most environmentally unfriendly brotherhood since the demise of the dodo itself, was about to be unleashed. Trees of all species and sizes, that had done no harm to anybody - other than as monstrous anthropomorphisms from the pens of demented fairy-tale writers - were about to be decimated. This yearly, uncalled for, unskilled and unsupervised pollarding reduced some of the most precious of nature's gifts to but quivering shadows of their former selves. Bonfire mania spread throughout the neighbourhood like an outbreak of rabies. Hydrophobic adolescents, foaming at the mouth, could be seen dragging their intractable cargoes from all points of the compass. How the countryside ever managed to survive those perennial ravages is beyond comprehension. Suffice it to say, that survive it did, if only at a later date to be covered by brick and concrete and surrounded by ring roads and flyovers. But that's another story.

In the large field bordering our estate two of the most important bonfires in the area grew, like wigwams, from late September right up to the emblazoned night itself. One, for the sake of clarity, we will call Linford's. The other - at the opposite end of the field - we will call, in deference to its eponymous builders, Bates'. Wigwam was the appropriate metaphor. Usually on friendly terms, at that particular time of the year the tribes divided into two separate warring factions. The pilferage of hard won timber and the likelihood of premature ignition were constant hazards. Any forced absence from the danger zone entailed coming to terms with the neuroses creating symptoms of uncertainty. At school, concentration on the 'Three-R's' - always difficult - was next to impossible. Bedtime - that plague of all right-minded infants - become worse than the little death it was already reputed to be. One wanted, and needed to be on perpetual guard. The honour of the clan was at stake. There was a difficult problem to resolve concerning those autumnal proceedings so beloved by the pyromaniac. One of my most special friends belonged to the opposing camp. Eddy Bates, now there's a name to conjure with even after all these years. At the risk of mixing my already mixed metaphors even further, I would have likened us to the infatuated offspring of rival ranch-owners. You've all seen the movie. You know the scenario. The difference in our case - as you've no doubt guessed by now - is of being of one and the same gender. Now don't get me wrong, this isn't turning into a story about rampant youthful homosexuality. We'd been known to indulge in the trousers round the ankles, willy-waggling bit. What healthy young buck of the wildwood hasn't? We had even - in the sight of one and other I must add shame-facedly - experienced the wide-eyed, breath-convulsing guilt of un-climaxed masturbation. "Forgive me father for I have sinned." But I can say in all honesty that our relationship was of the good old-fashioned dib-dab-dob, help an old lady across the road, platonic variety. Those of you looking for more spice would do better to find a second-hand copy of this book. The relevant pages will become instantly apparent owing to their dog-eared, dowdy, well-thumbed accessibility!!! No, the problem was simply the one of reconciling our year round blood brotherhood with that seasonal breakdown of tribal relations. Somehow we managed to. Nothing could stop us coming together in the name of such unutterable delights as penny-for-the-guy, pseudo begging, and in my case profanity to boot - or the equally enjoyable but far more dangerous pursuit of gunpowder, treason and pre-festivity pyrotechnics. In general the guy was a sorry looking affair, something of a cross between a drunken scarecrow and a pile of dirty laundry. Artistic endeavour and sartorial elegance were not on the agenda. The sole function of that poorly trussed bundle of rags and screwed up newspaper was an extortive one. We trundled that lolloping sprawl of an effigy on the top of the rusty chasis of a squeaky wheeled, tyre-less old pram, down to the local hostelry. There, in the dark, dank, alcoholic fug of beer-swilling, smoke-billowing autumn, we set up shop. "Penny fer the guy mista!" "Piss orf!" came the slurred retort. Undeterred we kept up a barrage of persistent banter in the face of every insult imaginable. In the end - as we always knew it would be - victory was ours. Those, half-cut and teetering on the borderline of sobriety, were soon to become imbued with the spurious bonhomie long associated with the company of John Barleycorn, and stagger merrily across the Rubicon. In that newfound state of stupefied philanthropy, pennies in the bright alchemical wonder of bleary moonlight were miraculously turned to silver. Those once insensitive, hostile brutes were themselves transformed into earthbound Agnus Dei - Whatever the plural for that is in Latin! Along with the money, an unquenchable shower of crisps and lemonade came tumbling from the hands of saints. "Hallelujah Eddy! Hallelujah!"

What was to be done with the accumulated bounty? Sweets were always an option and would be succumbed to, but the futures to be most invested in were fireworks. Legendary names at the forefront of the market - then as now - were Paynes, Brocks and Standard. Whether in boxes with star-spangled, volcano erupting lids, or under glass and loose in irresistible rows - like lessons in a multicoloured Euclidian geometry - they were the prizes valued above all others. In the middle of a tumbledown parade of shops, in what was euphemistically known as the High Road, there stood an emporium of dusty old-world splendour known by the less than politically correct name of The Jew Boys. The proprietor, a long-suffering, skinny, rheumatic wheeze of a man, was the living denial of the oft-cited, much fabled, symbiotic relationship between wealth and Jewishness. There, there was poverty in extreme. And what did the cowardly multitudes of local reprobates do about it? I'll tell you. Like the very plagues of Egypt itself, we descended upon him. We mercilessly tormented that man at every available opportunity. And worse - like the voracious locusts that we were - in one way or another we took the unleavened bread out of his deserving mouth. If anything in my despicable past should sentence me to the thermal depths of eternal suffering, the treatment meted out to that poor, defenceless upholder of the Sabbath should be at the head of the list. The details of our many taunts and jibes shall, out of a sense of shame and genuine atonement, remain unspoken. All that needs to be related here are the bare incriminating facts of our sweets-cum-fireworks subterfuge. Expensive fireworks were kept in a display-cabinet at the front of the shop. For some unknown reason, squibs, jumping-crackers and tuppenny-canons were stored in tin boxes behind a curtained door leading on to his living quarters. He tried his hardest to keep his eye on all of us at once. He was aware that whatever our motives were for peering and poking around his store, they were certainly not honourable. Once we felt that we'd raised him to the necessary pitch of suspicion, one of the assembled throng would ask for a half-a-crown's worth of tuppenny-canons. As quick and backward glancing as he was in his efforts to fulfil the order without losing sight of us, there was always that heart-thumping seemingly infinitesimal moment when observer and observed were eclipsed. In that blinding instant pockets were stashed with blackjacks, fruit-salads, liquorice-pipes, gob-stoppers and anything else that would stick like an accusation to our sugary fingers. He must have known. The look of feigned innocence simpering across our un-scrubbed faces must have been as transparent to him as the centuries of unjustifiable persecution suffered by the descendants of Abraham and the twelve tribes.

Having acquired sweets and tuppenny-canons on occasions such as those - whether *en mass* or in ones and twos - that

33

virtual Diaspora of insensitive gentiles scattered like chaff to the four winds. Wherever they settled the sound of peardrops and spearmint-pips being ground between ruminating molars pervaded the atmosphere. And of course, the black, saltpetered grist to their nefarious mills bristled with fuses from the bulging precincts of their explosive pockets. For Eddy and myself - near inseparable partners in the pursuit of crime - the first objective was the procurement of milk-bottles. To that end raids were carried out on the unsuspecting doorsteps of innocent plotlanders. From there - with our best scrumping jumpers full to overflowing with their vitreous contents - we made our way to the secluded acres of our own private atoll. Testing was about to begin. First, one banger was lighted and dropped into the open neck of a bottle. We retired into cover and awaited results. The fuse caught and a shower of sparks issued forth. A liquefied white smoke spilt from the lip of the bottle like the ghostly dregs of milk drunk long ago. Bang!! A somewhat muted and hollow explosion admittedly, but interesting enough nevertheless. Next, two bangers were inserted with a blob of clay as a stopper. Poohf! Even more muffled, and clouded by the confinement of vapours. But at least the bottle had cracked. That was far more promising. Finally, three bangers were used, sans clay. Crack!!! Splinters and shards of glass were blasted in all directions. Exciting? Perhaps. But for experts in the arts of warfare it was still too tame. Eddy suggested that we repair to his father's workshop. That brick-built, asbestos-roofed shed - connected to the house by a glass-covered walkway - was an Ali Baba's cave to the more than forty thieving rascals who lived in that unsavoury neighbourhood. Eddy's father was a bit of a whizz when it came to tinkering. To us children he was a Merlin of the machine shop. It seemed that he could make or mend anything, and the fixtures, fittings, and variety of tools lying about in that den of mechanical demonology, proved it. Everything that we needed was there. Half-inch diameter gas-pipe, block-ended bends, three-eighth threaded metal plugs, a vice and a power drill. Considering our tender years we were as adept and efficient as any indentured gunsmiths. If our existence had been more widely known, I'm sure that the Birmingham Small Arms Factory itself would have made us offers of employment. Tubing was cut to the required lengths, one end of each section being died, greased and bound with string. Tapped and threaded bends of the correct diameter were then screwed tightly into position. Those - by now weapon-shaped artifacts - were clamped one at a time into the vice to have a small aperture drilled into the top of each bend. That was all there was to it. The resultant six-inch pipe-guns were deadly. Wadding was crammed into them. The fuse removed from a banger was inserted into the small, drilled hole, and then the powdery black contents of the firework were poured carefully into the barrel. More wadding was added, followed by one of the three-eighth metal plugs. Finally, just enough more wadding was inserted to hold the metal plug firmly in place. Everything was ready. All we needed now was a target. A galvanized bucket was secured and set up at the end of the garden. I held the gun at arm's length - just as I'd seen the duelists doing at Saturday morning flicks - and Eddy lit the fuse with one of those wonderful, green-glowing matches so redolent of the Guy-Fawke's season. Crasssh!!! The explosion was deafening and reverberant, and the instant recoil as near as damn it bone shattering. Hopping around in a hot-footed, foul-mouthed manner, shaking and blowing my sizzled fingers, whilst at the same time shrieking with gales of nervous laughter, I moved off with Eddy to inspect the damage. A starburst with a half-inch aperture was emblazoned where the projectile had entered the bucket. On the opposite side a great, gaping, jagged orifice had been rent completely out by the secondary impact. That was the firepower afforded the most undisciplined army to have ravaged in the area since the drug-crazed Berserkers of our infamous past. Nothing, whether furred or feathered, scaled or skinned, would be certain of safety while there was enough powder to charge the muzzles of those unchallengeable weapons.

35

At last the big day arrived. Sometimes on those longed-for occasions the weather was kind, those classic November days fondly remembered and yet somehow nostalgically enhanced by the deficiencies of memory and distance. Those misty and sun-hazy autumnal days, followed by fog-frosted, potato-roasting, buttery, starlit nights. Invariably however, November the Fifth was the culmination of the longest period of web-footed inclemency since St Swithin slipped on the bath-soap and flooded the entire bishopric. It was one of those days, a squelching, soggy, rain-slanted morass of a treasonable day. It was the quintessence of damp-squibedness. The clouds oppressed with their continuous weight of southwesterly nimbostratus. That unwanted cargo of $H2O$ multiplied to the power of infinity, extinguished the fires of our hopes with an incessant, down-streaming, diagonal drench. Forlorn behind my hand-wiped, rain-runnelled window, I looked out upon the dismal scene. It was the Jewish shopkeeper's revenge. In my childish imagination I could almost hear the rending of cloth. Very God himself had deserted me. It was indeed the fate of the damned.

By late afternoon the rain had eased. A light, all moistening drizzle dampened my hair and trickled down my face with all the effectiveness of Japanese water-torture as I prodded about at the sodden edges of the bonfire. The chances of Guido-Fawkes being engulfed in celebratory flames seemed further away than the combustive brandy on the Christmas pudding. The day continued to drag its soaking feet for what seemed to the impatience of youth an eternity. Eventually darkness fell and adults were pestered into becoming a part of something that they had up until now been totally excluded from. They were the combustion men, the ignis fatuus - the spontaneous jack-o-lantern men performing their miraculous duties. Those can-carrying torchbearers were for once in their lives heroes to be admired. Forgiven were all the cuffs and cantankerousness suffered throughout the preceding months. Wads of dry newspaper were thrust with long poles into the heart of the bonfire. Petrol liberally sprinkled into and around the circumference of the sacrificial piles. Torches were thrown and results waited for. Usually after a number of unsuccessful and disappointing attempts - accompanied by sighs and the re-charging of dry paper and kindling - the flames would hold amidst the cheers of the surrounding war party. Boxes were opened and children admonished for getting too close to them. Unknown to the guardians of our safety most of us had our own secret supplies concealed about our person. While parents concerned themselves with setting light to fireworks and the serious business of policing the perimeter of the bonfire, the warring factions sent out their scouting parties. The favourite weapon on those sorties was the Roman candle. They could be held in a gloved hand and aimed purposefully at the enemy. Like the popular song of the same name, 'Great Balls of Fire', their heavenward trajectory curved like tracer bullets across the night sky. Unfortunate warriors struck down by stray rounds out of the meteoric rise and fall of that deadly Dameon Shower were to be seen rolling around in the wet grass screaming for mercy. White flags were for wimps. No namby-pamby suing for terms would be tolerated in this man's army. The first assault was followed up swiftly by a barrage of tuppenny-canons, jumping-jacks and ear-splitting squibs, intent on their own serendipitous trajectories. While that was going on the oohs and aahs of the less rebellious children could be heard in the wake of star-scattering rockets and diminutive Mount Etnas spitting and spluttering through their streams of lava and smoke. The night was a riot of sound and unaccountable colour. Despite all the previous rain-soaked fears it was to be considered as a success. Except that is for one poor lad, who in the absence of the necessary years required for the build up of practical knowledge, had decided in his naivety that Swan-Vestas and bangers could share the same pocket with impunity. Events were to prove him mistaken. On tripping over while frantically waving handfuls of sparklers in the air the offending pocket and a knob of hard earth made acquaintance with each other. On impact the Swan-Vestas ignited, these in turn - as is the usual sequence of events in

37

such matters - did ditto to a pocket-full of bristling fuses. Fortunately for the boy - who was by now writhing around on the ground giving a fair impression of the verbal restraint exhibited by stuck pigs – quick-witted adults had the presence of mind to pull his trousers down over his unforgiving boots. The sight of that lad slithering bare-arsed across the wet grass closely followed by his exploding trousers was a vision never to be forgotten. The iconoclast has not been born who could shatter the deep, spiritual satisfaction associated with that sacrificial image. The fiery immolation of the guy itself - with all the undertones implicit of paganism - could not compete in kind with that striking portrayal of a juvenile Via Dolorosa. Luckily injuries sustained - other than those to his pride - were negligible. To this day warnings about the dangers of fireworks pervading the air-waves on the well-meaning voices of TV pundits, brings vividly to mind not only that lad's trouser-less, knobbly-kneed embarrassment, but also the thousand and one blue-eyed indiscretions committed in the name of gunpowder, treason and plot.

The days following the event - especially if of the school-less variety - were almost as exciting as November-the-Fifth itself. The surrounding countryside was scoured for the burnt out remains of the once majestic bonfires. Within the rocket-falling, banger-throwing radius of those sacred ruins were often to be found the relics of the previous night's festivities. Working on the maxim that you can't get enough of a good thing, the season of sun-propitiating ritual, was prolonged for as far into the distance as possible. Trophies were collected and disposed of in the traditional ear-shattering, smoke-belching manner. Embers were stirred, fuel added, and fires revived. Around the rekindled flames - flickering with the lambent glow of smouldering memories - parleyed the indigenous worshippers. Talk of burnings at the stake, smoke-signals and baked hedgehogs proliferated. Mention was made of the walking on fire initiation ceremonies performed by certain exotic tribesmen. Someone suggested a reenactment in the name of authenticating our proclaimed savagery. The potential headhunters amongst us prepared ourselves by war dancing in the peripheral puddles. Those too young or thought of as unworthy - for whatever reason - to participate in this particular rite continued to occupy themselves by raking out the hot, glimmering coals. Words of encouragement were offered, strongly laced with insults for those thought to be tardy in the performance of their sacred duties. The task proved to be well within our capabilities and a number of runs were made. Sparks flew and cheers followed. Not satisfied with the effectiveness of wet-shoed magic a bare-footed attempt was proposed. I for one thought it rather unnecessary. But not wishing to lose face in front of the assembled multitudes, agreed to give it a whirl. That day I came closer than I have ever been to achieving the Olympic qualifying standard for the hop-skip-and jump. I have since received correspondence from articulate kangaroos complimenting me on my near marsupial agility. The sound of my post-ceremonial feet sizzling through the grass was no less sibilant than the noise to be heard coming from a nest of disgruntled vipers. The sight of pustulant, discharging blisters has the same mortifying effect on me now as it did then in the days subsequent to that inflammatory event. Slippers and a footbath are now my constant companions.

Somebody else tormented to distraction during that season of witches and whizzbangs, was a poor, wretched, dishevelled old lady known locally as Topsy. To all of us children she was definitely a witch. Whether or not she wore the tall pointed hat that my reminiscing mind so richly adorns her with is hard to say for certain. But the long black cloak, from its silver clasp at the neck, to its frayed edges trailing along the ground, is without a doubt no imagined garment. She lived in a house about mid-way along the bridle path between Pitsea and my own estate. If you saw it now you wouldn't believe that anyone could have lived in it. Although brick-built and slate-roofed - a rarity thereabouts - It had as they say, seen better days. Windows were either cracked or non-existent and hung with rags of hessian. The roof had as many slates missing as it had intact and was neither impervious to light or rain. One corner of the house had split open from the eaves to the damp course and the equally derelict character of its insides could be seen through the gaping brickwork. Set in its own copse, comprised mostly of elm and hawthorn with a couple of stag-headed ancient oaks for company, it had all the appearance of a setting for a story penned by the Brothers Grimm. Down the bridle path there was a general store known locally as the back shop. One of my not too infrequent chores was to visit that shop whenever my mother had forgotten anything on one of her own shopping expeditions. The dread of bumping into Topsy on any of those excursions was constant. I've run faster past that house than Roger Bannister's shoelaces. Once, at full-pelt, I met her coming towards me on the curve of a sharp S bend in the path. Unfortunately, at that point, the path cut its meandering way through a blackthorn thicket. Veering off at an angle - and in need of a machete and a pith helmet - I left a boy-shaped hole in the hedge only to come out on the other side streaming with blood and as prickly as a porcupine. On another occasion - being more courageous than usual - owing to Eddy's older brother Reg being with us - we crept into the copse and taunted her from behind the relative safety of the trees. Much to our terrified surprise she was much quicker on her feet than we expected. She came screeching out of the woodshed - axe in hand - like a reincarnation of Boudicca. "I'll kill yer, yer little barstards," she croned. Before our legs - in my case and Eddies, very little legs at that - could overcome the lack of traction, she let fly with the axe. To my heathen amazement, my swift and extremely breathless supplications in the direction of my Maker were answered in full and the hurtling weapon bounced harmlessly of the bole of a life-saving tree. "May the saints preserve us!" as my mother used to recite in moments of high anxiety. Needless to say, our shocked selves, and the far horizon, were soon to become acquainted. It was rumoured in the neighbourhood that this old lady and water were natural enemies and that periodically she was taken into

40

hospital by the authorities to be scrubbed, fed, and checked out in general. During one of those enforced absences, we decided - cowards that we were - To take revenge. We 'acquired' a couple of short scaffold-poles from one of the building-sites on our estate and made off in the direction of demolition. It was easier than we thought. The mortar had lost most of its adhesive properties. Very little in the way of ramming and levering was necessary before the cracks in the brickwork became crumbling holes. That was just another episode in the sorry history of my childhood that I'd far sooner forget. If anyone was a candidate for Bell, Book, and Candle in those days, then it was I. It seems strange to me now that I didn't even think of it as wrong. I made up lies in the confessional, inventing mere peccadilloes because the priest wouldn't believe in my pleas of innocence, yet it never occurred to me that I had committed enough real sins to keep the staff at the Vatican on overtime until well after The Second Coming!

To my remembering mind the culmination of that season so resonant of the 'Old Religion' always coincided with that other recusant activity - mushrooming. The emergence of those mysterious subterranean entities - whose phallic symbolism though not fully understood, was nevertheless immediately recognized and commented upon - signalled the commencement of a form of worship more associated with the Twentieth Century than anything to do with our mythic past. Money! What else? My idolatrous relationship with 'the root of all evil' started at an early age and mushrooming was one of the highlights of the fiscal calendar. Some of the less scrupulous local greengrocers were prepared to buy them by the sack-load. How much they paid for them I can't recall now, but you can rest assured that it was considerably more than the starvation wages offered by that scourge of the under-aged and oppressed classes; namely, the newsagent. The Essex marshes in autumn - and in my opinion at all times of the year - were a wonderful place to inhabit. Before the ravages of Dutch-Elm disease those tall, stately, undulating, top-heavy trees added a rhythm to the otherwise more monotonous music of the level deltas. Rooks and jackdaws joined in with the pitch of their raucous voices and the shallow pools of standing water were replete with the echoes of a sky-wide symphony. Redshanks tewked, curlew fluted, and shelduck curved into shrieks of eerie laughter. Creeks were sinuous, dykes deliberate, and fleets feathered with whispering reeds. On the slightly drier meadows - much grazed by cattle and nibbled by horses and rabbits - grew the desired crop. Sometimes the harvesting would be a mob-handed affair but on other occasions I would work alone. Although I had no shortage of friends - even when I was quite young - I often felt the need of solitude. The uncharitable amongst you might think that that had something to do with wanting to keep all the mushroom money to myself. How dare you, think such a thing! No, the truth is that even at a tender age I communed with nature as easily as I do today. I did not have then, or have now, any need for guru or priest to instruct me in the arts of spirituality. Any sense of alienation suffered in my life has invariably found its cause in other human beings, nature and myself have always existed in continuum. When out and about in God's great wilderness the only time I'm affected by the meaning of the word vacuum is when my spiritual refreshment needs supplementing with a cup of coffee from the flask. Spontaneity of response and oneness are second nature to me. My only fear is, that the void - some would say abyss - between my then spiritual awareness and my then intellectual development may have unwittingly been the cause of much of my secular misery. To me all mushrooms look alike. To unscrupulous greengrocers - perhaps with enemies in the community, or long-suffered nagging wives - field-mushrooms, yellow-staining mushrooms or destroying angels are all - give or take a stomach-pump or two - substantially the same. Sell them I did by the hundredweight. But eat them - never! Even now when walking through that marshland cemetery - with the quaint nostalgic name of Dicky Bird Hill - The memento mori of the ubiquitous skull-and-crossbones transubstantiate in front of my guilt-ridden eyes into the cups and stipes of highly toxic fungi. R.I.P. until we meet again!

A Scottish friend of mine tells me that where he lives people from Essex are 'affectionately' known as Clay-Kickers. Some may take umbrage at such nomenclature, not I, I for one am proud of my somewhat tacky heritage. It seems that Essex clay was the main reason why the area had relatively few large working farms and was more suited to smallholdings, plotlanding and other forms of pseudo bucolic endeavour. Due to the Depression - and other things best known to students of agricultural economics - farmland was not in as great demand as was usually the case. Consequently, the best land got sold off first - and as is the way with supply and demand, or so they tell me at the Adam Smith institute - the worst land failed to reach the asking price and was either left fallow or taken out of agriculture altogether. Far-sighted speculators - who were obviously in dire need of the services of an optician - bought thousands of acres of that potential hard-pan and divided it up into plots to sell to Londoners looking for somewhere to build their summer dream-homes. In conjunction with The London Tilbury and Southend Railway, weekend excursions were arranged to show the prospective buyers the advantages of country living. For some reason, whether it was to do with the ague, the infertility of the soil, or a surfeit of inbred, indigenous idiots, sales were slow. In fact they never really gathered momentum at all. And that accounts - I think - for the miscellaneous patchwork of thorn-thicketed, grass-tufted territory that I was to become heir to. Those who did buy, build and stay in the area - whether for purposes of tax-avoidance, family evasion, or even genuine agricultural interest - were soon to find out, as all of us unsuspecting immigrants did eventually, something of the intractable nature of Essex-clay. In summer it was a rock-hard, dust-blowing desert. Owing to shrinkage it formed a reticular moonscape of interlinking chasms. Some of these were so wide and deep that newcomers could be recognized by a grimace and a hobbling gait. It's rumoured that one smallholder lost a gaggle of geese and his mother-in-law down one of those abysmal trenches for a week. But that could be the elderberry wine talking. Sufficient to say that for those interested in market gardening, you'd probably find more tilth on a greengrocer's scalp! With regards to the season that concerns us now we have to shift into the diametrically opposite mode. Wet, cold, claggy, and pretty near impervious to rain, is a fair résumé, I think. But for my fellow agrarians and me this was the ideal soil-profile. To walk across those late autumn-cum-winter fields was as to step into your father's shoes. The accumulated weight of the adhering clay built up to the point where the equation of legs + boots + gravity = dry feet, became untenable and was as insoluble as infinite regression itself. The leaving of boots behind and squelching off into the mire was all part of the ten-toed, mud-oozing, morass of mathematics. "Take that," splat! One of the boys having grabbed a handful of clay from his retrieved boot had scored a bulls-eye. "You filthy pig!" I responded. Throwing an even bigger handful back in his direction. Somebody else would join in and before you knew it everyone present had got in on the act. Between the sucking sounds of mud and the wet slap of direct hits, expletives buzzed through the air like black satanic bees. "Shit!" "Damn!" "Bollocks!" "Sod it!" It would end in tears. And it did. It always did. One of us, or two of us, or all of us, would fall headlong into the glutinous furrows. Then the heart-stopping realization of our predicament would dawn on us. Another tricky arithmetical calculation would have to follow. Wetness + mud + clothes + parents was as near an insoluble problem as that of infinite regression or even Zeno's inscrutable arrow itself. Though not the time of year for skinny-dipping desperate situations required equally desperate remedies. Water over grass was usually the answer. Cold, but at least mercifully clear. Stripping off, scrubbing clothes and flesh, turning blue and purple, was all part of the teeth-chattering excitement. We never got fully dry or clean. We always ended up with thick ears, hot-baths and runny-noses. Lying in bed - earlier than usual - sniffing and whimpering, you swore to yourself that

44

you would never, never, ever, do such a stupid thing again! But of course you did, you did........

Fog was another perennial joy. Schools have been known to close early because of it - guardians to be confused by it. Literally and metaphorically to my un-fathoming mind it is one of the most obscure and obscuring of nature's miracles. How by subtle shifts in temperature, invisible water-vapour - which to me is something of a contradiction in terms anyway - can become visible water-vapour is like having your cake and conjuring it out of thin air at the same time! Having tentatively dabbled at the keyboard of a microprocessor I'm patently aware that you don't necessarily have to know anything about the scientific principals lying behind something to gain benefit from it. So it is with the word-processor, and so it was with invisible water-vapour. "Where are yer Eddy?" "Over 'ere, where d'yer fink?" So it went on. Like binary black holes we revolved around each other, spared only from the crushing weight of oblivion by virtue of our equal and opposing gravitational influence. Along the bridle path a muted, indivisible cloud of overhanging branches mimicked the ways of rain. At the slightest breath, the once intermittent drops altered their frequency. As in the lull after thunder they gathered their strength and spattering momentum only to descend *en mass.* "Bloody 'ell Eddy, I'm drowned!" "Me an' you bof mate. Let's get out of 'ere!" Coming together again, like twin apparitions newly evolved from the diffuse unknown of the astral-plane we ran along the path as the sole inhabitants of our own grey bubble of thoughtlessness. "What shall we do next Merv?" enquired Eddy. "Let's go an' look at the one-eyed man," I said. "Not me!" replied Eddy in quivering castrato. "What's a matta," I taunted. "Not scared are yer?" "Who me? I aint scared of nuffin," he countered. He was though, and so was I. One of the greatest games of do-and-dare in our neck of the woods was that of confronting the one-eyed man. This - as I see it now - shy, reclusive, old soul, lived on his own in another of those near uninhabitable dwellings scattered about the plotlands. In the deep, hushed unwelcoming dankness of that foggy, late November day, that lopsided box of a home made up of little more than pebble-dash and tin reminded me of the immortal - but ill-remembered words - of that much anthologized and much quoted poem by Thomas Hood - November. No sun, no moon, no gas, no coal, no light, no warmth, no way! "Praps we could do somefink else?" I suggested. "Scared are yer?" came the triumphant response. Rather like the atmosphere itself there seemed no way out. "All right then," I said, "Let's go!" Just how that poor old man came to have the terrible disfigurement I'm about to describe, I don't know. What I do know is the spine-chilling effect it had on all of us children. One side of his face was red and blotchy, and hung with loose wattles of folded skin. Above that was a dark unseemly orifice, which drew us in with its hypnotic power to the very brink of corruption. If a wriggling mass of worms and maggots had come spilling out of that eyeless orbit we should not have been surprised. The closer we got to his home, the further we were from sanity. All sorts of imagined disasters crept in to our distraught minds. Looking through the bushes into his front window we could see him at his table carving a lump of meat. To me that lump of meat could have been the carved remains of any of my erstwhile acquaintances. Unaware of our presence he began to eat his meal. The sucking sensation of canines and incisors tearing at my goose-bumped flesh was as real as it was electrifying. "Ow! yer little bastard, get yer teeth out of me arm." Such was Eddy's juvenile sense of humour. Whether or not it quite compensated for the reciprocal blow to his ribs, I wouldn't like to say. All that can be said is that the resultant yell was enjoyed far more than the preceding laughter. This of course had the less than desired effect of attracting the attention of Vulcan's feasting Cyclops. His swivelling one-eyed glance had all the force of an impacting thunderbolt. The smithy's contract between Vulcan, Jove and himself had been fulfilled, and we were the unfortunate recipients. If running away could by any stretch of the imagination be called an art-form, then it goes without saying that we'd perfected it. We were once again about to experience that strange and somewhat disorientating thrill of high-speed fog jogging. To see one's pursuer in the light of day is frightening enough but to be continually looking over one's retreating shoulder into the fog-shrouded world of monstrous possibilities is petrifying. Waves of diffusing sunlight entered the space-time continuum of the enveloping foliage. Throughout the hurtling track of our converging trajectories the constelled glitter of condensing droplets followed our ill-starred progress. At a certain point in the proceedings the combined force of our accelerating mass crossed the horizon of that meteoric event and we vanished into breathless singularity.

After the fog came the first frosty days, those hoary outriders of the big snowed battalions themselves. Short-lived substitute that they usually turned out to be we nevertheless made the most of them. In those days of hot-water bottles and single glazing, winter windows - so our memories seem to tell us - were always opaque. Waking to a yellow painted bedroom and white frosted glass, I often fancied myself as the coiled element in a particularly drowsy light bulb. Having been switched on and illuminated by the wonders of whiteness, getting up was easier than usual. Rubbing the fern patterned glass with benumbed fingers the world outside was soon to be exposed. Gardens at that time of year were very much the domain of Brussels sprouts. Come on admit it, when you think of frost don't Brussels sprouts come leaping to mind? And if not, why not? They should do if for no other reason than Christmas dinners depend on the coincidence. I digress. Out there in the beak-bending answer to the name of grass, worms - with all the elasticity of six-inch nails - were for once in their wriggle-less lives safe from the marauding instincts of blackbirds and thrushes. That resplendent, shivering expanse -denied the luxury of deckchairs and daisies - was to minds of the lowest degree - of which I include my own - portentous of frozen puddles. They in turn conjured the rosy, glissading images of those scarf wearing and be-muffled skaters so inspiringly and eagerly depicted by

47

the Victorian artist. Where I lived there existed some of the biggest puddles in the universe. Even the ever-revolving swathe of the Milky Way itself paled into insignificance when compared with those hyper-galactic watercourses. Understandably breakfast was some thing to be skated through. "D'you wan't 'ot or cold milk wiv yer cornflakes," queried the lady of the house. "Cold please," I blurted. "But yer always hav' 'ot milk," she continued. "Well yes, but I fancy cold fer a change," I mediated. "What on a frosty mornin' like this," she challenged. What was the use, how could you tell a grown-up that that was precisely the reason why! Our two minds had the same polarity. On the surface there was everything in common but the closer and more often the contact the greater the repulsion. Age and understanding continually strove to drive us apart. The great Magnet in the sky had deemed it necessary that attraction was okay up to a point but that eventually every little iron filing had to find its own place in the pattern of things. "Yer can't go out yet, yer hav'n't finished yer breakfast," she implored. But alas the glint, Boreal frost-smith of the Pole had drawn my southern soul towards his craft. "I won't be long," I remonstrated, while all the time gathering my frictionless momentum. At the end of the long slide the Aurora awaited. And who was I to deny the charge of that particular electronic power?

The redoubtable Eddy and I found ourselves in that proverbial winter-wonderland so pertinent even now to the Peter Pans amongst us. The fairy-dust of a glittering winter's night had transformed the bleak reality of a dull and leafless landscape into the dazzling intensity of a glacial Never-Never-Land. A dispersing mist had left its frozen residue on the trees and hedgerows. The bifurcating tips of white-furred branches bristled in the diffuse sunlight. Spicules of shimmering ice drifted like dust-motes in the wake of alighting birds. Along the hedgerows the radial spokes of shivering cobwebs shone into infinite regression with all the sparkle of a set of diminishing solar-wheels. There, in that eerily candescent world of blue and white and gold, was the El Dorado so often found in the gilt-edged dreams of the eternal slide-maker. As always when one travels along the slippery paths of nostalgia, wish and outcome are bound to coincide. In the shape of the innumerable corrugated ruts to be found in the unmade roads of that bucolic yester world the Promised Land was encountered. Like manna from the very heavens the Ice Queen had performed her perennial miracle. The slides already in place were both long enough and wide enough for our slithering purposes. All that was needed was polish. Something that has to be said - that in our case at least - was in rather short supply. However, the attempt was made. Tentatively at first, like apprentice tightrope walkers, arms outstretched, in a teetering file of two, we inched along the frozen rut. Slowly, on gaining confidence, we gathered pace. Our erstwhile vacillations were forgotten. A run-up was selected and the trampled grass partially defrosted. From a flying start, ice and shoe-leather came together in unison. At first two-footed with the occasional twirl, then at a crouch, then on one leg, and then inevitably head over heels in a temporarily ego shattering tumble. Soon, inured against any amount of derisory laughter, an unwarranted optimism regarding one's capabilities concerning the *sports d'hiver* was attained. The fairy-dust itself was about to be transformed into a shower of shooting stars as the headlong giggling speed skaters inevitably became head-bumped sprawling imbeciles in an avalanche of tears. Those two bruised and battered athletes of Olympian stature were ready to settle for bronze. Peter Pan was in danger of growing up, El Dorado had been confused with iron pyrites and the golden beginnings of that crystalline day of enchantment had ended up by being tarnished with blood and abrasions.

Chapter 4 - Christmas Past.

If we were really lucky the first snows of winter came before Christmas, or even more rarely during the holidays themselves. But in truth they hardly ever came at all. The prevailing misery of North-Atlantic depressions and warm fronts were the unwanted and dispiriting prophecies of gloom precipitating from the despised mouths of meteorologists. Rain and wind, wind and rain. Rain and more rain. Wind and more wind. That was the continuous sorry track of our southwesterly existence. Respite came in the form of fitful ridges of anticyclonic hope, tantalizingly promising, but never delivering one speck of frost from the blue-moon rarity of their starlit nights. In that evergreen, ever remembered, time of year, grass occasionally grew, trees budded-up for spring and winter-greens sprouted from the gardens like the mocking tongues of self-righteous Martians. But Christmas was coming and the clangorous honking from the fat-yarded, feathery smallholdings proved that the geese were portentously aware of the fact. My major solitary pursuit of the season was window gazing. Whether the windows in question were the tree-lit and tinselled ones of the domestic hearth or the eye for the main-chance glittering transparencies of commercial insincerity, it didn't matter much. Whenever freed from the shackles of familial restraint and allowed to venture out into the darkness on my own, I could be seen wandering the sublunary December streets like the lost and fallen image of Bethlehem's most celebrated astronomical occurrence. Even now, thinking of such simple things as coal-eyed, carrot-nosed snowmen, puffs of cotton-wool, stuck and askew, against plate-glass windows, or star-spangled revolving mobiles, brings the whole ethereal event sharply back into focus. Then, there was wonder indeed. Walking those magical streets I inhabited a dimension only to be returned to fleetingly in those moments of heightened awareness that age and a surfeit of alcohol allow. Without the aid of any known stimulant to man, other than the innate

50

hallucinogens of spontaneity and relative innocence, the gateways of perception were open. Angels were indeed possible, conceptions could have been immaculate, and even the enforced dogma and doctrine of my hair-shirt upbringing seemed for once founded on some unshakable truth.

The time for wishes had arrived. Kitchens themselves partook of the season and became just as otherworldly. The spice-laden mixtures were stirred. Eyes closed and supplications made. If the letter to Father Christmas failed, this would surely do the trick. Puddings the size of cannonballs were swaddled in muslin and immersed in great bubbling copper cauldrons. Ovens were racked from top to bottom with mince pies and sausage rolls. Smells were exotic and intoxicating, cinnamon and sherry, brandy and cloves. Smells that any self-respecting Bisto Kid would follow unflinchingly to the ends of the universe. Drunk on the yuletide elixirs I watched as the icing was poured, patted and scrolled onto the cake. I sang as the red-lettered words of greeting were inscribed and the sprigs of artificial holly thumbed into place. My mother took on a new countenance. Gone was the neurotic ear slapping she-devil of old. Here was the apotheosis of womanhood. Man was relegated to the blubbering ranks of the newborn or to a bumbling, white-bearded, stuck up the chimney sort of avuncularity. This was the time of the Goddess and for this brief period at least - not forgetting that other season of celebration, namely my birthday - I worshipped at the adored feet.

The begging-bowl of Guy-Fawkes was about to be changed for the more respectable collection plate of the caroller. Eddy and myself, with his older brother Reg for protection, and other too numerous to mention imitations of the Dickensian waif descended, like a flock of discordant cherubs, onto the hapless population. Partakers of pre-Christmas, drug-induced snoozes, were about to be rudely awoken. After a nerve-shattering volley of knocks against the intervening door, a perfunctory chorus of Adeste Fideles rang out from the cracked bell of our tremulous voices. Suspicious bleary eyes peered from the chinks in the curtains, then disappeared again. A nervous shuffling of feet ensued. "Shall I knock agin Merv," inquired Eddy. "Praps we should try annuva chorus first," I said, sheepishly. "Alright then afta free," said Eddy's brother. "One, two, free!" .... "Why don't you effing kids piss orf," countered the staggering, light-bathed, apparition in the rifted doorway. "We're singin' fer the church mista," I profaned. "Yer don't look like choirboys te me," said the unusually astute low-browed adversary. "It's the truf," I muttered. "We're collectin' fer the old folks Christmas party, aint we lads." "That's right mista," came the for once unified, and as it happens, somewhat ecumenical response. "Clear orf, 'fore I set the dog on yers!" was all we got by way of charity from that legless representative of Proto-Christianity. If alms were to be obtained we should have to try elsewhere. As we left the lamp-lit streets of the estate and moved off into the outback our beaming elf-like faces dimmed accordingly. Don't for one moment think that we were the acme of carol-singers. We weren't. To have been rigged out in scarves, gloves and tossel-hats, would have offended our sense of sartorial decorum. Well-scuffed, grey-flannel trousers, frayed wooly-jumpers smelling of mothballs, and the navy-blue balaclava were by far the most favoured apparel. If you're thinking in terms of swinging lanterns swung from the ends of beribboned poles – beware, you may well be romanticizing! Candles we had in plenty, matches by the pilfered box-full. But matches, candles, and damp December winds are not - it would appear - allies! Tenacious little brutes that we were, we persevered. The striking of matches, the flickering into life and guttering out of it again of candles, intermittently illuminated the darkness. During the blacked-out eternities, made almost palpable by this unreliable source of light, could be heard the snuffing pinch of licked and sticky fingers and thumbs as stubborn wicks and hot wax took their toll. Eventually, sheltered from the wind by an enormous privet-hedge, we stood in front of one of those desolate plotland properties. Matches were struck again, candles lit and throats cleared. We decided to be more traditional and sang a verse or two before we knocked. This had the desired effect. The old lady of the house was actually pleased to see us! She asked if we'd like a glass of ginger beer and a mince pie each, which we gratefully accepted. " And who are you collecting for dears?" she asked, and in that season of 'peace and goodwill to all men' - and old ladies, incidentally - I drew on the latent wellspring of my as yet unfathomed humanity. "Fer ourselves," I gushed. Could it be true? Were all those parables to be believed? She gave us thruppence each and wished us all a very merry Christmas. Doubts had been cast and that age-old struggle between good and evil was to commence anew. To be, or not to be - honest - that is, that was the question. We came as close as a rabble could to taking a vote on the matter; and for the sake of our newborn - as opposed to born-again spirituality - honesty was decided upon. But in actuality - as all liberal, freethinking philosophers will concur - every case had to be treated individually. Moral philosophy - even then - was a treacherous subject. To this day I am still susceptible to its many pitfalls. To my mind the only really black and white issue - existentially speaking - concerns the renewal of my television licence. But that's another story, as the bishop said to the lady in the detector-van! Whatever, whether requests for alms were based on truth or falsehood, faith or doubt, carol singing was as much a part of the season as tangerines and red-nosed reindeer. That glimmering band of hopeless youth travelled the shadowy byways of December confronting remuneration or rebuke in the same wholehearted manner. Christmas was coming. Yea, verily I say unto to you; Christmas was near upon us!

According to custom, decorations should not be put up until Christmas Eve. As my parents will tell you this is a custom that's pretty near impossible to adhere to. I think I first started to pester my mother with regards to this seasonal activity - in those less than liberated days fathers had little to do with the process - sometime around Bonfire-Night. Her way of coping with such insistent demands was to shut me in the spare-room with a toppling stack of those coloured strips of paper gummed at one end. There with a tongue as taut and tacky as a glue-maker's jockstrap, I licked my way through seemingly endless miles of paper-chains. Most of which were never to come into contact with the ceiling, by the way. But I didn't care. This was an important task. Christmas depended on me. The time came of course - long before the date traditionally adhered to - when the decorating began in earnest. Little of today's dazzling array of mass-produced metallic gimmickry was available. Coloured coils of frilly crepe paper were to be unfurled and twisted into spirals. Chinese-lanterns were to be concertinaed into position. Balloons, long and thin, round or pear-shaped, were jaw-achingly puffed into existence, then pinned to the ceiling to display all of their titter-inducing, Phallic similitude. The tree - then as now - was the centrepiece of that extraordinary pagan ritual. On arrival it was immediately potted and set on a small table. This was the *pièce de résistance.* Like an ancient Druid in his sacred grove I communed with the spirits of Christmas past, and even earlier. It was a shrine to the god Pan. The Holy Babe but a contemporary manifestation of a far older, far deeper, spiritual hunger. The spirit of the wildwood was indoors. The faint atavistic echoes of tree-bound dryads exuded from every resinous needle. I danced goat-footed around that tree. I poured libations of cherryade and Tizer. I placed gift-wrapped, symbolic offerings at the roots of my shamanistic inheritance. Tinsel was cheap and skinny in those days - and still somehow appropriate to the chilling memories of our ghostly antecedents - but even then the flickering shadows of our future opulence fell from the flashing beacons of electric fairy-lights. But as yet the past was still with us as Christmas and Yuletide strove between carols and wassails to authenticate our mysterious origins. As I struggled on tiptoe to equip the tree with its surmounting star, I could feel the accumulated weight of different wisdoms as magi and priest vied for ascendancy.

For those to whom Christmas Eve is just the culmination of a prodigal season of humbug and hypocrisy, it would perhaps be advisable to skip a paragraph or two. For me Christmas Eve was the quintessence of a delirious, emotional, and imaginative unreality. Even the dreaded mass took on a new, and magical, midnight significance. The day started in a dream and ended likewise. There was no place for ambivalence. Belief was to be absolute. The house was aglow with expectancy. The grate was banked higher than usual and out of the glimmering embers flames of gold, amethyst, and methylated blue roared up the air-sucking chimney. Why I never made the connection between ascending flames and descending Father-Christmases I'll never know. Imaginative truth, I suppose. Decorations spun and swayed and twinkled in the heat. Misted windows trickled with glittering condensation and strings of greetings-cards displayed their compliments in various styles of red and green calligraphy. Holly prickled from the picture-rails; fruited in scarlet for that stirrup-cupped, horn-blowing revelry of a fox-bolted gallop of a day. Mistletoe was pendulous with impending kisses and I was at my long-spitting and lip-wiping best. On that day of delectable days even the once detested chore of helping with the shopping was volunteered for. At that slaughterhouse of a shop - euphemistically known as the butchers - carnage, carnivorous and carnival all came etymologically together in an unspeakable display of fur, feathers and flesh. Hung turkeys with scraggy necks glared their belated disapproval. Peter Rabbit's less literate and sophisticated cousins were closer that they'd ever been to a relationship with Baby-Bunting. Geese were honk-less, chickens devoid of cluck, and pigs without bodies grinned inanely at the expiring bite of sour apples. All of that meant nothing to the worm-slicing, wing-plucking, environmental scourge that I was. What to others might seem a veritable charnel house was to me no more than some vague unutterable statement of human supremacy. Feeling no need whatsoever to justify the ways of the world, meat tasted far better to me then than it does now. The excuses I make nowadays are rather abstruse, to say the least. Alas, my predatory past remains firmly with me and I lay the blame squarely at the door - or should I say, trap - of my dental configuration. What to blame when the need for dentures arises, is the subject of much devious rumination! Fortunately, unless one is squeamish about vegetables and their rights, the greengrocers shop is far less problematical. Here, in the world of the legume and the tuber, I feel much more at ease. In my youth however - as indicated earlier - it didn't matter much one way or the other. Butcher or Brussels-sprout merchant - both were unquestionable heroes in my book. To me the greengrocers shop held something of an all-round appearance of Christmas. Where in these northern temperate latitudes could one find such a tropical temple of colour and delight? If a humming bird flew off of the shelves and hovered over a potted-hyacinth, who would be surprised? But at Christmas the already sumptuous exotica was augmented. There, was the geography of the real world, and the geography of an inventive childhood. From exactly what corners - if corners, is not a contradiction in terms - of the actual globe, those fruits came from, I couldn't have told you. But in the forests of my imagination I knew every shrub, bush and tree. I lived in one of those vivid two-dimensional worlds so excitingly recreated in the paintings of Henri Rousseau. It was a tiger-striped, kaleidoscopically leaved world of chromatic intensity. Bananas were yellow tusks, walnuts, the fossilized brains of pygmies. Tangerines were the crazed orange eyes of long-extinct creatures haunting the frog croaking, bat-winged, under storey of a dripping rainforest. There were succulent figs, tempting apples, and the 'Spick-and Span' cleavage of round, ripe, juicy melons. I was in the grip of the serpent. It was paradise and I was soon to lose it. Still, as Milton said, what's lost can be regained, and who was I to argue with Milton?

As the evening approached the atmosphere was saturate with anticipation. Dew point was nearing. Soon the air would be precipitate with laughter and merriment. All weather would be good weather and even the rain-reviled forecasters themselves would be temporarily forgiven their meteorological sins. In the kitchen things were hotting up again. Squat and trussed in its baking-tray sat a plump, pink-fleshed capon. Turkey was out of our league at that time. But the capon itself was enough of a rarity to turn our minds away from the do-gooding, middle-classed, gobble-gobble-did -a lots on Snob's Hill. That's Clay Hill Road Vange, for those of you with an interest or a degree in ordinance-survey and cartography. A joint of beef as big as a battering ram was already lodged and sizzling in the oven; strange to think of the overdraft now incurred for even the slightest nibble of a salt-beef sandwich! Home economics and farm subsidies are still a closed shop to me, I'm afraid. In the living room, bottles of beer, spirits, port-wine and cordials were lined up along the clean-clothed and festive sideboard. Below, on the floor, was my domain. Lemonade, cream soda, Tizer and many another effervescent, bubbles up the nose, burp-inducing vintage awaited the frothing palate of the budding connoisseur. Loose sweets, fruit and nuts, nestled in glass and china bowls. Sugared-almonds - like clutches of new-laid eggs - were almost too much for this particular tree-climbing nest-robber. But all was to be left alone until after midnight and the traditional boot up the backside was the last thing I needed as an additional gift. Letters to the North Pole had specifically avoided mention of such unwanted presentations. To occupy ourselves before churchgoing we sat down in front of the television. That haunted fish-tank had already begun to take over the role of entertainment. Between my grandparents and myself, seemed to lie the transformational hinterland separating self-creativity and other more passive, vicarious forms of existence. Some parents, some aunts and uncles, some cousins even, could still play a musical instrument, sing a song or recite a poem from memory. Sadly, the indoor arts were gradually being lost and the fun of the great outdoors - which I so richly enjoyed - was soon to follow suit. Once our parents biggest problem was getting us in, whereas now they find it difficult to prise their offspring away from the magnetic influence of the flickering screen. How can they convince them that there is a world beyond the pixels, and that virtual reality is no substitute for the experience of the real thing? For all its claims towards modern technology the fuzzy 14" black and white set in the corner of our living-room had something of the air of a dishevelled, antiquated aunt about it, when seen in comparison with the otherwise bright and bountiful surroundings. The post-war sociological shift towards greater and greater prosperity for the working classes seemed inexorable. Who would have believed then - with the ration-book coming to a welcome end and the National Health Service already the envy of the world - that the Nineties and the Thirties would find themselves with so much in common? Crash! Bang! Wallop!

"Let us pray." .... The time for midnight mass was nigh. Church was never one of my favourite places. Not only did it represent hours of unrelieved boredom, but the apostolic order in its infinite wisdom had decided that we were to be bored in Latin! But on Christmas Eve even religion in a foreign tongue was tolerable. The ear-scrubbing, boot-polishing, tie-straightening preliminaries were as tedious as ever, but this was the holy night, the spirit was undaunted. Our church at that time - known as the Church of the Sacred Heart - was at the top of an unmade road leading on to Vange 'High Street.' The large brick-built church of St Basil's had yet to be constructed - more of that later. The Church of the Sacred Heart was no bigger than the prefabs we had left behind in London, and if my memory serves me well, made mostly of the same materials. I think it had asbestos side panelling - though on reflection they may have been pebble-dashed. It definitely had the luxury of a wooden roof though, with a cross to match. Inside at that time of year and especially at that time of night the atmosphere was decidedly ecstatic. In such a confined space, the ringing of bells, the shaking of incense burners, and the waxy fumes emanating from Advent-candles, combined to focus one's deepest spiritual attention. Before the mass proper there was carol singing, some in Latin and some in English. Drunks were not unusual and in fact greatly augmented the otherwise patchy congregations. Alcohol, swaying, and songs it appears, go together. Unfortunately, so do snores, belches and other unmentionable outlets for excess gases. Priests were used to this yearly outbreak of scurrilous profanity and took it in their reverential stride. Personally I was always torn between the seriousness of the occasion and the ensuing bathos that the involuntary bodily functions seemed to provide. Outright ribald laughter was out of the question of course, but the tittering escape of suppressed mirth was unavoidable. This too - in deference to the momentous events being symbolized - was excused. It seemed to me that the licence afforded at Christmas was something that should be granted to the rest of the year - although I never mentioned it as such. One doesn't to push one's luck too far, does one? What with the voices, the crib, the gold, frankincense and myrrh of it all, if Caspar, Melchior and Balthazar had come sailing through the nave on their ships of the desert, I for one would not have been taken aback.

On returning home through the moon-silvered and starlit Christmas streets, that sense of difference so much associated with that one night of the year was almost tangible. Windows for once, as well as receiving light were returning it in a multicoloured brilliance. Strings of illuminated bulbs looped from the eaves of the houses of the better off like nocturnal rainbows. Fairy lights winked from trees in coy corners and the glass-chinking, bell-ringing, riotous welcome to the joys of the Nativity rang out from shack and villa alike. Back indoors, the metaphorical ribbon of out tacit understanding was invisibly cut and the proceedings formally opened. Having fasted in preparation for Holy communion I was more than ready for my first sampling of the seasonal delights. Sausage-rolls and pickled onions were scoffed at an irreverent speed, closely followed by a cheek-bulging mountain of mince pies. The first gulp of Tizer - the juvenile equivalent to a slug of whisky - found its mark. Eyes watered, breath exploded, and a shower of froth and soggy crumbs plastered the surrounding revellers. Bed was suggested and not wishing to offend the Spirit of Christmas Future, I complied obediently with the request. Father, staunch Protestant that he must have been in the eyes of Rome – although, not in his own I hasten to add - hadn't been to church. His major role in the festivities was yet to be performed. Having never caught him in the act - so to speak - I couldn't tell you whether or not he dressed appropriately for that theatrical event. Suffice it to say that the sherry was drunk, mince pies were eaten and stockings filled. No further evidence would be needed on my part to validate the existence of that jolly old man of the north. Before one could delve into the expected treasures, the unwelcome dream-ways of a few hours sleep had to be negotiated. From my bedroom there was a clear view of St Michael's Church across the fields and copses. It was a typical Norman church, built out of Kentish ragstone. Perched on the top of its hill, floodlit and encircled by tall elms, it was the epitome of all that's sentimental in the British Christmas-card. In those days sentimentality came easily to me and I felt no need of shame in the face of it. Cynicism is something I've developed since and I'm not sure that I'm any better off because of it. Above the clock tower the prismatic sparkle of an auspicious star hung from the hook of a recumbent moon. Into those hopefully polar skies I cast my believing gaze. Many's the time in that borderland between sleep and wakefulness that I fancied I saw the desired configuration. The powers of the unfettered mind are indeed miraculous. Out of the rarified atmosphere of that heart-pounding starscape, sleigh and reindeers would materialize. St Nick himself could be clearly seen. Beard streaming and diffuse in the firmament like the tail of a glittering comet. Both hearts and chimneys it seems were large enough to accept that symbol of universal benevolence. Would, that it were always thus. If only, if only, if only.......

Morning - as is the quotidian way of things - arrived as usual. Although, usual in this case would be something of an understatement. In the light of today's wealth of high-tech gadgetry our treasures may have seemed somewhat tawdry.

But treasures they were and the mere act of remembering them fills me with excitement. The hours of fun and frustration gleaned from such simple things as those small metal Chinese puzzles would be an enigma to the screen-glued, button pushing conquerors of space amongst us. How would the whizz at the word-processor see the attempts of trying to un-jumble the letters of the alphabet just to get them in order in their tatty plastic frame? Little toy animals and people made up of pop-together segments. Black jacks and fruit-salads. Five-stones. Nuts and tangerines. All these and more poured from the bulging stocking while the main present still sat firmly beneath the tree orbited by a solar-system of baubles and beribboned packages.

Before long the world was all soda pop and liquorice. "Don't eat too much, yer won't be able to eat yer dinner," advised mother. Her lack of understanding concerning the insatiable appetites of children still amazes me. Okay carrots and greens and the likes might be difficult to eat wholesale, but chicken and stuffing and roast potatoes? I ask you! Let alone sweets and jellies and cakes! I spent most of my childhood trying to educate her about these matters, but her programming was almost robotic. "Didn't I just tell yer not to eat anyfink else?" she continued, somewhat predictably. My appetite wasn't affected. As dinnertime approached - we didn't have lunch on council estates in those days, by the way - if anything my hunger had increased. Setting the table, all thoughts of humble origins were forgotten. To my mind the spread wouldn't have been out of place in Buckingham Palace, Balmoral or Sandringham, or wherever the figureheads of state were going to pull their crackers and celebrate the occasion. Hand-made, home-crafted, artificial centrepieces sprouted their spiralling red candles. Holly-trimmed, paper serviettes from Woolworths had the look of the finest Irish-linen. Crackers, fresh from the gaudy stock of market-traders completed the illusion of nobility. For once in the year at least the Jones' had been surpassed, and I knew it. Pride bubbled from my pigeon-breasted, angel-throated strut through the carol-singing, all-praising kingdom of my princely heritage. Mother's head - held high in accordance with the customs of haute cuisine - stooped down to our level and with a voice like a gong reverberating through the serving-hatch, announced that luncheon was served. None of the gastronomic rules commonly adhered to in polite society were observed. Separate bowls for vegetables, gravy boats and the puzzling outside to inside cutlery arrangements were readily dispensed with in favour of the trough. A good nosh was what was wanted and the colloquialism received full and unequivocal justice. My only major complaint about the grand repast in general was the subterfuge resorted to by my parents on the thorny issue of the respective merits of legs or breasts. They were insistent that legs were by far the best part of the bird, and as a consequence of this - peerless benefactors that they were - the children were given them as a special treat. I didn't believe it then, and I don't now. I suspect that the scam is universal and that many of my readers carry out the same deceitful practices on their own suspicious offspring. "Heaven forbid!" I hear you say. "Heaven forbid!" Always, it seemed, when dribblingly engrossed with the most finger-licking, bone-stiffened morsel, mother would say, "Let's all pull our crackers." I warn you, repartee of the sort you might have in mind, was not, I emphasize, not allowable! If the matriarch wanted you to pull crackers, then crackers you pulled! And, I add, with as much good grace as you could muster. Greasy digits not withstanding, bangs were banged, sparks were sparked, and contents and mottoes scattered across the table, and beyond. "What's green and hairy and goes up and down?" "Don't know, tell me," "A gooseberry in a lift!" Laughter...... "What's red and round and rides a white horse?" I haven't got a clue, what is red and round and rides a white horse?" "The Lone-Tomato," more laughter....... Such innocence! Such simple pleasures! We all put on our paper crowns and bishop's mitres - the spirit of Saturnalia descended again and the unread, unknowing Lords of Misrule somehow mysteriously knew it to be so. Christmas pudding - never a favourite of mine - was not what you would have called a flaming affair in our household. Tradition dictated that it came in great steaming wedges, covered in lumpy custard. I was allowed jelly and canned-fruit as an alternative and was more than thankful for its wobbling merciful weight. Christmas pudding, carrots and cooked onions, all had the same retching affect on me in those days. If forced to try them - for my own good, I might add - my sympathies went out to the fat-livered, gagging geese of the Dordogne.

What did the nuclear family do on a Christmas afternoon? It was not the same as the extended affairs experienced at their headlong best throughout the protracted festivities at Granny Kerns'. If I were lucky in those days we'd go back to Canning-Town on Boxing Day and stay overnight. Sheer heaven! But this was Christmas afternoon in Pitsea and a child's need for continuous excitement was not to be catered for. The propensity that adults have for the mouth-wide, high decibel doze astounds me even now. For me sleeping is very much a horizontal phenomenon. How right-angled, chair-sprawling bodies can achieve anything more than a drowsy, irritable state of restlessness is beyond me. And yet, my parents were masters of this near transcendental art form. Catching flies would have been child's play. A flock of wood-pigeons would have disappeared just as easily down those pink, gurgling throats as they would have in a vast acreage of Brussels-sprouts! I was in Christmas limbo-land. Between the feast and the picking of the tree. Between the early morning trinkets and the expected enormity of my main present. Descriptions of purgatory so ardently given by nuns and priests alike moved out of the doctrinal shades into the realms of a sharply delineated reality. As yet, the Chinese puzzle had produced nothing more than frustration. Their fiddly interlocking curves defied all my problem solving and manipulative skills. The fun to be ascribed to the final solution of those inscrutable devices was a form of satisfaction yet to be attained. I threw them away in disgust. What next, my parents asleep, my brother elsewhere? That end of the rainbow world of glistening trove was mine for the taking. Permission was neither needed nor asked for. Once again I was torn, this time with trans-Atlantic associations - between the temperance league and the speak-easy - so to speak. The prohibited alchemical elixirs beckoned me in all their Faustian glory. I was about to sell my soul to a spirit, or at least to a fortified wine. The times I'd heard ladies ask for port and lemon, and never having seen them any the worse for sipping the concoction, convinced me of its so claimed medicinal benefits. I poured myself the required measures of lemonade and Portugal's answer to red-biddy and took a swig. In that scintillating emporium of all that makes for Christmas, I was about to discover that 'all that glisters' definitely isn't! In a relatively short period of time walls became malleable and the ceiling distended and contracted seemingly at will. Decorations, designed to spiral gently in the heat, took on the aspect of shimmering tornadoes. The lines of communication between stomach and epiglottis were fully opened and a dash was made for the toilet. The old joke about never eating carrots - a fact in my case - but always finding them in one's vomit was more than apparent. After making my emergency call down the white telephone I was astonished to see so many goldfish bobbing about in the viscous waters. The heaving echoes had woken both my parents who were instantly by my side with words of sympathy. "I told yer not to eat so much, yer stupid git!" was my mother's contribution to the annals of compassion. "Yer useless bleedin' cowson, yer give my arse the 'eadache you do!" was father's attempt at sound parental guidance. Fortunately, the speed of the poisoning so closely followed by its emetic consequences left me with nothing worse than a bad taste in my mouth and a balloon-like form of light-headed-ness. If suspicions there were about the cause of that sickening episode of alcohol and deceit, they were never mentioned. I suspect that a sense of rough-justice and lessons learnt was sufficient to satisfy the larruping instincts of my beloved guardians!

Now we come to the main event. Before tea we would unwrap our 'big present' and then pick the tree. If ever proof were

64

needed that anticipation and its object-in-reality were disappointingly dissimilar, then cast your minds back to some of your own Christmases. No doubt there were some absolutely wonderful presents but the ones that spring to mind are the real jaw-droppers. My own example concerns a pair of roller-skates. Santa Claus couldn't be blamed totally of course, and whilst ripping the paper and ribbons from the package, I was already gliding effortlessly along the boulevard thumbing my nose at all and sundry. How to describe that sudden hollowness in the pit of the stomach when they were finally revealed is a job for the poet - alone! Prose has not the linguistic resources for such a gargantuan task. It was there on the box, I can see it now, that dreaded logo so despised and repugnant to all eight-wheeled hopefuls. 'Jacko Skates'. Think of a Rolls-Royce Silver Ghost, then think of a Ford Popular. Even then you wouldn't be anywhere near to perceiving the difference between those ponderous prehistoric artifacts as compared with the latest models on the market. Metal wheels, as opposed to rubber, a pouch for the toes, and a leather strap and buckle for the ankles instead of lace-up - all in one - boots and skates. If being seen in them was a knock to one's credibility, then it couldn't be avoided. They were a present. They had to be used - or else! There was no such thing as a quiet pair of 'Jacko-Skates'. Anonymity was impossible. The clicking of metal wheels over the cracks in the paving-slabs was a dead give-away. Boxing Day would be a nightmare. Heads would turn, eyebrows would be raised and jibes proliferate. Our roller-skating rink in those days seemed to have been purpose-built - as was soon to be the case with all the individual estates making up Basildon *en masse* - a parade of shops had been constructed, and not just shops! More to the point as far as we were concerned were the wide paved areas, the long slopes - with prams in mind - and the hazardous stairways. I can see them now, the lithe Head Boys and Monitors burning rubber. I can see the pirouettes, the leaping splits, the crouches and the long glides. And most of all I can see the poised perfection of their rubber-toed athletic breaking. And there was I, clattering along like a lumbering

Blackpool tram, stopped only by brick-walls, unexpected flights of concrete stairs, or slow-footed perambulating mothers and pedestrians.

I felt sick again but what could I do? Kisses had been given and received, smiles exchanged and grateful thanks expressed. Such is the hypocritical side of Christmas. Not confined to the young alone, however. Any visit to the four-ale bar after Christmas and you could be forgiven for thinking that the assembled throng dressed in their latest woollen attire were all members of the Val Doonigan appreciation society. The un-matching ties and socks are also to be seen as testimony to the extent to which fawning insincerity has become an integral part of the gift-giving season. All was not lost. There was still the tree to pick. I could still salvage something from the wreckage of disappointment surrounding the 'Jacko-Skates'. First down and eagerly unwrapped was a gift from a formerly favourite aunt. Socks! Next - from another relative about to lose out on brownie points - white initialled handkerchiefs! Surely it couldn't get worse? A neighbour - with a dubious sense of humour; or else totally lacking in the skills required for present giving - decided on a pack of multicoloured soaps! This was getting ridiculous. Would I be able to contain my grief, my sense of outrage? Could fist clenching and foot stamping be avoided? I have to admit that in my ungrateful reckoning most of the presents received were more utilitarian that enjoyable - a hangover from wartime frugality, no doubt. Even my own parents didn't seem to know the difference between the gratuitous pleasures of frivolity and the dour solemnities of education. New-fangled, scratchy fountain pens, ink and erasers, were considered more important than cowboy hats or chocolate-money, see-through instruments for use in geometry lessons, rulers and exercise books, of greater necessity than matchstick firing toy field guns. Last to come down from the tree was an ominous looking cylindrical package. Yet another exercise book perhaps, or an indispensable list of dates and facts pertaining to the British Empire? No, that particular festive

66

day at least was to end on an up-note. It was a colouring-book and crayons. If nothing else Christmas Day would pass away under the blankets bathed in torchlight and accompanied by blue trees, green-skinned fairies and red-recalcitrant seascapes. My somewhat surreal approach to life was already gaining momentum!

Unless you're a cold meat and pickle freak, you may think of Boxing Day as something of an anticlimax. For me it entirely depended on whether we stayed at home or went to the wide-eyed wonderland of Granny Kerns in Canning-Town. Being as this book is - ostensibly, at least - about Pitsea-in-the-Marsh and memories of childhood concerning said parish, I shall confine my descriptions of the feast of St Stephen to the pseudo rusticity of that emergent New-Town. Regardless of the homebound locality there would still be diversions, even despite the fact that wren hunting was becoming more and more frowned upon in those unenlightened days. Non-educational presents were in need of exercise and the epicurean side of my nature was still cognizant of leftover confectioneries. Whether or not the unexplored pit of my abysmal stomach could cope with the sugary intrusions of any more of those sticky-fingered, liquorice-booted potholers, was another matter. Whereas Christmas Day was devoted more or less to indoor activities, on Boxing Day the outside world was once again to re-assert itself. Slowly at first, the spoked chromium glitter of a new bicycle would tick its freewheeling pride and superiority past the front porch. Then, the occasional blatancy of a promenading cardigan closely followed by a brum-brumming pedal-car. Before you knew it scooters were scooting, drums drumming, and of course miniature prams - in their own infallible skate obstructive fashion - perambulating. The high-pitched sounds of "Look what I've got," pervaded the post-festivity atmosphere. Excited children pedalled, pushed, and generally paraded their prized collective wares in all directions. I - as it happens – un-strapped my iron-wheeled appendages and went dejectedly back indoors. The next thing to be endured was Boxing Day dinner. Another of my feared culinary enemies was about to take the field in the form of lumpy mashed-potatoes. Those blanching dollops of sludge and fibre, mined with the offending and potentially explosive throat-blockers and encompassed by mounds of red-cabbage and piccalilli, had all the appearance - and who knows, taste - of battleground carnage. You may by now be well on the way to thinking of me as an especially difficult to please sort of individual. I wouldn't argue with you on that point. The psychological legacy of anticipation and subsequent disappointment lives with me still. Any tendencies I may have towards nihilism and cynicism can be traced back to certain formative experiences. 'Jacko-Skates', monographic handkerchiefs and lumpy mashed-potatoes, amongst other things, must take their share of the blame for my near pathological inability to confront the world with any sort of optimistic purview. Behavourists amongst you will be well aware of the effects of such early conditioning on the developing personality and will no doubt forgive me accordingly. No amount of latter-day good fortune has been able to extricate me from those incipient psychic patterns. If the worst can happen, it will. And if it doesn't, then it can only be the prelude to an even greater disaster. As I believe the famous American poet Robert Lowell once said 'If there's a light at the end of the tunnel, you can rest assured that it's that of an on-coming train!' or to quote my not normally aphoristic self, 'if money grew on trees, I'd have a wallet full of leaves'. My psychotherapist has done her level professional best to rid me of this almost paranoiac mind-set, but as yet the rationale is willing but the emotional responses are still unthinkingly triggered by the programming of the past. Tablets and the patronizing smiles of psychiatrists are still the closest approximations I have as regards to the ramifications of the word hope - let alone optimism! Although, if you've found yourselves thus far into this desultory and impenetrable book, you won't need me to tell you about the debilitating effects of 'Largactyl' and other mind-numbing anti-depressants. And of course the self-contradictory occupation of textual deconstruction will be of absolutely no help to you whatsoever. Better to try and understand the tenets of sub-atomic particle physics than to attempt a study of the inscrutable microcosm of my neuro-cellular instability. Just think of it as a breakdown in the Grand Unified Theory of literary appreciation and try to enjoy yourselves. What's all this got to do with Boxing Day - you're asking? Nothing, I reply, nothing. But if, as I'm assured by quantum physicists, that one thing can be two different things at the same time, that a theoretically spinning particle has to show the same side twice before you can see it once, or that in the beginning there was nothing - nothing mind you, not space, not time, not anything, absolutely nothing - and then a big bang and hey presto, the potential for everything. Then who cares? It's not worth worrying about, is it? After the rigours of lunch - or dinner as we so quaintly and unscientifically called it - the sense of the winding down, or to continue the insanity, thermodynamic decline of the Christmas Holiday, was all too depressingly apparent. Not for us the joys of a twelve-day binge. The decorations would be kept up out of loyalty to the spirit of ecclesiastical law, but the letter of it was - if not already - pretty close to being dead. Epiphany may have been all right for The New Testament. It may even have been a good story; but as far as we were concerned in that mass-produced, post-war Christmas of ours, it was the partridge that had gained ascendancy. The twelve drummers could go rat-a-tat-tatting all the way into obscurity along with the twelfth-cake and all other vestiges of arcane reverence! The pear tree had definitely been defoliated. All I had to look forward to was New-Year, and even then, the chances of someone of my age seeing anyone first-footing it over the midnight threshold with a lump of coal in one hand and a glass of whisky in the other were minimal, to say the least. In fact there would have been more chance of finding the Eleven Pipers Piping at a Burn's Night temperance meeting! No, that was it. The fun had been had and the sweets eaten. School loomed and so did the dentists, the addition of fillings and the subtraction of teeth only to be mitigated by the miserly visits of a parsimonious tooth fairy. As my fears for the future multiplied my division from the past was creating its own equations of doubt and alienation. None of which were to be fully resolved. The wooden stairs to Bedfordshire would have to be climbed again. The sandman would come only to fill my dreaming eyes with handfuls of grit! Winter had surely come, but would spring be far behind? I doubted it - oh - how I doubted it!

Chapter 5 - 'If Winter Comes'

Being aware by now of the vicissitudes of my temperament you will not be surprised to find that my lack of optimism was invariably rewarded by the answering of my most fervent prayers. All this of course added to my secular and spiritual confusion. I'd prayed for snow, therefore it would probably rain. I awoke to the beginnings of another year, and what do I find? The country had come to a standstill under the drifting immensity of my crystalline wishes! More important than that, school itself had become victim to the self-same slithering good fortune. Much to the chagrin of my warm-blooded - and in this respect at least, soulless, kith and kin - snow and yours truly have always shared an affinity. I can still be seen - by shiftworkers, insomniacs and cat burglars in the main - tramping the snow-laden streets in the early hours of January mornings as if in reality my growth hormones had been bypassed and what you see now is the magnified and illusory image of my diminutive former being. Snow! Snow! Snow! What is it about the stuff? There is nothing quite so featureless in the whole of creation - unless you're prepared to include the minimalist movements in art and literature - as snow. Perhaps the innate hyperbolism that I suffer from has need of its muted and unifying influence. I don't know! But love it I do now, as much as, and perhaps even more than I did then. Or is it just some sort of slippery time warp, a sort of tin-tray, downhill hurtling towards a collision with the sensibilities of my erstwhile wintry self? It's a chilling thought isn't it? When you think about it, this very paragraph that you're reading now, suffers from all the same timeless, ever shifting juxta-positions exhibited by the incongruities of tense. Where was I, by the way? Ah! Yes! I remember, now.

Snow had been falling all night. An anticyclone over Scandinavia and low-pressure over Northern France had ensured that by way of an easterly gale the aforementioned falling was in fact somewhere between 45 degrees and the

71

horizontal. To the literary snow-freak the synopsis and the denouement's measurable results were as near perfect in relational terms as is possible. This was white-out weather! The blank page of all my textual dreams! I could see through the obscured glass of our front door the curving drift of the longed-for inclemency. The Eskimo in me was aroused. I would even have been able to rub noses with Violet Elizabeth herself, share my igloo with the Pope, or cut a hole in the ice that formed periodically in the parental ocean. Dressed in my best imitation Nanuk of the North cast-offs I mushed my imaginary huskies and cold-footed it out across the Arctic wastes. Eddy had already speared his third polar bear and was about to make a start on the penguins. I didn't like to tell him that they lived in different hemispheres; Eddy had a thing about smart-arses! Anyway, it was far too good a day to be wasted on pedantry and squabbling. Snow was being lifted in swirling gusts and carried like smoke on the back of an icy wind. In places, drifts had surmounted the wooden-pailings of the garden fences. Paradoxically, those parts of the field taking the full brunt of the blizzard were bared to green, springlike patches of grass. But spring it certainly wasn't! In the lee of the trees and hedgerows snow was knee-deep. Brambles were lagged with the stuff. Ditches were choked and dangerous in their seeming absence and where that raging Arctic sea had sprayed and spumed through gaps in the hedges, or had crested over high banks, it left in its wake a streamlined jumble of weird Boreal sculpture. Now like the colourless flukes of submerging whales, then like the slit-gills of great white sharks. The feathery weight out of those sagging pewter skies continually tumbled and drifted as it whitened and transformed my shifting reality. Heads down, inclined against the cutting blast, we struggled towards the North Pole. If ever I was to come to face with my arms akimbo, Ho! Ho! Hoing! benefactor surely my chances would never have been better. Like two abominable apparitions, lost and alone and happy, away from the prying eyes of priests, parents and Sherpas we began the obligatory snowball fight. Anyone who has ever indulged in such Siberian antics must know from experience that there is an inevitable progression involved - by the action of some infallible Parkinsonian law, the more compacted and swiftly thrown the snowball, the more immediate and violent the response. "Yer put a stone in that one you did!" complained Eddy. "Not me!" I protested. "Your just jealous because yer can't frow as straight as what I can!" Whack! "You bastard, that's an effing white 'ouse-brick, that is!" I cursed. Even now in middle age, if I hear children ner-ner-ne -nerring, I instantly feel the urge to thicken their insensitive ear lobes. "What's a matta wiv you then, don't yer like yer own bleedin' medicin'!" jibed Eddy. It was unavoidable. In the absence of seconds all pretence to the decorum bestowed by the Marquis of Queensbury were abandoned. Like a couple of white-furred blubbery seal-pups we rolled about in the snow, filling the air with our high-pitched prepubescent blasphemies. Throughout all our years of friendship, Eddy and I never really worked out our respective places in the pecking order. The unfortunate corollary of this fact was that our fights usually ended more through exhaustion than seniority. The resultant cuts and abrasions being far more serious and long lasting than they needed to be. If when being threatened with physical violence nowadays, you saw me grovelling and whimpering, whilst engaged in a cowardly back-stepping retreat, at least now you'd know the reason why. We have a lot to learn from our furry cousins, I think. They know their place and are happy with it. Effort should be expended in more profitable directions, I'd say -like writing books maybe?

From one white expanse to another, the struggle continues, the page waits patiently. It wasn't always just Eddy and myself as sole companions on those polar expeditions. Sometimes we would join forces with other frost-bitten explorers and like foraging polar-bears get up to mischief on the outskirts of town - especially under the cover of darkness. Even the collective wisdom of our community elders was not sufficient to put a spanner into our icy works. They thought that they were up to all our wintry ruses; we knew differently.

From our prone positions on garage-roofs, unsuspecting pedestrians - were to quote my poetic hero, Thomas Hardy - 'inurned by a volley of dislodging lumps'. Unable, after the event, to calculate the angles of trajectory they naturally assumed the assault to have come from ground level and reacted in the obvious rational manner. Had they have had the benefit of Edward De Bono's perceptive writings in those days the chances of discovering the perpetrators of those shivery crimes would have undoubtedly increased. As it was they ran around in ever-decreasing snow-blind circles issuing threats and ultimatums to their unseen, uncaring adversaries. On one occasion, Eddy's brother - and if my memory serves me well, mine also - rolled up one of those gigantic balls of snow so defiantly seen after a thaw inhabiting the opulent greenery of parks and gardens. A misdemeanour was about to be committed, accomplices were asked for and a number of large snowdrifts were levelled in the rush. There was no one-step-backing in those days. Where dirty deeds were concerned we had volunteers in plenty. The King could keep his rotten shilling, we'd join just for the hell of it. "Afta free!" said Eddy's elder brother. "One, two, free, lift!" and the deed was done. There it sat, a hundredweight of freshly tainted snow denting the roof of a bubble-car. Considering its more than grounded nature it seemed somewhat inappropriate to me in the circumstances that the vehicle in question should bear the appellation 'Mescherschmidt'. But without doubt being - as we were - so close to the end of The Second World War it certainly eliminated the need for guilty consciences.

Winters like those are not I suspect a thing of the past. I'm not in this instance just talking about global warming and the inferred ameliorating effects on our climate. Those of us in environmental greenhouses will always throw our conservational stones whilst driving our unleaded dreams or stacking more logs on the fire. No, it's the universal winter that I'm talking about. That white inviting wilderness of youth where everything takes on the colour of innocence except for the ruddy-faced urchins who inhabit its mischievous corners.

Children will always find more to enjoy in winter than the adult. Bound by the supposed freedoms of our supposed civilisation we lose contact with the icy realities. Weather is something to be endured. Mastered even. We seed the skies, dam the rivers, and insulate our homes and ourselves against the dreaded onslaught of an ultimately - we hope, or should I say some hope - controllable nature. But deep inside the human heart - for the searchers of truth, questers of the Holy Grail, brimming with rejuvenating liquor - still falls the snow of a white-enlightening childhood - a reminder of that naked confrontation with the dangerous elements that we so much fear and yet unaccountably desire. Snow! Snow! Snow! That all engulfing oneness of our innermost necessity, that outward sign of inward grace, that chilling link to the past of all pasts, still so tacitly adhered to by the child in all of us.

One last recollection of my earliest winters may serve to illustrate the differences between the childlike acceptance of things as they are and the later habits of the theoretical and categorizing mind that we're all so debilitatingly heir to. Having no Catholic schools or churches of any size in the area in those days, when I volunteered for something with supposedly civilizing attributes; namely, the cubs, I had to join a Protestant group. On a bitterly cold winter's night, after rain having turned through sleet to a dusting of snow, then clearing to a frosty and starlit sky, I arrived outside St Michael's church hall. Already there, were a group of slide-making, capped and toggled, cavorting veterans. In no time at all I was made to feel welcome. With all the lack of self-consciousness so often found amongst young children I was soon absorbed into the fraternity. Without the need of questioning anything other than things of immediate consequence an outsider would have thought I'd known those boys since birth. Things, as you may have already gathered, were about to change for the worse. The Cub-Master opened the doors and invited us in. That smiling, friendly man asked us to form a circle and to start the proceedings by reciting The Lord's Prayer. Foolishly, because of my own prejudicial

75

brainwashing, and the consequent fear of sin, I admitted to being a Catholic. "I think that you should go and stand in the corner until we've finished praying," he pointed. "But I aint dun nuffink wrong," I protested. "We are a Church of England pack," he continued. "I'm afraid we can't pray with Catholics, it's a sin." "Yer could always go ter Confession," I said, innocently. I'd suffered and contributed to all the Cat-lick and Proddy-dog banter before, but there was something particularly despicable and demeaning about that memorable episode. Seldom had I felt so lost and alone as I did then. I left that hall and went out into a cold night air that seemed far, far colder than it had when I was larking around with the rest of the boys earlier in the evening. I never returned. But the form of religion I already knew and feared took on - as well as the one I'd just become acquainted with - even more sinister undertones. Dib-dib-dib! Dab-dab-dab! Dob-dob-dob! .... Load - tup three! Aim - tup three! Fire!!!

Although still in the depths of winter, Candlemass (February 2nd) seemed to me to be the beginning of spring. Formerly 'The Purification of the Virgin' it was the time in the Roman Catholic Church when all the candles needed for the coming year were consecrated. To us they were symbolic of Jesus Christ himself so often referred to as 'The Light of the World'. In the vicinity of where I lived it was about that time that you could find some of the earliest wild flowers. Along the ditch banks celandine shed their early galactic light. From cold, clay verges, coltsfoot thrust their premonitory stems and yellow, crew-cutted heads. Nettles, groundsel and chickweed sprawled amongst the shivery hints of their own unfurling colours and the miserly shepherd got ready to fill his purses. If you were lucky, confused bees or prematurely woken tortoiseshell butterflies, could be seen drinking from the gentle, toothless jaws of the much maligned dandelions. The occasional blue-eyed speedwell turned its iris to the sun and periwinkles did what whatever it is they do best from the shadowy bottoms of the plotland privet hedges. In the aspiring cottage-gardens themselves, crocuses opened their golden mouths and sparrows - unable to resist the gape-like nestling insistence of them, I assume - snapped them shut, or shredded them, or ate them, or whatever else it is that witless sparrows do when springtime urges get the better of them. Snowdrops nodded their white whispering heads as if parleying on the fortuitous change in the weather while at the same time superstitious enough to want to keep the news to themselves for fear of wintry reprisals. Aconites offered solar warmth and the primroses were budded and ready to respond. Elders were showing their first green fists of leaves and the blackthorn waited to bloom with the spurious gift of winter wrapped in its crumpled flowers. Into that newly woken world I wandered around as aimlessly as possible. I sat in the sun-warmed glades under thrush-singing skies and waited for absolutely nothing to happen. And it did, for uneventful hours on end. It was there that I acquired the habit of idleness that I now prefer to call meditation. No such guilts in those days. If there was nothing to be done, then I was prepared to do it; or not to if you see what I mean? I've always been a solitary soul and I think that's why I eventually took up fishing. As any angler will tell you, the skill required for sitting on your own, motionless for inordinate periods of time with a free-floating purposeless mind, is staggering. The lessons learnt in those far off lazy days have been invaluable. Not for nothing was I once ridiculed as the laziest man in the universe. Little did the profferer of that insult realise that I would consider it as more of an accolade than a rebuke. Or that he would be thought of forever more, not as a foul-mouthed devil, but as my own, my very own, admonishing angel.

Spring, when 'the wise thrush sings twice over' and a young man's - or boy's in my case - fancy turns to thoughts of pancakes! The time for shriving had begun. Shrives, I committed in plenty, but alas, very few of them would be confessed. So absolution was not only unlikely, but in reality, impossible. Since cock-fighting was no longer considered a laudable pursuit, other equally exciting activities would have to be sought out and tossing the pancake was one amongst many. The humble pancake was not just a form of pre-Lent licence but also a religious rite in its own terms. Eggs, for creation, flour, for the staff of life, salt, for wholesomeness, and milk for purity. I couldn't go wrong. If I could eat enough of them without taking too much notice of the sugar and lemons, I would surely be saved completely. That's how I saw it anyway. My mother was an ace when it came to making pancakes. Being a religious woman she saw it as not only pleasurable but as a God-given duty. That of course made my ravenous task that much easier. If I could convince her that I was eating them on spiritual grounds - not an easy proposition in itself - I could more than line my limitless stomach with them. For your edification - sorry, I'm smart-arsing again - the word Lent comes from the Saxon. They called March the lencten monath (month) because of the lengthening days. Lent became lencten faesten because of the fast. Are you still with me? Now, I didn't know anything about that at the time but I did know about the forty days and nights Jesus spent in the wilderness and that that was why we fasted more than usual during Lent. If I promised - with no thought of keeping the promise, obviously - to give up sweets or some other such unliklihood for the period of mourning in honour of the time our Lord spent in the desert; and if my mother believed my intentions, then I would be on a winner. I suspect that I was never really believed, but the opportunity to get me to promise anything - and to see me grovel to boot - was something not to be missed. Whatever, the pancakes came, and they kept on coming. Thin ones, thick ones, doughy ones and airy ones. Lemon was squirted and sugar sprinkled. Teeth ground, lips dribbled and the roof of the mouth got claggier and claggier. Milk was drunk, burps burped, and eyes narrowed to the familiar refrain about their size in comparison to that of the consumer's belly. Thus was I fortified for the purgatory to follow. Laying in bed with a stomach ache to end all stomach aches, I pondered once again on the dubious wisdom of indulging to fully in the culinary side of religious festivals. Sleep that night was a fitful affair. A sweaty, sickly, tossing and turning between the realms of opulence and frugality. Behind me lay the joys of Christmas, and ahead the looming terrors of the crucifixion. In that feverish half-sleep suffered by all who over-indulge I felt as though I had been trampled underfoot by the Four Horse-Riders of the Apocalypse. I was to awake eventually to a world where the days may indeed have lengthened, but where light as I knew it was about to dim through the cock-crowing of Gethsemane, and the agonizing slopes of Golgotha, all the way to the darkness of the very tomb itself. The words Lent and Death are to me almost synonymous. School and church in those six weeks of hell-fire and the Passion were pretty near unbearable. It started ominously enough when a balm made up of oils and ashes from last Palm Sunday's palms were thumbed crosswise onto our wretched foreheads. Any flickering of light I may have found in the church before had now been completely snuffed. Candles remained unlit. Statues and crucifixes were covered in purple drapes. My knees were to be punished daily by The Stations of the Cross. Prayers were to be prayed more fervently than ever, and gloom in every form imaginable to the prepubescent sinner was about to descend.

Outside of school and church there existed that other, older more heathen environment where spring was still to be worshipped for its own sake. Where symbols of death and rebirth didn't require the wearing of a hair shirt, and prostrastions were reserved for staring into ponds and ditches. Newts, frogs, toads and sticklebacks were to become the unfortunate receivers of my inquiring attention. What amphibians and fishes have done to deserve the wrath of humankind I don't know. But wrath, and worse, they suffered. Being no protector of creaturely privacies, I thought nothing of peering rudely at their most intimate activities. Croaking male frogs clinging on - inconsiderately and most unceremoniously, I may add - to distended spawn-laying females, were sure to rouse my interest. Prodding, poking, squeezing and leg-pulling those ghastly copulators, I found near orgasmic. Handfuls of black-spotted jelly were scrunched between slimy fingers and offerings made to deities of the anti-tapioca kind. Necklaces of toad-spawn were lifted and lowered and swirled. Hapless ambling toads were encouraged against their better natures to hop. Wide-mouthed, pop-eyed stares were picked up purposefully, then ogled and grinned back at. Talk of poisonous warts was talked and the necessary 'hubble, bubble, toil and trouble' recitations were made. Newts in Essex - and elsewhere no doubt - come in three varieties: smooth, palmate and great-crested or warty. I can't remember whether or not we had palmate newts in our neck of the woods - or ditches - but we definitely had the smooth and the great-crested species. We always called the smooth ones simply newts, and the great-crested - more exotically we thought - salamanders. Exotic they were, especially the males in the breeding season. Deep olive brown on top, silvery sides with a band of silver along the tail and bright orange underneath. They were also covered in black spots and for their crowning glory they had a crimped, rippling crest along their sinuous backs. What had they done to deserve us? What indeed! Strands of wool and wriggly worms were all you needed for equipment. I can see them now, waddling suicidally up from the murky depths. Gulp, and out they came with an inane smirk on their surprised faces! They were tenacious little brutes nevertheless. Once they'd got their greedy little gums into a worm they certainly didn't want to let go. Naturally, encouragement was forthcoming. A gentle squeeze was all that was required. Mind you, the sight of a lip-puckering salamander disgorging a well-bitten worm is not, I would say, a particularly pretty one! I have to say in all honesty that the zoological interest was negligible - probably a good thing.

Had I known their ability concerning the regeneration of lost limbs my twitchy fingers may well have been tempted to put them to the scientific test! The intrusion into their lives was normally kept within the bounds of - what seemed to us in any case - reasonable behaviour. The odd salamander race did nobody any harm, and they were probably grateful for the much needed additional exercise. And what salamander wouldn't relish the chance of seeing the world from a never before experienced tail-swinging vantage? No, compared with other creatures of my acquaintance newts definitely had an easy time of it. Perhaps even then I was dimly aware of that intemperate maxim that I was later to become staggeringly attached to. Pissed as the proverbial! Jam-jars replete with newts and tadpoles in various stages of development and other forms of wriggling subaqueous life, wouldn't be complete of course without the ubiquitous stickle-back. In spring these normally drab fishes change colour. For the female this means just taking on a yellowish tinge but for the male the transformation is nothing short of miraculous. The once dullish blue-black upper parts become a clear translucent green. The pale silverish undersides are set on fire by a vivid orange-red throat and the swivelling hypnotic eyes turn into a deep, electrifying shade of blue. Did that technicolour dream-coat of a fishy transubstantiation save it from our predations? No, without doubt it made it even more desirable. Did the fact that it made a nest for the female and guarded the subsequent eggs and hatchlings teach us anything about compassion? Sadly, the answer must again be in the negative. That glittering prize was hunted ruthlessly and strands of wool were replaced by threads of cotton and bent pins. The arts of real angling were to be experienced for the first time, and it has to be said, the frustrations also. Hooked fish don't always, alas, remain so. To see that quivering jewel sparkling in mid-air, only to flip, release itself and plop back into the water was near intolerable. To see it happen time and time again was infuriating. Patience being a virtue in rather short supply where any form of prospective booty was involved, the more subtle arts of the piscator would have to be abandoned for the time being at least. Water was scooped and spilled in frenetic handfuls. Splashing about in the shallows was resorted to. Eventually, knee-deep wading - and the accompanying danger of an unwanted baptism - was succumbed to. Unfortunately, fine-meshed nets on the ends of bamboo canes were the accoutrements of wealth. Socks on the ends of twigs were tried. Unsuccessfully. Caps were commandeered for the purpose -equally useless - and incidentally, the millinery theft leaving the petty criminal open to an immediate thickening of the labials! Finally, by hook or crook - as the saying comes so conveniently to mind - some of the iridescent quarry made their way into our glassy prisons, only to be distorted by both the refractive properties of water and the tall-tale inventiveness of our leviathan-like imaginations.

In due course the grinding solemnities of Lent were to be temporarily alleviated by the religious respite offered by Palm Sunday. The triumphant entry of Christ into Jerusalem coincided with our own English version of the palm: pussy willow. This was probably most frequently the goat-willow but there were many willows growing in the area, variously known as osiers, withies and sallows, as well as palm. Whatever the names they all added brightness to that otherwise religiously glum season. Their ritual pruning was always something eagerly looked forward to and to bear the palm victoriously was a temptation to be paradoxically yielded to. Boys and girls were to be seen as if in torchlight processions carrying them home in both hands. As well as the precious vases, jam-jars and milk-bottles were brought into service. From window after window could be seen the flickering yellow flames and the puffs of silvery smoke fuming from their feathery fuses. Also around that time that othere explosive event - at least as far as the taste buds were concerned - took place. In baker's windows those one-a-penny, two-a-penny, mouthwatering sticky-buns appeared as if by magic. Why they should have tasted so different to other buns of the same consistency scoffed all year round, I do not know. Some would say it was the spices, others would put it down to the zest. I should like to think that in my case the reason was of a more spiritual nature. But as my mother was so often heard to say, "You know what thought done don't yer?" Still a mystery to me, grammer aside! There was a pub in our area where a hot cross bun had been nailed to the ceiling every year for centuries. I'm not lying, I've seen them with my own eyes – honestly! The basic configuration seems to have been timelessly adhered to, although, social historians amongst you could have deduced something about the vagaries of agricultural boom and slump by the difference in sizes. I personally thought the fifties a mite slumpish but that may well have more to do with my greed than agrarian economics. The most amazing thing about those admittedly desiccated, rock-hard, long-baked Bumblies stuck on the ceiling, was the fact that there was not one iota of mould or fungus to be seen! Considering the furry green and black jungles of the stuff to be seen on white bread nowadays just after the sell-by date has expired, I find that somewhat remarkable! The only problem I ever really had with hot cross buns was their ill-timed proximity to Good Friday. If Lent in general was to be seen 'through a glass darkly' then Good Friday in particular was somewhere lurking in the dregs at the bottom of the said glass! If that sounds sacrilegious or even blasphemous then there is only one person who can forgive me. And I'm sure that if His Holy Word were to be rewritten, then He in His infinite mercy, trailing clouds of glory behind Him, would allow a few more jokes in the religio/biographical account of His earthly doings. Good Friday was gloom indeed. The very gloom of the very veriest of all glooms. Grooves were being worn round the aisles of every Catholic Church in the land. Hail-Marys and Our-Fathers were being susurrated to the topmost rafters. Confessionals were on overtime and self-flagellation was not only deemed necessary but was masochistically admired. As if all this was not enough, self-denial in the form of fasting was taken to extremes, and rumbling-stomached, light-headed cherubs were expected to stay awake for as long as possible on the following Saturday Night to partake in the all-important vigil.

I for one was never happier than when the metaphorical stone was rolled away from the allegorical tomb and I could get my pale, starved face into the awaiting Easter-Eggs. This account of Lent and its outcome at Easter must stop here before my contritional tears swamp the very, very, page itself and bares the fibre of my innermost being to your harsh and disapproving gazes.

After Easter, in both the secular and spiritual realms, things took a turn for the better. Thoughts turned from Easter-Eggs to the real things. What had befallen the earlier amphibians was about to befall our feathered friends. Bird nesting was a way of life. Even in those unenlightened days of wholesale egg collecting certain of our religious and temporal guardians tried to show us the evilness of our ways. Lectures on the harmlessness of their feathery little lives and the care lavished by God on even the merest of sparrows were listened to in disbelieving silence. Appeals to our better natures were made in earnest, only to be totally ignored. Threats of punitive action were treated with sniggering comtempt. The more that was said against this springtime *raison d'etre,* the more red-ragged and bull-headed we became. Nothing short of The Day of Judgement itself could dissuade us from this tree-climbing, hole-delving, bush-barracking pastime. Like stamps, picture-cards and matchbox-labels, bird's eggs were at the top of the list as far as swoppability ratings were concerned. The options were seemingly endless. Elms were steeple-jacked for rooks and crows eggs, in spite of the dangers of their snapwood fragility. Holes in timber or brick - or anything else for that matter - were widened and delved into for the red-flecked whiteness's of the tit family. Old boots, tin cans, kettles and other discarded kitchen equipment were painstakingly searched as prospective homes for refugees from the Christmas Cards. The gigantic, yearly added to abodes, of the legendary 'light-clawed' magpies were to be found in hedgerows and trees of all types and sizes. Swans were foolhardily waded towards in the fleets and the rare bearded-reedlings - soon to become even rarer - were stalked through the swampy margins of any of the marshland waterways. The sky-blue, black-speckled eggs of thrushes and the blue-green, mottled brown ones of the blackbirds were retrieved by hands and arms, trickled and beaded with blood, from the prickly hearts of bramble-bushes. The nests of pigeons and doves -

seen latticed from below, like a game of Chinese-sticks - were pinpointed for future reference. Linnets, greenfinches, bullfinches, redpolls and dunnocks, all in their turn suffered from our predations. Jackdaws, house sparrows and starlings, chacked, cheeped and wheezed at us from the crumbling remains of derelict buildings. Sleepy owls hooted, terrified pheasants rended metal and jays shrieked as only jays know how. We were unstoppable. Not a rat or a mongoose alive was as adept as us in the ways and means of egg pilferage. How any birds managed to survive the ravages of our springtime assault, let alone find the strength to go on for a second or third brood is beyond all reasonable attempts at explanation. Like all hobbyists worth their salt, justifications were sought to rationalize - to ourselves at least - the disputed extent of our deprivations. If you only take one or two eggs the birds will continue to lay, was one of the favourite excuses. It never crossed our minds that a thousand and one other scuffed-kneed, snotty-nosed individuals were quoting the same hogwash. A calcium stuffed regiment of mass-producing battery hens couldn't have kept up with our demands had their oviducts been greased and their heads squeezed thirteen times to the dozen! I tell you, we were to eggs what the Great White Hunter was to the tiger. Our much loved and admired trophies were - as I see in retrospect - just as despicable. If you'd ever pierced both ends of an addled egg and blew, you'd know exactly what I mean. But did it bother one then? Not in the slightest. The pink, barely pulsating foetal flesh inside its freshly peeled shell was regarded with as much indifference as a cat might show to a trapped and injured mouse. I'm ashamed to say that even now when I see the clutches of eggs nestled in cotton-wool in natural history museums - far from taking to heart the attached messages stating that these are all old collections and that bird nesting is now against the law - I'm immediately overtaken by feelings of ambivalence, as nostalgia and the wonder I felt in the presence of those multicoloured ovalarities lifts me to the rustling boughs of my alas, deciduous childhood. I can only say in my defense, that like many a hunter turned conservationist, I have since seen the error of my ways and repent on a daily basis.

Another of our - genuinely more innocent I feel - decimations of the countryside came in the form of blue belling. This was decidedly more in the Beatrix Potter, Alison Uttely mode. Unlike bird nesting it was then considered the proper way to conduct oneself in the vernal season. Flowers and flower arranging, though somewhat sissy, were nevertheless acceptable. Moreover, parents thought that the participation in the gathering of the garlands was a good sign as regards to one's developing character and maturity, and therefore treated you accordingly. Points so easily lost in yolk and albumen could be more than made up for in the dusts of pollen. In our environs bluebells were to be found in abundance in the vicinity of the quaintly - but misleadingly named - One Tree Hill. Being somewhat distant it necessitated the use of pedal-power and my Gresham Flyer was eminently up to the job. Eddy, with even less wealth to show for his heritage than mine, had to make do with a homemade, rusted and rickety death trap, laughingly referred to as a bicycle. As we made our way, squeakily along the country lanes, all the flora of late spring was there to be enjoyed. Jack-by-the-hedge reared itself up to its garlic-headed height and plucked orange-tipped butterflies from the blue emblazoned sky. Primroses punctured the darkness of hedge banks and sweet-violets - like miniature purple-emperors - stared out from their odorous corners. Stitchwort constellated in the grass. Cuckoo-flowers listened for the resounding two-note ring of their namesakes and honesty was as trustworthy as ever and at its pre-moon-silvered flowery best. One-Tree-Hill is part of a series of sand-capped and gravelly ridges that overlie the London clay and are characteristic of so much of southern Essex.

I'm no geologist but I remember well the variety of habitats, from the dry, loose sandy tops, through various stages of water retention, down to clay-bottomed, claggy, spring line hollows. It was a mixed evergreen and deciduous woodland. I

86

can't remember the predominating species now but oak there was in plenty and hornbeam also. There were definitely wild-service trees, a rarity in other parts of the country yet relatively common in parts of southern Essex, some wild cherry, beech, hawthorn, blackthorn and holly. Silver birch, larch, Scots pine and some cedar of Lebanon, sycamore, ash, sweet chestnut and field maple. I could go on and on: crab apple, hazel, rowan and various - for me at least - unnamable firs, pines and cypresses. It was a paradise at any time of the year but in late spring in that dreamy-world of the unfurling canopy, shadows, and the diagonal flood of incoming striated light, it was breathtaking. Eddy and I hitched up our respective metal steeds to the fence and like two of the chosen people entered the enchanted wood. It was a misted sea of bluebells. You could have easily have drowned in them and been glad of the loss of breath. In the open glades and by the shaded edges, campion, both red and white, some early foxgloves, yellow archangel and the strange cowled spathes of the cuckoo-pint beckoned us hither and thither on our nectar-drunk botanical investigations. Bluebells – sacrilege beyond redemption – were ripped up by the billowing armfuls. Their pale, ghostly lower stems drooping on air like a tangle of etiolated recriminations. Campion were snatched, archangels wrenched, and foxgloves snapped. Those, and whatever else could be gathered from the wayside on our homeward journey, would be offered in propitiation to our goddesses of the hearth in hopes of better times ahead. But hopes, like the flowers themselves, were prone to withering looks and the driest of comments. No matter what we did it seemed that we could never satisfy the demands of the women in our lives. We either brought home too many or not enough. If we managed to get the balance just right and presented our loved ones with perfect sprays of springtime beauty the invariable response was "What are you afta." Will it ever change? Will feminism save us from the heart rending slight of such ingratitudes? One can only hope! One can only pray!

Something needed to be done to cheer ourselves up a bit and what better than money-back-on-the-bottles, collecting? Eddy and me and a flea in the ear - as the old song goes - were not so easily put off. We'd knock on any door at any time and with all the cheek of a dewlapped granny would ask the residents for their empty lemonade and beer bottles. If asked what we wanted them for, any well-known local charitable cause would be quoted with a bare faced, do-goodedly aplomb. I wouldn't have believed us and to be fair nor did many of our potential donors. But the law of averages being what they are - and were - the soft touch was always a distinct possibility. Little old ladies with no money - and sad to say, even less sense - were often so impressed by our charitable endeavours that we were invited in for drinks, biscuits and many another free-loading handout. Not all of the bottles came from people's houses. Many were picked up from the hedgerows and thickets where the plotlanders had dumped them along with any other unwanted household waste. In the more accessible spots where the council refuse carts could get to, there were rows of flip-top, galvanized rubbish bins all connected by an iron bar strung between two upright concrete posts. These were duly rifled through and bottles covered in all sorts of unmentionable gunge were retrieved and added triumphantly to our treasure trove. Transport was invariably the base of an old defunct pram rigged out with a wooden box. If we were lucky we'd find a pram that still had its carriage affixed, but that was a rare occurrence. Having taken the loot back to Eddy's place we'd fill a tin bath with water and scrub and rinse those bottles not fit for an immediate refund. It was never a wholly successful enterprise. Stubborn tidemarks remained inside, like the ghostly dregs of their erstwhile full-bodied contents. Labels were peeled off and those bottles that were supposed to have stoppers, but hadn't, were re-fitted from our stock of ill-matching replacements. Local shopkeepers became sick of the sight of us. A motley collection of bottles - in most cases unrecognizable as to their proprietary brands - were lined up along the counter. "Not you two again," complained the shopkeeper. "How many times have I told you, I don't need you or your junk in my shop, I've got customers to serve." "It's not junk mista, honest," I lied. "It's all our bottles left over from Christmas; mum said they all came from 'ere." Whats happened to all the labels," he quizzed. "And why are they full of muck?" "they've bin out in the back-garden," I ad-libbed. "Maybe the rain dun it!" The bartering began. "This one's not mine," he said. "Yes it is," I replied. "It's a Leddicots." "No it isn't," he countered. "Leddicots are made from white glass not green!" So it went on. Eventually a bargain would be struck. He'd take a few of the bottles, give us a penny each, and be glad to see the back of us. "It's a penny on each bottle aint it mista," Eddy would say, enterprisingly. "Don't push your luck," was the usual business-like reply. So we didn't. The rejected bottles were put back on the cart and pushed off towards the next unwelcoming entrepreneur. I can still remember some of those magical names. Apart from Leddicots there was Corona, Harringtons and R Whites. R Whites still being very much with us of course. Amongst the beer bottles Allsops, Mann, Paulin, and Crossman and Taylor Walkers spring to mind. Taylor Walker's trade name has been revived recently. In deference to Camera, real-ale and the rustic image, perhaps? One of our favourite scams at the time took place at the local off-licence. In the yard round the back of it the crates of empties were stacked. That vitreous convertible form of currency was guarded on one side by a ten foot set of steel gates, and on the other by a free roving, fanged and slaverous, throat-ripping alsation. Eddy would go into the off-licence from the front and with an air of uncharacteristic likeability about him would proceed to charm the manager. "Nice day aint it," he began. "got any jobs yer want doin', I'm an 'ard worka and it won't cost yer much." The manager - not needing any work done but admiring both the enterprise and the polite approach - warmed to the hireling. "Well there isn't anything I need doing at the moment," he confided. "But it was very kind of you to ask; would you like a sweetie?" "That'd be nice, fank yer very much!" said Eddy, effusively. "By the way," continued Eddy. "Where's yer luvly dog? I aint seen 'im

89

fer a long time." "He's probably in the store-room or round the back," answered the manager. "I'd love to stroke 'im," pleaded Eddy. " 'e's me favrite 'e is." "Well I don't know," hesitated the manager. "Go on," urged Eddy. "Please, I really luv dogs." The manager acquiesced and the dog was summoned. "Here boy, here boy, there's a nice young man to see you." It doesn't need saying what was going on out in the yard. Gates were scaled, walls were tiptoed along and empties lined up along the asbestos roof of a shed in the next-door yard. Eddy, timing things to a tee - as always - made his farewells to the manager and came round the back for me to pass the bottles down to him. All that remained was for me to go into the off-licence and collect my ill-gotten gains! That particular ruse lasted for a very long time and was a valuable source of income. How he eventually sussed it, I don't really know. I suspect that we were not the only bottle bankers in the neighbourhood and it must have got to the stage where through a mixture of stock-control and Mr. Micawber-like reckoning he was finally persuaded to see red in his unaccountable figures. Whatever, by the cunning application of vee-shaped nicks along the bottom edges of the labels he was - at last - able to recognize his own stock. The game was up. On my last attempt deception I too was persuaded to see red. My own red-handedness, caught in the very act!

Chapter 6. A Totter's Redemption.

Rubbish was definitely one of our major preoccupations. Although, we never saw it as rubbish as such; one person's garbage-tip is another's cornucopia after all! Pitsea-tip was developing nicely thankyou. Apart from the throw-aways of the indigenous inhabitants themselves, the gradual influx of Londoners into the newly built estates was helping to create a much more diverse and interesting habitat as far as refuse was concerned. The dump itself - to use a cloacalism - was interestingly situated, being surrounded on all sides by creeks, fleets and marshes. Along its western edge ran Pitsea-creek, which branched off into Vange-creek. If you turned left - or is to port? - at that particular confluence and followed the waterway passed the wonderfully name Fobbing Horse - a wide bend between two reaches - you came eventually to the junction of East and Hole-Haven creeks. From there one direction led you to Benfleet and the other to Hole-Haven, the River Thames and the oil-refineries. Spread out along both sides of most of those creeks - especially the closer you got to Vange, Pitsea or Benfleet - were a rickety assortment of 'houseboats' and a number of long-abandoned fishing and sailing vessels slowly rotting away. To my land-lubbering shipmates and me this was our version of the Spanish Main with Pitsea-tip our very own Treasure Island. A parrot squawking, pieces of eight, paradise, where wooden legs, gold earrings and the Black Spot were all the rage. What the resident seafarers thought of our piratical excursions into their nautical domain is probably not printable. But swashbucklers we were and despite remonstrations from the Governor's lily-livered lackeys; swashbuckling, free-booting and buccaneering were partaken of to their loot-gathering fullest. Ah! Jim lad, belay thy tongue! Stow e gab! And other references to the diction of Davy Jones spilt from the gunnels of our well-pitched voices. "Splice the main brace! Haul the sheet! Hove to! And many such unfathomable phrases dropped on the anchors of our weighing words. There it was that we fired our volleying broadsides. Where grapples were thrown and the full-sailed, cannonading men-o-war were boarded. Palm trees were hawthorn bushes. Silver, foam-washed sands were silt and broken cockleshells and the crosses on the top of poles marking the passage of subterranean electric cables were x's on the maps of our many-pacing minds. The oozy, grey glutinous mud in those creeks was the home of serpents and mermaids, turtles and octopuses - or is it pi? On one occasion, having had enough of keel-hauling and yard-arming for the time being - we disembarked from the furled sails of our square-rigged fantasies and drifted to landward on a quest for booty. Close by the entrance to the tip there had been erected a veritable shanty town of wooden-framed sheds, walled and roofed with corrugated-iron. How would we have survived without that precious rain-deafening material? The smaller sheds were used as makeshift offices, canteens and toilets, while the larger ones housed such things as drotts, refuse trucks and whatever else was required in the way of machinery to run a tight - if somewhat smelly - ship! The shed that attracted our attention more than any of the others was the totter's shed. That was where anything of value - mostly in the form of metals - was retrieved from the rubbish to be sold to the local scrap-merchant and the proceeds shared out amongst the refuse workers as a much-prized bonus. On that occasion - a Sunday - Eddy and myself and the rest of the dastardly crew made for the presumed, deserted compound. Inside we headed straight for the totter's shed. At the back of the shed we found that one of the sheets of corrugated iron had come loose at the bottom. Bending it backwards we managed to make a gap large enough to effect an entry. Once our eyes had become accustomed to the whispering darkness, we began to look around. Coils of stripped wire lay all about us like so many nests of slithering vipers. Disused gas and electric cookers were stacked in haphazard heaps, their unhinged doors lolling tongue-like from the jaws of those seeming robots. Piles of lead, copper and brass, materialized in all directions, their ponderous hundred-weights, lightened by the thought of bunce. And then I saw it, the two-foot curve of a sharp, steel-sleek cutlass, replete with guard and spiralling handle. It was unbelievable. Hanging from the yardarm of a rusty six-inch nail was every young pirate's dream. How did it get there? Did it matter? I grabbed it by the hilt and swung it round and round above by head, while all the time issuing loud-mouthed salty challenges to jolly jack tars and excise men alike. Unbeknown to us we hadn't, as we'd previously thought, been alone. A watchman, alerted by my timber-shivering tirade, came crashing through the front door of the shed. Like piss through a porthole we poured out through the gap in the corrugated iron. No way was I going to leave that blood-curdling weapon of war behind. Still clutching it firmly in my landlocked fist, I raised myself to my full sub-tropical height and ran like hell towards the reefs and the waiting ocean. The watchman wasn't going to give up that easily. Like the scrawny, wide-eyed, hair-raising image of Ben Gunn himself, he set off after us spitting, wheezing and cackling in a half-crazed manner. The weight of the cutlass began to get the better of me. My shipmates were drawing ahead and the madman abaft was gaining on me all the time. Running along the edge of the creek, legs tiring fast, heart pounding and the first signs of the stitch beginning to alarm me, I realized the futility of my efforts. Looking out across the creek, towards the ooze and the rippling silver of the incoming tide, I decided - as many a spoilt brat has done before - that if I couldn't have the prize, then nobody else would. I threw the cutlass as hard as I could out over the creek and watched - as in slow motion - as the spinning blade fell from the felonious sky and sunk like Excalibur beneath the mystical waves.

When I think back to the inordinate amount of time we spent rummaging around in the rubbish on that tip, it's little wonder that none of those concerned are to be found in the egregious pages of 'Who's Who'! Mind you, I dare say that honorary professorships in the deliquescent properties of comestibles are rather thin on the ground anyway. Still, if there's ever room on the lucrative lecture circuit for an expert on the aesthetics of twentieth century garbage, then I'm definitely their man! For those of you unfamiliar with the joys of domestic waste, perhaps I should make an attempt at some sort of description. Are you sitting comfortably? Are you still the proud owner of a Mickey-Mouse gas mask? Is there a spittoon to hand? Good, then we'll begin. Picture this if you can. If you dare even! You're standing in the middle of a veritable moonscape, made up of paper, rags, proto-plastics and many other offensive items of household refuse all gelled together by the putrefying pulps of equally unmentionable detritus. Here and there - probably due to the effects of spontaneous combustion - smouldering craters belched - and I use the word advisedly - pustules of acrid smoke. The air is thick with seagulls, cascading seagull shit and a stench beyond the describable reach of even the most lyrical of poets. At ground level, with each squelching footstep, the circumference of an imaginary circle moved with you in the scurrying shapes of not so imaginary rats. Not your idea of heaven? Well it was ours! It's all relative, as any modern waffler will so philosophically tell you. In that pong-perfect paradise - excuse the plosives - we scavenged unwholesomely. You could smell my picture-card collection at ninety paces and people were known to swoon at the merest whiff of my salvaged display of matchbox-labels. No amount of peg-nosed ridicule dissuaded any of us from the odorous pleasures of garbage gathering. One of my greatest finds was a wind-up gramophone complete with spare needles and a stack of scratchy, foul-smelling 78's. What did it matter? They sounded sweet enough to me! I can't remember all of the titles now, but most of them were along the lines of 'When Father Painted the Parlour' and 'The Laughing Policeman'. And naturally, I've had a bit of trouble with 'music appreciation' ever since! The most modern piece of music I heard on those rank-cum-formative airwaves was 'Singing the Blues' by Tommy Steele. The legacy of it exhibits itself as an extreme form of synaesthesia. Nobody, but nobody, can hear the blues as odoriferously as I can! The edges of the tip-crumbling cliffs of rubbish were eroded into slime covered stagnant pools of water. It was there that we washed our grubby little mitts - unknowingly running the gauntlet of Weil's disease - and proceeded to eat any fruit or sweets that we'd found and considered in our dubious wisdom not to be too far beyond their sell-by - or perhaps less euphemistically - typhoid date! I can only say that whenever I'm dragged kicking and screaming by my junk-foddering associates into a fast-food restaurant I'm exceedingly grateful for the immunity I built up in those early tip-foraging days.

Before we leave the miasmic world of refuse, mention should be made of the inhabitants of the houseboats moored in the creeks bordering the tip. Now, I didn't know any of those people personally, but nevertheless had a natural affinity with anyone who had the aesthetic foresight to live in such close proximity to a garbage mountain. Whenever I encountered any of those marsh-dwellers I felt an immediate kinship. They appeared to me to be followers of the same sort of scruffy existentialism so favoured by myself, Eddy and Co. They had a dishevelled olfactory air about them that one admired instantly. One quaint eccentric old lady, well known in the area for her matted coiffure, great-coat and stylish Wellingtons, was an ardent rescuer of stray dogs. She could often be seen trundling along from the butchers with a pram-full of flyblown lights, closely followed by a mange-ridden tribe of mutts and mongrels. To us it was the next best thing to a carnival. Whether she appreciated us tagging on behind banging our air drums and practicing our raspberry-lipped embouchure is debatable. But we felt it to be our bound duty to follow in the train of such a kindred spirit. In retrospect of course it's easy to see how cleanliness - with only creek water for ablutions - must have been a near impossible feat. What they did for drinking and cooking water on those boats never crossed my mind in those days. But thinking about it now, what limited freedom they had, was hard-won indeed. If it was difficult for the plotlanders, they did at least have a well or a pump in the backyard to help them. How the marsh-dwellers ever supplied themselves with all the water and fuel they needed to survive on those houseboats is pretty near unfathomable. But survive they did and no doubt still do in the odd pockets of nonconforming individualism. *Vive la resistance!* That's all I can say.

I don't know whether its got anything to do with marsh-fever or just a lack of suitable material to make up the expected literary linkages, but as my mind takes me back up that hill from the marshes and past the rook-roisterous elms surrounding St Michael's Church in late spring, thoughts of Whitsun and First Holy communion descend pentecostally upon me. You would be forgiven for thinking that religion has had a rather rough time of it so far in this account of a somewhat sinful pre-pubescence. But the pious amongst you will be gratified to hear that not all of my early religious experiences were negative ones. Even Stanford-le-Hope lives up to its last syllable and the dreaded St Josephs itself is bathed in the light of the Dove when I recall participating in my second major religious rite. I can't remember the first. From being too wet behind the ears - no doubt! Being dressed all in white was something of a novelty for me and my equally irreverent school-friend Jethro Buckley. It can only be said that we rose to the occasion. When we had a mind to we could process with as much solemnity as the rest of them, and on that particular day we certainly had more than our share of psychological-cum-spiritual purpose. I think we fervently believed - even though we didn't understand the word - that this was our chance of redemption. All our former sins - we hoped - would be forgiven by virtue of the sincere observance of that transubstantive act. Maybe all the cannibalistic talk of bodies and blood had something to do with it, I don't know. But I definitely felt holier than I had ever felt before, and like the feelings evoked by our childish blood-brotherhood ceremonies, I had that overpowering sense of becoming part of something of far greater importance than my otherwise small and worldly self. The added excitement of a drop of hitherto illicit wine was undoubtedly the supplementary grape on the gateaux. After the hymns, the prayers, and the rite itself, I seemed to float angel-like out of the church and into the assembly hall for the First Holy Communion breakfast. By now I was growing accustomed to the penitential pleasures of self-denial and the waiting feast was to be all the more enjoyable because of my - assumed - abstemious superiority. Nuns with uncommonly radiant smiles on their otherwise hell-fired faces, served us with boiled-eggs, bread and jam, and brimming glassfuls of cool, quenching milk. After the repast, white First Holy Communion prayer books with names and the date inscribed, were given to each of the assembled initiates. I still have them to this day along with my first catechism and whenever I feel the need of some God-bothering nostalgia I get them out and gaze longingly at them whilst all the time fingering my mother's rosary. 'Hope springs eternal'!

Chapter 7. The Willow Pond.

As the summer began in earnest so did my love of fishing. Across the fields from where I lived - in the middle of a network of unmade roads and flowery meadows - was to be found the Willow Pond. Whenever I think of childhood it's invariably that one watery oasis that springs immediately to mind. The eponymous tree in question was a magnificent spreading willow. Some of its immense boughs - splintered under their ancient weight - hung out across the pond. Its thin linear leaves cascaded in a grey-green shower. At certain times of the year a blizzard of seeded down drifted on the whispering breezes from both the willow and the surrounding poplars to settle like white, ecstatic words on the water's rippling pages. Crowsfoot sprawled out across the surface; lilies held golden cups in their green palms and yellow-flags hoisted their signals from the shadowy margins. Marestails swished amongst the blue-green metallics of flickering demoiselles and the erratic needles of darting dragonflies, stitched and cross-stitched over reeds and rushes. More than anything else before or since it was that pond and its environs that fired me with the love of books. Initially words were not as important as pictures. In the library at Vange hours would be spent gazing dreamily through colour-plates of insects and wild flowers. Drawings would be sought out and studied in rapt detail. My favourite book at the time was - naturally enough - 'Mr. Crabtree goes Fishing'. For me it was the perfect mix of text and illustrations. It was the first book to both delve and tap my emotional well springs to the full. I was hooked. Explications of tackle and tactics required for individual species of fish were suitably arcane. Types of bait and their preparation bordered on the alchemical. This was the sort of esoteric activity that I'd been searching for throughout all of my short life. Jargons and shibboleths have always been indispensable to those who feel the need to highlight the ignorance of others! My new-found piscatorial knowledge would surely mark me out as someone very special indeed. I

98

would be the envy of all dried-up and drought-ridden intellects. Unfortunately, the gap between theoretical knowledge and practical expertise was as wide then where fishing is concerned, as it was to subsequently become in most of the other departments of my jack-of-all-trades existence. It must be said though - by way of an excuse - that in those days the means were not available to equip oneself with the standard of tackle so lovingly depicted in the Mr. Crabtree series of books. Split-cane, greenheart and Spanish-reed had to be substituted with materials of a far lesser order. The exceedingly supple - as opposed to subtle - withy was a favourite angle of mine. Not 'Allcocks' or 'Hardy' admittedly but what was lacking in quality was more than made up for by the resolute plummeting test-curve of my imagination. Reels of course were beyond our very limited resources and no more than the revolving subject matter of our deep and fishy dreams. Nylon mono-filament was unheard of in that big-fished, small-ponded environment and any found thread, thin enough and strong enough, was picked up and ravelled into service. Hooks, once purchased, were prized and treated with the care and reverence they deserved. Split-lead shot had a value in our eyes comparable with that of the gold-standard. Home-made floats constructed out of corks and quills and then painstakingly painted and varnished were considered to be works of the highest artistic achievement. Baits, prepared at home from secret recipes consisting of dough, custard powder and infallible essences such as pilchard oil - the divulging of which still smacks of heresy - were squeezed, sniffed, tasted and discussed by the assembled fisher folk. The best swims were always argued over. If short-strawing, or one potato - two potato - three potato – four, were not sufficient to resolve the issue, then trials of strength were resorted to. Needless to say the biggest boys caught the biggest fish! Such is the discriminatory logic that governs this cruel world of ours. Although the ultimate purpose of our visits to that pond was to catch as many crucian-carp as possible, having once secured a swim - hopefully one of comfort in amongst the rushes with a stretch of unweeded water within casting distance - you were likely to be just as preoccupied by whatever came into the view of what Jack Hargreaves so rightly called 'the angler's other eye'. Long legged pond-skaters dented the water's surface tension with the poised tips of their slender limbs, and then all of a sudden skittered around erratically in all directions, as if balance had finally deserted them. Whirligig beetles, whirled their gigs, and back-stroking water-boatmen sculled aimlessly around seemingly unconcerned with the strictures of upside-downéd-ness. Countless filmy-winged ephemera rose and fell through their short-lived fluttery lives over the sun-shot glances of irradiating ripples. Occasionally the upended tail of a great-diving-beetle could be seen as it rose to the surface to replenish its air supply. These ferocious insects were the piranhas of our Amazonian fantasies. Both in the adult and larval stages they had jaws capable of dealing with newts, tadpoles, small fish, and even the fingers of unwary children - and if needs be, each other! Captured prey was injected with digestive juices and the resultant bodily fluids siphoned off for lunch. In spite of their less than refined table-manners, much else about them was worthy of the finishing school. They were - like many a product of charm and elocution - little gems. The male of the species was a deep brownish black colour. Seen from above its entire perimeter was banded by a thin red stripe and two more stripes of the selfsame colour formed parallel lines across the top of its head. The female was of exactly the same configuration but her body was a rich-olive green and the stripes were an almost fluorescent yellow. Nevertheless, like so much else in the world of apparently ownerless value, if one didn't want one's fingers severely burnt, they were best left well alone. If they were our piranhas, then the grass-snakes - with or without half-swallowed frogs protruding from their dislocated jaws - were definitely the anacondas of our steamy jungle waterways. To see their zebra-striped sinuous bodies undulating through the margins was enough to raise the hackles of the most seasoned of hunters. At first sight of one a gaggle of disconcerted tribesmen would gather frantically in the shallows throwing both spears and curses at the unfortunate serpentine intruder. Exertions of this kind together with the fatigue built up during prolonged periods of motionless float watching required the revivifying effects of nourishment. Ideas of a feast in those days were vastly different to our present day epicurean expectations. My basic roughage usually consisted of teeth-grinding bread and sugar sandwiches washed down with a sun-warmed swig of Adam's ale. In honour of high days and holidays, rancid, sock-sweaty cheese and tomato sandwiches were consumed, and for those children lucky enough to have botanically minded mothers, ginger-beer could be quaffed with all the aplomb that superiority confers. None of this seemed to matter that much, as long as a hole was filled and a throat quenched, affairs of the body remained stodgily subservient to the necessities of the soul. If the Gods needed nectar and ambrosia then I can only think that we must have transcended them. How to experience the quintessence of crucian-ness was the one and only grail-like purpose of our watery pilgrimages. Fortunately for us, although they were somewhat small and stunted fishes, the pond held a massive population of them. If we could stay late enough - after the heat of the day when the breezes died and the shadows lengthened - they would often come on feed. Primitive as our equipment was it was more than adequate when it came to coping with those diminutive leviathans of the shallows. In fact, the extremely pliable willow switches that we used were perfect for the job. A hooked crucian was a formidable little creature. They ran and wriggled and shook in all directions and a more rigid implement in our less than capable hands would have undoubtedly resulted in their getting away. It would be impossible to explain to the anti-fishing fraternity the heart-pounding, adrenaline-soaked ecstasies involved in playing a fish. Being connected physically to two different dimensions in our concrete reality by the already arm-shuddering excitement of rod and line was compounded by the near primal impact of the conscious and subconscious mind making similar multi-dimensional connections in the abstract. I can honestly say that few other

101

experiences in life - if any - have affected me as deeply and with the same all-embracing sense of communion and continuum as much those related to angling. Even now, just writing and remembering, the palms are beginning to sweat and the pulse quicken. Not a thought in the rational universe can compare with that peerless sensation of being wholly alive to the experience of unadulterated nature. Ecology lived as opposed to being understood. I'm aware of the complaints to be made against such expressions of romantic idealism but I'm afraid I just can't help myself. The feelings were felt and the rationale can never negate them. After the victory came the spoils. There are fish and there are my favourite fish, but like the very seasons of the year itself, my roll of honour in terms of preference are prone to ambivalence. The joys of the moment it seems are always unsurpassable. Imagine a golden muscle. Ponder on verdigris, on sheens of shimmering bronze, on rubies. Hold in your mind's impossible hand the pulsating jewel of everything you've ever desired, set in the sense of an insurmountable wonder. There you would have the crucian-carp, the willow pond, the pathos and bathos of every noble and ironic blessing bestowed upon the alchemical seekers of eternal youth. Being close to dusk you would also have the mosquitoes to contend with, but that's another itch without a pearl to justify the scratching; wouldn't you say?

I've always considered myself to be part of a minority group of one. This powerful sense of social alienation has its benefits though. It has throughout my life enabled me to empathize with the outsider. I can honestly say that xenophobia is a stranger to me! Differences of race and religion have always been topics more appropriate to the exercise of my curiosity that they've ever been subjects of fear or loathing. Certain of the eccentric characters who inhabited the mansions of my earlier more superstitious mind, did admittedly create pulses of trepidation along my neural networkings. But even then I feel it had more to do with the deeper fears and anxieties that their physical appearances symbolized and evoked, than anything to do with speculations on innate individual or collective evil. I would have no more joined an organization devoted to the abolition of witches or one-eyed men in those days than I would now. My life was enriched then - and still is to a lesser degree - by the eccentricities of others. In these high-tech days of instant communication throughout the global village both subject and object seem to be becoming more and more indivisible - sameness being the rationalizing virtue, user-friendly consumers, the purpose. One of the minority groupings we were encouraged to fear and despise in accordance with the accumulated tenets of folk-law, were the Romany's They were supposedly thieves, murderers and kidnappers. Were cruel to their horses, cooked live hedgehogs over open fires, and had direct clairvoyant links with the Devil. We were told - for the sake of our very lives even - to steer well clear of them. I knew differently. As you may remember one of my earliest school-friends - Jethro Buckley - came from such stock. I even had a smattering of traveller's vocabulary myself - cacka-chavi and mooie springing immediately to mind. So for me Romany wagons under the elms at Craylands were more to be welcomed than reviled. What young boy - or girl for that matter - has not been smitten by the thought of joining the circus or taking to the open road? Romantic perhaps, but freedoms like these - so vehemently railed against by the mono-culturists - are in my opinion expressions of the human spirit to be both cherished and rigorously defended against the deprecations of bureaucracy. I spent many a happy hour of my childhood in the company of travellers and throughout all of those lavender-bunched, wood-whittling hours, I never once felt to be threatened in any way whatsoever. Lurchers lurched across the fields, horses browsed through chain-rattling circles and black-bubbling cast-iron pots hung from the trestles over wood-scented fires. The meticulously painted flat-topped and bow-roofed caravans were a delight to behold. Always spotless and replete with polished brass ornaments and racks of gleaming porcelain. To turn a penny the Romany's would turn their hands to almost anything. The traditional occupations of flower-selling, peg-making and

103

fortune-telling were supplemented in season by back-breaking work on the surrounding farms. Hoeing, beet-topping and potato picking were all strenuously partaken of, along with the harvesting of peas, fruit and strawberries, and much else besides. For the inveterate shirker that I was - and still am given the opportunity- the variety and extent of their industry was something I found quite astonishing. Like so much else from those days I'm left with the memories only. The horse-drawn way of life has virtually disappeared and if the authorities get their way most forms of independent travelling will be legislated against as well as just frowned upon. Except perhaps for the package-tour there seems to be little space left for the home-grown wandering spirit at this end of the twentieth century. Alternative life-styles may understandably produce feelings of unease amongst the landowning classes but why they should cause such violent reactions from townsfolk and city-dwellers is beyond me. As the world shrinks and first-hand experience of other cultures increases you would think that the parochial attitudes so characteristic of the xenophobe would be replaced by a wider and far more enlightened viewpoint. You would think!

Sadly, it has to be revealed that despite the capacity for juvenile philanthropy hinted at in the preceding paragraph not all outsiders were treated by me with equal tolerance. One species of outsider that I held in particular disregard was the bully. Living within begging-for-mercy distance of my former home lived an especially appalling example. For fear that he's still alive, and even worse has learnt to read and found a copy of this book in his moll's handbag. I shall have to be careful where nomenclature is concerned. The last thing I need at the moment is for him to come round to my house filling my boots with concrete and my body with bruises. He will therefore be known hereafter - and I use the word advisedly - as nasty-person x. Set in its own half acre of land beside a copse bordering the bridle-path was one of the first properties I remember having been vacated owing to the dictates of compulsory purchase. Whenever the need for solitude came upon me it was there - amongst other deserted places - that I went for refuge. I used to love sitting in the empty rooms of that bungalow just mindlessly staring out at the vacancy beyond. My potential for seemingly pointless cloud gazing has always been immense. I've spent an enormous amount of time just looking without really thinking. The pleasures derived from a free-floating associative mind are limitless. To survive in the world of real things and events we obviously need the combined sanities of logic and sequence. But to survive in the equally real worlds of spirit and imagination, too much rationality can be very inhibiting indeed. The ability to range throughout time in all directions and to juxtapose the incongruous or the impossible is grist to the cog-less mill of the creative sensibility. It was during one of these mental chaff-winnowing sessions that the wind was abruptly taken out of my intuitive sails. Nasty-person x was going through his High-Noon phase and being the bad hombre that he was, cultivators of poetic inspiration were always prospective candidates for Boot Hill. He burst in through the portals of his own imaginary space and the Parnassian slopes of my own idyllic musings were immediately transformed into The Golden Nugget Salon! "Stick 'em up," he said, leeringly. Seeing that he was toting an air-rifle at the time I thought it only right and proper that I should comply with his request. "Don't shoot," I stuttered. "I aint dun nuffink." He swaggered towards me. "This tahn aint big enuff fer the two of us," he drawled. "I'd be more than willin' ter stake my claim elsewhere," I replied, pioneeringly. It was all to no avail, the taste of fear was on his snarling lips and I was the ideal whimpering victim. He chewed his plug of tobacco then spat. "Pick up that tin-can and 'old it abuv yer 'ead." he ordered. "Please," I begged. "Don't make me do it, what if yer miss?" "What if I do?" was his heartless response. I stood there, jelly-legged, with a tin-can shaking in my upheld quivering hand, and he took aim. Wham! And the tin-can went ricocheting against the back wall. "Pick it up again," he yelled. And with my fingers still smarting from the shock I did as he asked. This went on until fear translated itself into tears and

105

blubbering. "No more!" I pleaded. "You've 'ad yer fun, why can't yer leave me alone?" He transfixed me with his meanest desperado stare. "Yer miserable no good cow-poke!" he bellowed. Pick it up before I put a slug between yer eyes!" Trembling, I did as I was told. Thwack!!! "Ou.......ch!" I excruciated. "Frigging 'ell! You've 'it me, yer stupid git!" Blood was oozing from my stinging hand and a bruise was already beginning to show. I could see from the expression on his face that he was having second thoughts about the Wild West and his part in the taming of it. Posses and lynch-mobs were galloping through the deserts of his sand-storming doubts. "I'm lettin' yer off this time," he bluffed. "But don't cross me agin; get on yer 'orse and ride!" Painfully, dragging my wounded pride along with me, I trotted off towards the adobe. As luck would have it Matt Dillon was in residence. "Dad! Dad! I've bin shot!" I whined. " 'Ho did it!" he asked, breathing on his badge and packing his holster. "It was nasty-person x!" I divulged, somewhat gleefully. "Where did it 'appen!" he continued. "Down the alley," I urged. "In the deserted bungalow," and he rode off furiously in the direction of Dodge City. It was on occasions such as those that my life-long conflict between the merits of mercy on the one hand and the need for revenge on the other had their beginnings. It also helped to develop an ambivalent attitude towards authority in general. I'd grown accustomed to the idea of my father being both enemy and persecutor. I could live with that, we all need something or someone to hate. But to see him as hero, and as a role model worthy of serious consideration, was way beyond the grasp of my childlike understanding. I'm still confused on the issue, as any local post-office counter-clerk will testify. Anyone - no matter how lowly - who holds an official position is treated by me with the same dualistic approach. At the slightest hint of disdain on their part I'll break into a paranoid rant about such things as '1984' and 'The Thought Police'. Petty officialdom doesn't seem able to cope in any way whatsoever with my Jekyll and Hydisms and astrological allusions to my privileged status as a Gemini are not taken seriously at all. When I'm a good five hundred yards away from any government department I could swear that I hear the shutters coming down already. And I'm convinced that the reinforced glass and the emergency alarms were installed entirely for my benefit. To use an unfortunate word! I must speak to my therapist about it. Anyway, I digress again. My father returned from Dodge City with the evidence of his encounter with the local outlaw. I'd never seen an air-rifle with the stock smashed off and the barrel bent double before, but would have to say that the effect it had on my down-trodden spirit was one of immediate uplift. On the scales of my infantile system of justice the balance was definitely in favour of revenge. Mercy seemed an altogether unsatisfying proposition. It transpires that my father had been threatened with the possibility of a family feud, but much to his credit - in my merciless eyes at least - had told the miscreant that he would shove the bent barrel of the gun up the first available orifice that presented itself. That's telling him, I thought, and proceeded to carve another notch into my underdeveloped wooden-headed ego.

That unfortunate experience with nasty-person x strengthened my already formidable belief in the power of arms. Once sufficiently healed, both physically and mentally, I summoned Eddy to a council of war and it was decided that our dwindling armoury should be added to. The close-range effectiveness of knives, bayonets and knobbly-topped trench-picks would need to be augmented by a selection of long-range weaponry. We could always get hold of air-guns if we needed them - both rifles and pistols. Although this in itself was dangerous being as they were usually the property of our elder brothers to whom sibling rivalry was something of a sadistic art-form. No, there was nothing for it; we would have to learn some new military skills. Seeing as air-powered and powder-charged ballistics were out of the question for the time being we would have to concentrate on the more traditional means of juvenile warfare. Catapults and bows-and-arrows fitted the bill perfectly. We didn't exactly suffer from a surfeit of yew-trees in Pitsea in those days so other forms of timber would need to be tried and tested. We experimented with most of the local tree species but none of them were particularly successful. Through reasons similar to those in homeopathy lighted on the idea of using the rose brier. Anything as barbarous as a thorn bush, we concluded, must have military potential. How right we were, a good sturdy limb from a brier was made for the job. They were difficult to get at first admittedly; and a lot of cussing and cursing went into the selective arts of the greenwood. But once extricated, stripped of bark, cut to length and weathered, Robin Hood himself would have been proud of them. Once notched, all that was needed was for them to be strung and arrows procured. One of my favourite shops in the area was Mence Smiths, the ironmongers, seed merchant and corn-chandlers. You don't find shops like those anymore. Wooden floored, dank and dusty. Trays of seeds and bulbs. Poultry and chicken mixtures in large metal bins. I can smell it all now, can see the brown-coated proprietor slick with Pomade and his refined servile civility. "What can I do for you, young gentlemen," he inquired, in a *retroussé* manner. "We'd like some garden canes," I ventured. He showed us some of the bamboo variety which were immediately rejected. "No," I said. "We'd like some of them there fin square ones, about free foot long." "What do you want them for," he quizzed. "Not for bow-and-arrows, I hope." "Corse not," I prevaricated. "There fer a school project, int they; and the teacher said we've got t' 'ave them ones." "Hum," he huffed, disbelievingly. But sold them to us anyway, having trouble it seems with his conscience-cum-profitability ratio. Finishing off our order with a ball of strong yet slender garden-twine must have added to his suspicions but nevertheless the draw opened, cash jingled and money changed hands. Perhaps the blind-eyed cynicism associated with capitalism and the arm's dealer was not such a bad thing after all. We were looking for the materials to wage a war and were duly grateful for the acquired ordnance. Back in the armoury - that for some strange reason Eddy's dad insisted on calling his workshop - we set about assembling the weapons. Grooves were cut into wood, loops tied in string, muscles flexed and bows bent and tautly strung. To be on the safe side thread was bound carefully around both ends of the bows so as to keep the bowstrings securely in place. Next, it was the turn of the garden-canes to receive our warmongering attention. It has to be owned up to that our knowledge of toxophily was not up to the required standard. Fletching of arrows was completely out of the question, the skills needed for such a task didn't come easily to our callow and artless hands. Still hitting a bull's-eye at a hundred paces was not our desired aim. General close-quarter mayhem accompanied by the occasional shrieks of pain and terror from our tribal enemies was all that was needed to make life worth living. Or dying as the case may be! The arrows would have to remain flightless - that's without feathers for the pacifists amongst you - and other means would have to be devised to maximize their trajectorial effectiveness. Through a process of trial and error we eventually came up with the ideal solution for tipping the arrows, the solution in question being a particularly messy and viscous one. Namely, tar from out of the road expansion joints. Not only did moulded dollops of the sticky stuff give the arrows the necessary weight and balance, but clout-nails could be pressed into it and dipped in poison if ever the need arose. Next on our agenda was the scourge of greenhouse-owners everywhere. The catapult. We purchased the rubbery means of missile projection from the same place we obtained the garden-canes. Although, I must admit, not being a technically minded sort of person myself, I could never work out exactly what gardeners wanted with ¼ " square lengths of stretchable elastic! I dare say that they could give you many a credible reason as regards to its horticultural usages. But I'm equally certain - that given the power of speech - more than a few night-mewing moggies would have a different tale to tell! Still, not being a fully paid-up member of The Cat Protection League I suppose I'll have to give them the benefit of the doubt. Catapults were easier to make than bows-and-arrows. Suitable Y-shaped branchings were everywhere to be found in the surrounding woods and copses. The species of tree or bush didn't matter that much and weathering was not necessary. Two one foot lengths of elastic were cut, one end of each being passed through slits in a leather pouch. The ends were then bent back on themselves and tightly bound with string. Notches were cut into the two uprights above the handgrip, elastic wedged into place and then once again bent back on itself and bound with string. Finally a binding of copper-wire was positioned above and below the notched elastic to prevent the wood from splitting. Ammunition was rarely a problem. Nuts, bolts and ball-bearings were to be found in reasonable quantities in Eddy's shed and if we ever ran short there was an endless supply of stones to be selected from in the nearby fields. Thus equipped we set forth in search of opponents. They were never difficult to find, the sound of battle cries in our area was more common than the cluck and crow of chickens, and I can assure you that anyone with a first-hand knowledge of the plotlands, would know exactly what I'm saying! Our first encounter was at another of the shacks already vacated because of compulsory purchase. From our hidden vantage we could see a couple of yobs clambering about on the roof, prizing off the tiles, and sending them crashing onto the ground below - nothing unusual for the budding demolition experts growing up in that unsavoury neighbourhood. We crept up on them slowly, then let fly with a couple of arrows. They both bounced harmlessly off the roof, but nevertheless had the required effect. The surprised militia dropped through the gaps they'd created in the roof and made for cover. Sensing possible victory, we moved in cautiously. How were we to know that they weren't on their own? They had older boys with them, and as already explained; older boys and air guns were almost synonymous. No sooner had we kicked the door in and rushed forward - arrows and elastic at the stretch - than the sound of guns going off, closely followed by the intimidating whine of ricocheting pellets, assailed us from all directions. Discretion was called for. Dust and ourselves were to be seen together! I don't even think that our screaming mach 7 voices caught up with us until we stopped for breath. Okay, it was a tactical error, but

110

at least we'd come out of it unscathed. Other targets would have to be sought. At that time the new Catholic church of St Basils was under construction and it was a field of combat much favoured by local warriors. Mounds of excavated earth, stacks of bricks, house-to-house-like half-built sections, and a network of ready-made trenches were ideal for their gladiatorial purposes. Eddy and I moved off in its combative direction. We were not to be disappointed; a full-blown battle was already raging by the time we got there. Guns, catapults, and bows-and-arrows were all involved in the deadly exchanges of fire, with the odd lobbed house brick thrown in for good measure. This was serious business we thought. Injuries were distinctly possible. All the circumspection of the time-served veteran soldier would be needed if we were to come out of this battle in one piece. While the assembled troops were preoccupied with the hostilities we made our way along the flank and holed-up behind one of the mounds of excavated earth. From the other side of the mound there drifted up the whispered voices of a group of boys discussing tactics. Not being one to miss such an opportunity, I picked up half a house-brick, drew the imaginary pin with my teeth, counted five, and then threw it over the top. I've heard some screams in my life but that one was definitely x-rated. I hadn't expected a direct hit and as a consequence the bottom fell straight out of my stomach and my world. Obviously, not wishing to be detected, Eddy and I took off at full speed under cover of the spoil-heap and hid behind a stack of bricks. Cautiously I lifted my head up and peered out across the top of the them. The hysterical casualty was in full view. He was holding his head and blood was streaming down his face. I can't tell you just how I felt at that moment; it's almost impossible to describe the mix of emotions experienced. I certainly didn't feel proud of myself. Not for the first time in my short life I found the results of my actions sickening. My self-recriminations were bad enough but on top of that the over activeness of my childish imagination convinced me that the lad was going to die and that I would be tried, found guilty, and hung for the dastardly crime. The weight of having

111

to take responsibility for one's actions was for once bearing heavily on my young shoulders. The image of that boy, blooded and in agony, in the midst of soon to be consecrated ground, was etched deeply into my pagan mind. If he had died it would have surely been for my sins! Trembling, fearful, and resolved never to commit such a despicable act again, I slunk off sheepishly in the direction of the confessional.

The scene of that bloodshed was soon to become the scene of much boredom. In due course the building work was completed and St Basils was ready for its inaugural service. If Catholic masses appeared interminable at the best of times, then the consecration of a church partook of eternity itself. It was a job for the bishop and a number of dignitaries would have to be invited so as to give added pomp to the liturgical ceremony. I can't remember who it was exactly but I think the guest of honour was a member of the aristocracy. Now, as it happens, St Basil's church was built at the end of a no-through road - or was it rood? - Anyway, not wishing the dignitaries to suffer the indignity of three-point turns they actually constructed a roundabout so that the chauffeur driven limousines could be graciously accommodated. If as much of the ratepayer's money was spent on the arts as opposed to being spent on such ridiculous enterprises as the one aforementioned, then this book would have been written in surroundings more conducive to literature than the old mother Hubbard's cupboard of a garret where one lucubrates *en ce moment*. I digress yet again. I do apologize; forgive me. It was about that time that I started going to a new school. Adjoining the church and the convent of St Basils the Roman Catholic Primary School of St Teresa's had been recently opened. My daily journeys to Stanford-le-Hope and back were at last over with and I could continue my schooling much closer to home. Coincidentally, my first schools in both London and Basildon had the very same name - although, that's where the similarity stopped. I probably only spent about a year at that school in Basildon but of all the places where attempts were made at educating me, it was undoubtedly there that I came closest to enjoying the experience. Not only was it a bright modern building but the enlightened policy of having at least as many lay-teachers as nuns added to the sense of having finally left the Dark-Ages and to have become acquainted with the twentieth century at last. When I peer in through the windows of primary schools nowadays they seem little different to me than the way St Teresa's was then. All available wall-space covered with paintings and drawings, bottles full of wild flowers, jars full of tadpoles, and enough misshapen plasticine animals to fill a dozen Noah's Arks. Lay-teachers - and it has to be said - even nuns, came across as friendly, caring, and genuinely interested in one's temporal as well as spiritual well-being. I remember not only enjoying lessons for the first time in my life, but as a corollary to that, feel that I may have actually learnt something in the bargain! Unlike my uncertain gender memories of St Josephs, St Teresa's was definitely a mixed school. Girls were still spit-worthy of course, vague, be-ribboned, ginghamy creatures haunting the periphery of my misogynistic existence. Okay, all that would change soon enough. But for the present it was still a man's world. Albeit a rather puny one! As is usual with me, what other people deem as pessimism on my part invariably turns out to be uncannily accurate foresight. Schooling as good as that just couldn't be real, could it? Something just had to go wrong. There were minor low points, such as country dancing. The Valetta and the Gay-Gordons never having been strong points of mine. But once again it was religion that was about to lower the spirits more than anything else. The nadir came with the preparations for the consecration of St Basils. Daily at assembly, for weeks on end, we were instructed in the arts of cheering, flag-waving, praying and processing. Not satisfied with the length of the inaugural mass proper, it had to be rehearsed and rehearsed and rehearsed ad infinitum. When the great day finally came it was great indeed. It was to be my first practical experience of Einsteinian relativity. If you'd witnessed the opening ceremonies, then went away for the duration, and came back just in time for the closing address; you would have been only six hours older, whereas I would

113

have had all the hirsute appearance of Methuselah's great grandfather. There were more yawns in the nave on that day than there are black holes in the universe. Any one of us would have been first choice recruits for training as test pilots for Sleep-Easy or Dunlopillo. There was enough holy-water splashed around in the aisles and slopping about in piscinas to have filled an Olympic-sized swimming pool. Candles melted imperceptibly through the endless hours, guttered, went out, were replaced and re-lit. Only to go through the same mind-numbingly slow process all over again. Latin was incomprehensibly Latinate. An organ droned, dirged and lamented in an appropriately doleful manner. Incense was even more incensing that usual. Even my dear old grandmother - specially shipped in from London to witness the devout spectacle - was seen to be nodding uncharacteristically in the pews. The service did come to an end of course, but not before I'd vowed at least a thousand times to search out a religion that espoused the virtue of brevity. Unfortunately I was not to be allowed to make such choices for myself until I had reached school-leaving age. So far from being able to adopt another system of worship, the one I already found myself entangled in, was soon to be reinforced. The time for 'confirmation' was nigh and I was expected to prepare myself religiously! The only possible advantage I could see to being confirmed in those days was that of finding oneself the proud owner of an extra Christian name. Not only that but I was allowed to choose it for myself. The choice was restricted to saint's names mind you. But then, there was no shortage of those in the Catholic Church! Naturally, I decided upon Peter - the patron saint of fishermen. It wasn't until much later that I discovered that it also meant 'The Rock'. For some strange reason it always brings a quaint old French maxim to mind - *'il y a un anguille sous la roche'.* There being no literal translation, the 'smelling of rats' will have to suffice. Having chosen the name and meditated for a few seconds on the magnitude of the spiritual step I was about to take, all that was required of me was that I suffer the ordeal of yet another marathon session of prayers

114

and genuflexion. This time though the solemnities were alleviated somewhat by the sound of me regaling the approbatory congregation with snippets of unaccompanied plainsong. So there you have it. Through absolutely no fault of my own, merely by an accident of time and space, I found myself a fully-fledged - if somewhat un-angelic - member of the apostolic brotherhood. Whatever freedom of thought I'd been invested with at birth had finally been banged-up by my ecclesiastical warders. And St Peter - rock that he undoubtedly was - smiled benignly and threw away the keys.

Chapter 8. Markets and Moving Images.

Although I was still friends with Eddy and would be well into my teenage years, I had begun to make other friendships. Of one in particular I have especially fond memories. Charlie Keens was the epitome of boyhood, albeit in a 'Just William' sort of way. Mischief and Charlie were never far apart. Trouble followed him - and anyone else who cared to tag along - like his own shadow. He was a short stocky little lad with fair hair and clear blue eyes. The potentially angelic look was kept in check by means of a crew cut and almost permanent grimace. He certainly looked at home in the land of the East Saxons (Essex) and one instinctively felt that he had made the whole of it his personal territory. I fought with him on many occasions. It was unavoidable. And although a head taller and slightly heavier than he was I never once defeated him. He was invincible. But for all his fractiousness he was - and still remains, although I haven't seen or heard of him for more than 35 years - one of my best friends. It was a case, as they say, of better a friend than an enemy. One of the first places we explored - not to say exploited - together, was Pitsea-Market. It was situated, in the then; still elm lined Station Lane and was comprised of a higgledy-piggledy collection of ramshackle buildings constructed out of RSJ's, timber and the ever-present corrugated iron. Three of the structures were large, green-painted and hanger-like. Between and around those nestled a variety of flat-roofed buildings, which housed food-arcades and a cafeteria. On two sides of the enclosed areas there were open spaces to accommodate the stalls and other sundry pitches. Right through the middle of the market - between two of the hanger-like buildings - ran a wide concrete thoroughfare like the fifties equivalent of the pedestrian precinct. Although the market itself only traded on Wednesday and Saturday mornings it could, and did, receive our attention on most days of the week. Our favourite day was probably Saturday though. We would get there early, sometime between 6 and 7am, and offer our services to the

116

traders. They were always glad to see us and would give us sixpence or a shilling for helping them to unload their vans and set up the stalls. We had a couple of regulars we usually worked for and would always go back to them at closing time to help them pack-up and reload their vehicles. In the meantime there was the market proper to explore. Where does one start when trying to describe such a veritable wonderland as that was? We were like foxes in the chicken-coop. We didn't know which way to turn for the best or what delectable offering was to receive our attention first. For the taste-buds there was the handmade sweets man. He stretched and spun and looped his sugary concoction, like a skein of wool between his two magical hands. Then rolled it flat and thin on a board and cut it into bite-sized lengths with the confectioner's version of the gardener's secateurs. All the regular fruit flavours were available but at that particular time I had a thing about spearmint and could buy a monster bag-full for just one thruppenny bit! In the food-hall, one of the grocers had a sideline in broken biscuits, and was always popular with Charlie and me. For mere pennies you could pig yourself sick on the crumbling remains of such delights as, ginger-nuts, custard-creams, chocolate-bourbons and jammy-dodgers. The cheapest buy was an indistinguishable mélange of what looked like sawdust and loose-chippings. Little different from muesli I suppose in its own ersatz fashion! The cafeteria was as much of a draw to us as it was for the dark brewing tea in the great double-handled teapots resting besides the steamy, spluttering 'stills'. It was a wooden-floored, spit and sawdust establishment that would have kept any self-respecting environmental health officer permanently white-coated and swabbed-up for action. I can still smell the place in my less savoury moments. Like the mugs of tea and the rank and sweaty cheese rolls it smelled something like a cross between creosote and athlete's foot! Just about the perfect surroundings for one of my disposition! If neither food nor drink were on the agenda - which was a bit of a rarity in itself - then there was much else besides to captivate the less salivary senses. The pet-stalls were always a great attraction

117

to us, obviously. It's a well known fact that children just adore animals. Whether or not the compliment is willingly returned is of course a matter for protracted argument. And being as the majority of the quorum - excluding parrots and the like, who only say what you tell them anyway - is naturally speechless, I don't suppose that we'll ever know. Poking bits of straw up the twitching noses of rabbits was always good for a lark. The way they jumped up and down or ran round in circles kicking out their back legs was well worth the fiddly concentration involved. Puppies and kittens were great finger-sucking fun, until for no apparent reason the ungrateful little brutes decided to sink their teeth into you. There may be good scientific reasons for calling such dental equipment milk-teeth but I for one wouldn't want to put my delicate nipples into their ravenous scissoring maws. We didn't have much time for birds in cages, unless they were of the hand-reared wild variety. Parrots were interesting in a squawkish, nut-cracking sort of way, but I preferred to crush my own grapes, thank you very much! As for budgerigars and canaries, well, you could keep them. The only time that I was ever remotely interested in budgerigars was when I heard the joke: 'what makes budgies bounce with health?' Answer - rubber boots! Okay, not hilarious perhaps; but then, I was only a baby cuttlefish at the time! And as for canaries, well, they're about as entertaining to me as whistling jaundice; and anyway I prefer my custard without feathers! After upsetting the animal kingdom in general you could always mooch off and find a stallholder to annoy in particular. We usually ended up the worse for these barracking encounters but as our gym teachers were endlessly fond of telling us it was playing the game that counted and not the winning. Some hope! In one of the hangers a large area was given over to household-junk. Nowadays much of that 'junk' would be considered *objet d'art* and some of it without doubt, antique. Present day collectors of china and porcelain, brass and bronze - and who knows, even gold and silver - would give their last backhander to a dealer's-ring to have a look back through that trove of so-called bric-a-brac. What was throw-away then would probably now take pride of place in the knocker-spotted windows of any parvenu haunted country town! While some it seems were unwittingly giving fortunes away, others it appears were busy making theirs. The spiel of the general trader could be heard above the rest of the discordant hubbub of a market in full swing, as it pitched to the point of another sale.

"Not five, not free, not two, not even firty-bob! Come on, 'ho'll give us a guinea for the lot!" He juggled with cups and saucers, spread plates like a fan, and even balanced a teapot on his head. "What's a matter wiv yer?" he continued. "Is yer all deaf an' dumb as well as stupid?" He looked across to his assistant. "I dunno what's wrong wiv 'em!" he said. "Chuck in some of them sheets! 'ere's what I' gonna do, though 'ow I'm gonna feed me kids at this rate, I'll never know!" His assistant lobbed over a few packs of sheets. "Not one, not two, not even free single-sheets, but five singles and a double frown in fer good luck, plus the dinner-set all fer a guinea! I'll bleedin' starve first, before I leave 'ere wivout sellin' suffink!" And of course he did sell suffink he always sold suffink. That most of his goods were as phony as his accent was well known. Everyone had been caught before and no doubt would be again. It didn't seem to matter that the plates got home cracked, that sheets were frayed, or that shirts sometimes had a sleeve missing. It was cheaper than going to the Palladium and probably far more entertaining. Regular traders would always exchange shoddy goods - for the persistent complainer - after a bit of good-humoured argy-bargying. As for the one-off illegal pitches, well you knew it was a bit of a gamble. You paid your money and you took your chances.

Something else that the market was good for was that it enabled us to replenish our stocks of 'smoker's requisites'. I'm not talking about the exchange of legal tender in the tobacconists though, what I'm actually talking about is the age-old childhood pursuit of 'finders keepers; losers weepers'.

For some unknown reason we were more likely to find whole cigarettes in discarded packets at the market than just about anywhere else. Some of the raw-throated, green complexioned, brand names that come dizzily to mind are: 'Craven A', 'Turf Airman', 'Weights' and 'Gold Flake'. If luck - oh yes, not forgetting 'Lucky Strike' - were against us in the lost and found department of whole cigarettes, then the time-honoured down-and-out- pastime of picking up dog-ends would be resorted to. In many ways under-age smoking was more frowned upon then than it is nowadays. You didn't see children lighting up as soon as they came out of school. It was very much a secretive affair and if caught in the act by a teacher or a policeman you were in for the high jump. In a busy market place a certain amount of cunning was needed in the surreptitious art of butt collecting. Many a thick ear was promised and occasionally achieved in the process. Having stocked-up on smokables a safe retreat would have to be sought. Our favourite place was the market roof itself. A three-foot high brick wall gave us the height we required to lift ourselves up onto a flat guttered area between two sloping roofs. After the market had packed-up for the day, it was there that we concealed ourselves, to puff away to our hearts - if not lungs - content. The unwholesomeness of it all is sickening to think of even now. Apart from the normal dangers to one's health associated with smoking, when I think of the soggy, salivary, potential of hepatitis B and tuberculosis attached to such depraved habits I'm inclined to rush towards the nearest bottle of expectorant! The only problem with our somewhat elevated smoker's den was that the evidence of our misdemeanours could be seen rising wraith-like into the blue-beyond. The market was patrolled and guarded along the lines of Colditz by a man and his two particularly savage Alsatian dogs. On more than one occasion our nicotine-induced tranquility was disturbed by the appearance of an admonitory head levitating leeringly above a drainpipe. "What yer up to yer little basstards!" the guard would inquire reprovingly. "Get dahn from there right now, or else!" The breath required for an impromptu escape was hard to catch through the engulfing asthmatic haze, but smoker's cough or not; blood, muscles and oxygen somehow came together and the distances conducive to bravado were affected. "Yer girt fat git," bellowed Charlie - somewhat lacking in respect for his elders and betters I thought - "Yer can't catch us!" The fact hadn't occurred to him that he had two well-trained salivating guard dogs and that both exits would be snarlingly covered. "Yer useless pratt Charlie," I 'whispered' accusingly. "Why d'yer 'ave ter call 'im names? We'll never get away now!" But we did, we invariably did. By means of diversionary tactics we could usually get the jumped-up sadist and his two demented canines in the same place at the same time, leap off the roof from the other side of the building and make a determined run for it. If we still had any matches left we could always set light to a pile of rubbish on our way out. If it was good enough for armies in retreat, then it was good enough for us!

Next to the market stood that other magnet to children - and lovers of Kilroy everywhere - the public convenience. As an added attraction the fruit-and-veg stalls were set up in front of them, and even when not trading there was usually some rotted fruit to be sorted through before the bin-men made their collection. The pleasures of sitting on the loo and cogitating were developed early in my case. Legs dangling, with trousers around my ankles, I would sit for hours avoiding the foetid bruises and black slimes on both apples and bananas, whilst learning by heart all the bum-buggering addresses of the local 12" erectile supermen. The terrible thing to admit is that even at that tender age there was very little by way of scurrilous information etched into those walls that needed clarification on my behalf. Maybe we didn't use such sexually clinical words as fellatio and cunnilingus but all forms of gentital manipulation, oral or otherwise, were known about in all their sniggering detail. Even so there were things that we were not privy to. There was much conjecture about the discarded sanitary towels we found in the lady's toilets. It was inconceivable to us that the market could be so dangerous to the health of female of the species. There was hardly a soiled bandage to be seen in the gents, so why it was that women seemed so prone to injury was very confusing indeed! It was a waste of time asking the girls about it because they were as mystified as we were. Even those who had got through the trauma of their first period, having been reassured that they weren't bleeding to death after all, were not very forthcoming. At the onset of menstruation it seemed that girls were automatically enrolled into the secret society of all things womanly. Pink faces and whispers were all that could be expected from them from that point onwards.

In amongst the bushes at the back of the public conveniences a deep overgrown ditch ran into a three-foot concrete conduit. I've never lived anywhere where there hasn't been local folk-law concerning secret passages. Pitsea was no exception and that particular concrete pipe was ours. It was said that one branch of it went to St Michael's church and that another ran down to the ancient Pitsea-Hall on the edge of the marshes. The purpose of its excavation, was as always, linked to the activities of smugglers. If perchance, there were as many tunnels as local story telling avows, up and down the country, we would all be in constant danger of disappearing into the bowels of the earth - to use another scatological metaphor. But for children of course all those subterranean tales of evil doings were very believable indeed. Not only believable but in dire need of authenticating. I can't tell you just how many times I set off down that dark, dank, echoing tube, only for fear to get the better of me and send me scurrying back to the safety of daylight. It was like a journey back into the womb itself. To make any headway at all you had you get into a near foetal position and claw yourself along by your hands on the slippery circular surfaces. It was heart-poundingly warm and watery inside there and how anyone can talk of the womb in terms of security is beyond all understanding. Cold sweats and claustrophobia is all it induced in me. I would have been far happier with a good world welcoming, arse-slap, anyway! Truth is it was probably no more than a rat-infested storm water drain and we were lucky never to have been trapped and drowned in there in the flash-floods following thunder and lightning. Suffice it to say that we never did find any contraband in those resounding watercourses, but we did find our fear, and to a certain extent at least, learnt to confront it.

At night the market was the haunt of tramps and lovers, both of which category as far as we were concerned, were ripe for our unwarranted intrusions. Tramps were in obvious need of rousing, nobody could possibly want to spend all night snoozing in a place as marvelous as that, And lovers - already roused beyond the point of no return - would, given time - nine months as a rule - be grateful for the coitus interruptus! It's always been strange to me how some of my firmest held convictions could be so vehemently disagreed with on the part of others. However, convinced of our moral right and the ultimate good of our actions, we continued to bang loudly on the corrugated iron and to throw handfuls of gravel into the unseeing blackness whenever we felt the evangelical need to do so. The joint sounds of very un-lady-like screams and the twanging of suspender-straps being most gratifying to the budding missionary. Mind you, thwarted male lovers - unlike your average shuffling bag-man - once readjusted in the clothing department could be pretty quick on their feet, and contingency plans were often put into operation at break-neck speed! So that was Pitsea-Market. Day or night, summer or winter, open or closed, there we could often be found idling about its alluring vicinity, planning or already having committed one sort of diabolical deed or another. Whenever I think of my childhood those commercial environs are as much a part of it as the bridle path, the willow pond or the marshes. There I made and lost both friends and money. I earned, stole, fought and ran. Much of what I needed to know to help me along the wicked ways of my depraved existence was learnt there amongst the catchers and the caught alike. Even now, the long engrained habit of kicking empty cigarette-cartons and rummaging about in rubbish plagues my otherwise sophisticated approach towards the arts of shopping. Perhaps, given time, I'll even overcome the uncontrollable urge I have to stoop whenever I come across a well-sucked, juicy looking dog-end. Perhaps!

Sometimes, between bouts of loading and unloading in the market, Charlie and I would succumb to the delights of that other Saturday-Morning institution - the flicks. I used to receive nine pence pocket money every week. That meant sixpence to get into the pictures and three whole pennies to spend on whatever else took my fancy. If we were lucky - included in our entrance fee - there would sometimes be a free bottle of Coca-Cola or a Palm Toffee Bar. We certainly knew how to live in those days, didn't we? Our local 'flea-pit' was known as The Century. I don't suppose it was much different to any of the small-town cinemas to be found in the rest of the country. Between the strip-glass frames displaying the stills of forthcoming attractions, three sets of double-doors opened onto the foyer. On one side of the foyer was the tiny ticket window and on the other side stood an ice cream and confectionery kiosk. At the far end two more sets of double-doors led on to a small flight of ascending stairs. From the top of those you could look down on three rows of seats separated by two aisles. From the back of the auditorium to the front there was a drop of some ten feet. The stage itself was raised to about six feet above floor level and behind the main curtain and the fire-curtain there was the screen. The commissionaire was a man we all knew as Uncle Jack. He was a tall, slim, mild-mannered man who always looked resplendent in his military styled uniform. His unenviable task on Saturday mornings was to keep in order, what could only be described as a cacophonous rabble. One method of crowd control practiced was that of separating us up after we'd purchased our tickets into three groups. One of the groups was allowed to go in through the front entrance while the rest had to queue up outside by one or other of the many fire-exits. One of those was situated at the back of the building next to a cage containing the emergency generator. I don't know how it worked but I well remember the way it cut on and off automatically adding its deep mechanical drone to the clamour of our already high-pitched impatience. "Why are we waitin'," we yelled. "Why are we waitin'," ad so ad nauseum. When the doors were finally opened there was a veritable stampede. Single file now children," demanded the usherette, unrealistically, before she dodged back out of the way and let us get on with it ourselves. Pandemonium could only be described as the last word in understatement as far as that cinematic experience was concerned. A ravening hoard of ragged trousered imbeciles, charged, bumped, shoved and clawed their way into all the available seats. Frilly-frocked and beribboned girls, along with delicate, pasty-faced boys, were mercilessly trampled in the rush. Imagine yourself ensconced within a beehive, the incessant hum and movement being amplified to the utmost degree, and you would then have some idea of the decibelic values involved! Why I ever went to that god-forsaken place I'll never know. I was no more a lover of noise in those days than I am now and I would have certainly preferred to both see and hear the films properly, which was in the event, next to impossible. One of the favourite scams at the time was to let people in without paying. When the general hubbub and confusion was at its height and the manager and his staff fully preoccupied with trying to achieve some semblance of normality amongst the screeching multitudes, someone would creep off and open one of the fire-exits. The invading chink of daylight would alert the usherettes to the danger immediately and they would make a determined dash to close the breach in their defenses. Whilst they were off battening down the hatches on one side of the cinema other little wags would be opening the exit doors elsewhere. How they ever managed to get all the doors closed, the children seated and the film to commence, is nothing short of miraculous. Even then there was no peace. All manner of rubbish was thrown up into the projector-beams to see what sort of effect it would have on the screen. Ice cream would be flicked from the tips of spoons to see how far it would travel, and more especially, exactly where its journey would terminate. Cigarettes would be lit and little girls would issue forth with squeaky voices, "You're not supposed to be smoking, I'm gonna tell the manager of yer, nur!" "Tell tale tit, tell tale tit, yer make me sick, yer make me wanna shit!" and other choice reprovings would ensue. Torches swivelled about like searchlights, closely followed by the mandatory blast, "Put that fag out!" As far as the films went, even then I think I preferred the cartoons most of all. They were easy to follow and funny. An infallible recipe in the world of entertainment I should say! Some of the B Films - especially those of the Edger Wallace variety - were boring to the extreme. If it had been quiet enough to hear them I don't think that many of us would have bothered to listen anyway. Cowboys, I never liked, I always preferred the Indians. Minority groups and political correctness were part of my value system even then. Why should the Lone-Ranger wear the trousers? Give me a man in a loincloth any day! Excepting perhaps, Tarzan - far too upper class for my liking. Cisco and Pancho were ideal for the black and white screen I suppose, but both the stereotypical plots and the back projection left a lot to be desired. And why did so many people wear masks in those days? What did they have to hide? Mostly their goodness it seems, which is rather encouraging in a perverse sort of way! It wasn't just cowboys either, even The Count of Monte-Cristo had to get in on the act. Perhaps even then there was a shortage of good-guys and one angelic actor had to wear the mask and play all the heroic costume parts? Nothing would surprise me where Hollywood film contracts are concerned! The Bowery Boys and the Bash Street Kids - or Gang? - were okay in their own way. They had the right mix of violence and anarchy to suit a discerning juvenile audience. And the hierarchical sadism exhibited by The Three Stooges appealed to the vicious streak in all of us; to some extent tempered, depending on which of the three one identified oneself with! There was one serial however that always got the better of me and had me ducking down behind the seats quaking with fear. 'Flash-Gordon'. Nowadays it would probably be his tights that would put the fear of God in me, but then it was the monsters he had to deal with, not to mention the sinister rulers of equally sinister planets. There were some good-looking women though, in a statuesque - not to say wooden - sort of way. Not that women interested me very much at that time. They were still very much creatures of outer space and inner-kitchens according to the laws of any egg-headed, inter-galactic, male chauvinism. If the world as it was then had been as concerned with equality as it is now, then undoubtedly the girls would have been the proud possessors of ray-guns and I would have been atomized a long, long, time ago. Between films there were prizes to be won. The manager would get up on the stage and loudly demand our silence. The chance of getting something for nothing was usually enough to quieten us down for a while. "The first one up on stage with a green tie will win this lovely packet of 'Refreshers'," enthused the manager. Not only was the prize on offer not likely to start a stampede, but green ties and grubby little boys were a mite antipathetic to say the least. One or two of the lads from the goody-goody-gum-drops school of film-buffery made their way to the front of the auditorium, gleefully waving their prize-winning apparel. Needless to say, the reception they got from the rest of us - girls excluded - had a somewhat wayward ring to it. Hoots of derision were lofted to the rafters and pink-faced, limp-tied boys, would scurry for cover like timid rabbits. "The first girl on stage with white socks," continued the manager undaunted. As is well known the ratio of white socks on little girls is just about diametrically opposed to that of green ties on loutish lads. As a consequence of this fact it seemed as though half the audience rose as one and made for the stage in unison. You don't need me to tell you about the problems involved with quarts and pint-pots! Toes were trod on; hair pulled and shins kicked. Those normally delicate little creatures could be seen climbing over the seats, knickers to the wind, clawing and scratching at each other in the aisles. What was it Rudyard Kipling said about the female of the species being deadlier than the male? I for one was already frantically making mental notes. Perhaps it's the associations I still make between knickers and violence that keeps my therapist and the

127

dispensers of chlorpromazine in the luxury to which they've grown so regally accustomed. The prizes were never worth very much, packets of sweets, peanuts, small toys - even water pistols when the manager felt like living dangerously - and ice cream. I don't ever remember winning anything. Perhaps if he'd asked for the first person with chewing gum stuck to the seat of his pants, or a pocket-full of sherbet-lemons and dog-ends, I might have stood a chance. There you are, some you win, and some you lose, or so some-such fatuous saying goes! Two things marked the end of Saturday-Morning Pictures. One was that cleanest-cut of all clean-cut cowboys, Hop-along-Cassidy. Saying such less than endearing things as: "Well now boys and girls, be good to yaw mom and dad, and don't forget ter drink yer milk," Some hopes! The other was something far more unpalatable and to be avoided at all costs, The National Anthem. If you thought that the entry into the cinema was dangerous enough then the exit would have to be seen to be believed! Patriots, we were not. The manager and his staff tried to instill some discipline, God bless 'em! But it was a monumental task and bound to end in failure. "When God Save the Queen has finished," the manager instructed. "I would like you all to move one row at a time into the aisles and then walk quietly in single-file, walk I said, not run, to your nearest exit point." Can you believe the faith of some people? No sooner had Hop-along-Cassidy faded away behind the fire-curtain than all hell broke lose. We turned biblical teaching on its head. We were the camels and those tiny apertures of daylight - otherwise known as fire-exits - were the needles' eyes. We threaded our dromedary and Bactrian selves at full hump, bump and bumbling speed out into heaven's diurnal kingdom, with our sides in stitches and not a pricked conscience to be found amongst us. Talking of stitches, that reminds me. What was it my mother used to say about God paying debts without money? Once, rushing from the flicks to get back to the market in time for loading up the vans, I had a head-long contretemps with a patch of stinging-nettles. I can see it now, frame by agonizing frame. Short trousers and a tee shirt are no match for that particularly venomous form of botanical defense, even though the pantheist in me still allows for a certain amount of anthropomorphic aggression. Whilst we still have proverbs in mind, insult should be added to injury, in the shape of a broken bottle secreted deep within the painful foliage. I don't think that I'd be making a rash statement that we are here back at the very root and stem of my pessimistic overview. Would not bare flesh and nettles have been enough? Did the balancer of life's equations have to break a bottle on my behalf and add it to his already one-sided calculations? It would seem so, simultaneous being the correct algebraic term I think I'm looking for. While writing this I'm studying the tip of the lech-man or medical finger of my left hand and the scar still clearly visible after nearly fifty years is over an inch long. The medical finger, mind you! What chance has a body got after falling victim to such an early calamity as that? Portentous indeed! I never did have it stitched up. All I had in the way of treatment for that traumatic experience - not counting the half-hundredweight of dock-leaves rubbed in a mite too enthusiastically by Charlie; the only available paramedic - was lint and antiseptic cream for the finger and a bucket-full of ice cold calamine lotion for the third-degree nettle-rash. If only I'd taken notice of Hop-along-Cassidy. Things would have been different. I'm sure they would!

Chapter 9. Bikes, Breaststrokes and Bandages.

Swimming was a much-loved summery pastime. Not without its own inherent dangers though, as we will see in due course. The first serious swimming I got involved in was at a pool adjoining Riverside Farm down by Vange Wharf. When I say serious, what I mean is that it was there that I both learnt to swim and nearly drowned at the same time! Both sides of the watery coin coming somewhat fortuitously together. As pools go it was rather a small affair. Even as a child it seemed tiny, and when I consider the discrepancy in size between my playground at Stanford-le-Hope as remembered and the postage-stamp that it now appears in reality, then it must have been minute indeed. My other major memory of that pool was the vegetation. We're not talking about tastefully arranged plants to give it a sub-tropical ambience. No, we're talking about the Unintentional - though quite natural - slimes and algae that tend to proliferate in stagnant water. It was there that my lovable older brother decided that I was in urgent need of a swimming lesson and sent me slithering slime-wards into the deeps. I must say that the sudden shock of wetness, warmth and invading bacilli did wonders for my doggy-paddle! Although, on looking back, it was that rich an organic soup, that to sink in it would have been pretty near impossible. If there's any truth to the walking on the waters type of miracle, then I have a rough idea of what sort of water was involved. Sadly, such bodies as the Health and Safety Inspectorate were not in full bureaucratic swing in those days. The bacilli didn't strike, but the poliomyelitis virus did. I don't know much about the water-borne infectiousness of viruses but a couple of cases were contracted locally and the pool at Vange blamed and duly closed down. What I do know about is the panic that followed and the vaccination programme that was brought swiftly into action. Another of our favourite swimming locations were what were known locally as the side-pools. I'm not sure exactly what they were originally, probably clay-workings connected with the Vange

Brickworks. Whatever they were, they made ideal swimming pools. There were quite a few of them, cut small and square and about four foot deep. They were spread out along the sides of the creeks and were replenished with seawater at every spring tide. In the summer - if the weather had been fine and dry for any length of time - they would become as warm as a bath and were very tempting indeed for potential skinny-dippers. My problem of course was one that I've come to regard with defensive irony as Linford's Luck! To find another broken bottle so soon after the last one, and with the other end of my naked personage to boot, is to feel oneself to be the receiver of direct missives from the Fates and Furies. I'd be lying again if I said that whilst writing this I'm looking at the two inch scar on my left foot - widdershins may have something to do with it - but I have just felt it through my sock and can assure you that my imagination is figmentless. It was a long walk home from the marshes with my dripping confederates, and to my eternal shame I broke down bloody and blubbering before I'd even got half way. Then for once in my life I had the sharp unmistakable taste of a silver spoon in my mouth. My piteous cries had been overheard by the Samaritan of all Samaritans - a nurse no less. "Oh you poor little mite," she soothed. What have you gone and done to yourself?" "I've cut me foot missus," I snivelled. "An' it hurts." "You come indoors with me and I'll make it all better for you," she promised. I should have known differently. Okay she was a nurse, but she was still a she, and she was an adult as well. Those are the sort of combinations I'd suffered from before and the ensuing experience was to do little to change my mind about such matters. What is it about nurses and iodine? Are they sadists or what? I bet you a pound to a pinch of the proverbial, that if that vitriolic gunk were to be analyzed by the top medical scientists known to humankind, it would prove to be near medicinally useless to either man or beast - or boy for that matter. I tell you, they enjoy dowsing you in the stuff. Whether or not it's their sly way at getting back at a patriarchal society I don't know, If so, perhaps there is a certain amount of natural justice on their side - perhaps.

131

But to a poor, sick, defenseless child? No way! That's taking the Hippocratic oath just a smidgen too far for my liking. The only consolation I had of course was that Linford's Luck had proved itself as infallible as ever and that my a priori claims to eternal gloom, doom and despondency had once again been vindicated.

Along with swimming two other things have become inextricably linked in my mind. One, due to the distances involved is cycling and the other owing to my then ever-increasing age and the developing need to impress those erstwhile detested creatures, namely girls, is clothing. Most of my friends who were lucky enough to have bicycles had the sporty drop-handle barred type with double-clangers and Campagnola gears. I on the other hand had a Gresham-Flyer. Even the name has a satirical ring to it! It was a hand or two shorter than the steeds most favoured by my contemporaries and had straight handlebars and the more sedate hub-gears. It was painted in an unfortunate, eye-catching shade of snazzy metallic mauve, and if that wasn't enough to negate the desired anonymity, the 'designers' had decided to put a racy curve in the crossbar where it dipped down under the saddle. I could usually be seen standing up on the pedals, blue in the face and rocking from side to side, about half a mile behind the rest of the heads down streamlined pack. The closest I ever came to wearing the yellow jersey - due entirely to the weight of the machine and natural forces - was when careering out of control down a 1 in 8 with the wind behind me! What I lost in street credibility because of my antiquated velocipede I tried to make up for sartorially. Black jeans, a pastel shaded Fred Perry, and blue bumpers were all the rage in those days. I was especially fond of my only fashion accessory; a black and yellow striped snake-belt. Why the girls weren't swooning at my elegant feet - young Adonis that I was - was a mystery to me, and I could often be found exchanging quizzical glances with myself in the full-length mirror. Fair hair - almost blond when bleached by the summer sun - and translucent blue eyes should have done the trick, but unfortunately they didn't. The fact that I was covered in bum-fluff and pimples, had a squeaky two-tone klaxon of a voice and looked very young for my already tender years may have had something to do with it. But the eyes of the beholder were untarnished and I put my relational problems down to the capriciousness and lack of taste in the unfathomable opposite gender. Battlesbridge - about five miles from Pitsea - boasted the closest open-air swimming pool of any consequence and was a regular haunt of ours during the summer months. It was a well-maintained pool and the blue-painted sides and bottom gave it something of a Mediterranean air when viewed through the clear, balmy, sun-sparkling water. On three sides of the pool there were sloping grass-banks - much used by nubile sun-worshipers - and at the far end there was a glass-fronted cafeteria that looked out over the pool. It was there that posing first became a way of life. I didn't think that woollen trunks were exactly *à la mode* even then, but felt that the tasteful addition of a snake-belt would counteract my otherwise unfashionable appearance. Charlie didn't look much better either but at least he had the added advantage of a crew cut and some almost rippling muscles. I was pitifully thin in those days and spent an inordinate amount of studying the adverts in the Sunday papers. But unlike Charles Atlas I wasn't fated to be a kicker of sand into other guy's faces. The only information in the adverts that could have been of any possible use to me was to be found in the small print, i.e., satisfaction guaranteed within three months or your money back! Of course this didn't stop me walking with a swagger and flexing my puny, bicep-less arms at every available opportunity. I may have stood more of a chance if I'd stuck a sausage down the front of my trunks, but as it was water and genitalia had naturally repellent properties, and I would perhaps have been better advised to have worn a two-piece swimsuit and tried my luck elsewhere! If fashion sense and bodily attributes were not to produce the desired results, then machismo would have to be achieved by other methods. I wasn't a very good swimmer and my diving skills were even worse. Nevertheless, having seen a striking young lady

133

looking in my direction, after I'd managed a superb belly flop with half-pike, I thought that I'd found the short-cut to romance. It didn't occur to me that the glances received were far from admiring ones. Not for a minute did I think that those derisory smirks were other than genuine smiles conferred adoringly with regards to my Olympian prowess. Me, make a pratt of myself? Never! From being no diver at all to becoming the high-diving champion of all time took but a matter of minutes only. I progressed from the side of the pool to the springboard and on up through the stages to the top-board itself in quick untutored succession. Nobody had told me that on impact with the water one had to raise one's arms so as to reduce the chances of diver and concrete making unadvisable contact with each other. On the one and only occasion I ever dived from the top-board in any swimming pool - an act of extreme bravery on my part I might add; despite the attendant folly - gravity and pool-bottom did unfortunately coincide! It was only a little bump and being as I'd entered the water cleanly I was sure that nobody could have seen my sub aqueous failings. On emerging from the pool I expected no less than rapturous approbation. I wasn't disappointed. Everybody, but everybody, was looking at me. Fame at last, I thought. I'd finally been recognized as the expert I undoubtedly was. I was so proud. Chest puffed out - another overstatement admittedly - I floated along the edge of the pool soaking up the unaccustomed attention. Yet I couldn't understand why the looks were getting so serious, awestruck even. I could only put it down to the fact that my mastery of air and water was so complete that it had left my audience dumbfounded. And then I wiped the water away from my eyes. Eureka! My hand was bright red and blood was streaming down my face and beginning to find its way elsewhere over my little athletic body. "Bleedin' 'ell Merv, yer must 'av' cracked yer skull right open," screeched Charlie, reassuringly. I wanted to say something like, quick help me I'm dying, but there were too many girls watching for that. "It aint nuffink," I bluffed. "It's only a scratch, where's the first aid post, they'll put a plaster on it for me." Well, they didn't put a plaster on it, they wrapped my head up in bandages until I looked like a stand-in for the Invisible Man and sent me off on the five-mile cycle ride home. As you can imagine the looks I received from motorists and pedestrians alike, were curious to say the least. I must have looked like a survivor from The Charge of the Light Brigade, but alas, there was no Florence Nightingale to come to my rescue. When I arrived home - shell-shocked and battle-weary in my blooded balaclava - Charlie, being the officer and gentleman that he was, did the right thing. He knocked loudly on my front door a couple of times, then scarpered! "I'll see yer lata Merv," he hollered by way of a valediction. "Let me know 'ow yer get on." By this time my parents were well beyond the stage of hysterics where my interminable injuries were concerned. In fact, it must be said that I found their phlegmatic, somewhat dispassionate response to my many painful traumas, not a little insensitive. I was already well scarred and fractured. Though once, whilst showing off on a slippery, wooden, sea-weeded slipway at Westcliff-on-Sea - you try getting as many alliterative S's and W's into a phrase as short as that! - I managed to dislodge my big-toe nail between one of the cracks in the planking. Far be it from me to be casting aspersions in the direction of The St John's Ambulance Brigade and the selflessness of its medical recruits, but applying Elastoplast directly to a split and bleeding toenail, seems slightly at odds with the assumed text of their first-aid manual. Needless to say when my father removed the offending plaster to get a better look at the wound for himself, there were complications. The blood had congealed solidly between the split nail and the main artery and when the plaster was ripped away in the time-honoured fashion, blood from the severed artery spouted gushingly upwards. Believe it or not, one or two drops of that precious liquid managed to do a Jackson Pollack on the ceiling! Not being a tachist at heart the random patterning of my abstracted corpuscles was not something that I could appreciate artistically or otherwise. My major concern was with mathematics at the time, and more exactly the permutation of whole numbers subtracted from the figure 8 and the possibly dire consequences of such life-draining calculations. Once again my father donned his shining armour and proved, that even in his difficult case, gallantry could occasionally outweigh his black-knighted heartlessness. After the application of a tourniquet -like Sir Prancelot of the Lake himself - he hoicked me over his shoulder and galloped off in the direction of the doctors, my mother all the while waving - in a maidenly fashion - her favours from an upstairs window. Even the dragon it seemed had been transformed.

The game of life was constantly being interrupted for injury time. On another occasion - once again showing off in front of the girls - I fell out of a tree. The tree in question was an ancient oak located in Luncies Farm. Being a solitary specimen it had not only grown tall and wide with a magnificent stag-headed crown, but the outreaching lower boughs were as thick as ordinary tree-trunks in their own right. There, like an arboreal Robin Hood, I bounded along the boughs with seeming impunity, while all the time potential Maid-Marions looked up and gasped at my squirrel-like agility. But unlike squirrels, who seem to be able in their cute, cheek-bulging, storybook way, to discern the difference between nuts and their own being, I it seemed partook of nuttiness to the full. What pride comes before is invariably followed by the fracture-clinic! But first I had to confront my father again. Still winded and unable to move the fingers on the end of my limply hanging left arm I whimpered into the living room one summer's evening. "I fink I've broken me arm," I blubbered, fearfully. "Yer stupid cowson, your the biggest bleedin' nuisance I've ever cum across" he said, somewhat accusingly. "Sit dahn there and shut up, I'll 'av' a look at it when Maverick's finished." He was something of a telly-buff my father and cowboy films were definitely his favourites. Considering his bar-brawling, lynch-hungry approach to life it's hardly surprising really. Where was I? There must be a thread in this desultory story somewhere. Ah! Yes, I remember now. I was doing my impression of the

Invisible Man as a result of my gold-medal dive at Battlesbridge swimming pool. "What agin?" greeted daddy. "Gordon bleedin' Bennett, aint we ever gonna 'av' any peace in this God-forsaken bleedin' 'ouse of ours?" Probably not, I mused somewhat painfully. I'd built up quite a good working relationship with our local GP by this time and felt that his skills had increased considerably owing to the practice I had so frequently and readily afforded him. I had even invested in him a certain amount of trust, something that very few adults were privy to. But like all adults before - and most since, I might add paranoically - that trust was about to be betrayed. "It's not too bad," he diagnosed. "But it will need a couple of stitches," he continued, by way of prognostication. Another visit to the hospital I thought. Still, not to worry I was quite used to it by then. Then the doctor started to fill his sink with hot water and took down a pair of scissors and a safety razor from one of his cabinets. Fear began to wriggle its worm-like way deep into the pit of my stomach. "What yer gonna do," I Blurted, in a lip-trembling, cowardly manner. "I'm going to shave a bald patch in your scalp and stitch you up," he said, clinically. "But surely I need to go ter 'ospital, dun I," I inquired, hopefully. "No, not for a little cut like that," he said. "It'll only take two ticks and you'll be as right as rain again." "But yer will giv me ana, ana, anaset, that stuff that stops it 'urtin'," I pleaded. "There won't be any need for that" he replied, while all the time looking more and more satanic from the viewpoint of my bulging, terror-struck, tearful eyes. "The flesh is very thin on the top of your head and there are hardly any nerves worth talking about; just be a brave little soldier and I'll give you a sweetie when it's all over." Who was this talking? Mild mannered Dr Kildare or the very reincarnation of the Marquis de Sade himself? "You hold on to him Mr. Linford and I'll get to work." Arggggh!" Doctors had finally been relegated to their rightful place in the scheme of things. They were, after all, no better than all the sadistic nurses I'd already encountered and a couple of letters after their names couldn't alter that undeniable fact. From then onwards the medical profession and myself would be players in a mutual drama of irresolvable enmity.

The last place to be mentioned, both in the context of swimming, and the inevitable remedial consequences of cycling back home from the watery location, is the open-air pool that used to be situated on the Westcliff seafront. It was without a doubt the most swish of all the lidos of my acquaintance. It was built into a hollow with changing-rooms all around it and a parapetted area above for sunbathing and refreshments. If we didn't want the bother of bringing our own trunks and towels all the way from Pitsea on our bikes, we could hire them from the locker-room deep within the chlorine reeking bowels of that dank establishment. Mind you, baggy navy-blue woollen shorts with Southend Corporation stamped on the back of them in large white letters were not exactly the requisite garb for serious posing! Although I loved swimming at that time and would have cycled almost any distance for a dip, there were problems attached. The major one had to do with *après swim*. After just one or two lengths of the pool and some precision aerial bombardment from the top-board, I was usually ravenous. The hunger felt after swimming was of a particular kind. No other activity I know of can affect the appetite in such a gargantuan manner. The problem alluded to, was of course the normal one of pecuniary embarrassment. Financial cramp was as crippling an affliction to me then as it is now. Accusations of short arms and long pockets were always hurtful to one so richly endowed with latent generosity. Had I had the wherewithal, doughnuts and candyfloss would have been distributed to the starving masses with largesse undreamt of even by such remarkable institutions as the Aberdonian Philanthropic Society. As it was I had to suffer the thin-ribbed indignity of watching older, wealthier boys, munching away in epicurean splendour with hot adoring girls draped across their bronzed and muscular shoulders. How could a wan, potless youth with a xylophone for a chest ever hope to connect with any of those smooth-skinned, gold-fevered cuties? Even slicked-up with Brylcream from the penny slot-machine, and speaking James Dean-like through the curl of a fag-dangling lip, could not it seems lure the libidos of those pulse-disturbing beauties away from the envied clutches of their well-stacked escorts. Dejected as always, Charlie and my ever-celibate self, made for the cycle-rack and prepared to burn some theatrical rubber. The journey back to Pitsea was never as enjoyable as the one in the opposite direction. What with the deflation of the ego and the vacuous expansion of the stomach, peddling became something of a breathless and mind-numbing effort. The downward 1 in 8 freewheeling delight of Bread-and-Cheese-Hill was always looked forward to. But as so often in my chequered - as opposed to chequer-flagged - career as a racing cyclist, what was so often looked forward to was invariably looked back on in a very different light. The day that Bread-and-Cheese-Hill claimed me as one of its many victims is not only etched into my memory, but was etched literally into my forehead by the loose-chippings that I and the road surface managed to drag between us for some considerable distance, before the palings of a wooden fence so considerately intervened! I don't know if you've ever fallen off a bicycle going at full-pelt downhill, but it has to be said that it's a somewhat surreal experience. After the front-wheel had struck the fateful pothole the inevitability of it all registered immediately, but one could do absolutely nothing about it. What probably took no more than seconds to happen in real-time became a drama of infinitely slow proportions. The handlebars began to rock uncontrollably from side to side. I glanced behind just as the back-wheel lifted and caught a glimpse of the Munch-like scream beginning to form on Charlie's terrified face. I looked back again and in front of us the rear doors of a GPO wagon were opening inauspiciously. As I hit the ground, facedown, I veered off towards the cinder-path and the waiting fence. Charlie on the other hand, unable to avoid my rider less machine was catapulted skywards and landed - safely as it turned out, somewhat miraculously - in the back of the stationary van. Fortunately for me my sprawling, spread-eagled descent, was halted by the fortuitous juxtapositioning of a fence-post and my

139

Neolithic cranium, thus limiting my injuries to a thick-skulled minimum. Gravel and the resultant friction had worn a few subcutaneous craters in various parts of my anatomy, with a particularly nasty one on the inside of my left elbow, and my ribs - as prone and thinly-fleshed as they were at the time - suffered their share of scrapes and contusions. An ambulance was duly summoned for me, whilst Charlie being pronounced fit enough to continue his journey, was given a lift home in an open-topped sports car by a generous hearted nearby garage owner. Charlie, of course, never let me forget his good fortune and regaled me constantly with tales of that Monte-Carlo experience for months afterwards. Our parents were not so happy, mainly as it was they who had to organize the retrieval of our bent and buckled velocipedes. But then, no matter what you said or did, no matter how much you grovelled, parents were just unplacatable. When the ambulance arrived at Southend General Hospital I was wheeled in to the Casualty Department. Knowing the way I already felt about the nursing profession you can imagine the extent of my anxiety. One again I was to be treated with almost total disregard in respect of my human sensibilities. Why for the sake of a couple of stitches in my arm should it be deemed necessary that I sit stark naked in the middle of an open-plan unit? I may have only been a child to them, but to myself and a growing number of my fans, I was a mature, sexually attractive, super-star. Sitting there in the buff - in full licentious view of all and sundry - was, I felt, unnecessarily demeaning to someone of my histrionic stature. My expected future career as a sex-idol was, I think, irreparably damaged by that early and unbilled exposure. Even now the strategically placed hand accompanies me on all my visits to the doctor's surgery and I wouldn't be seen dead outside of my three-quarter length velveteen smoking jacket and leather slippers when in the company of a lady. The only possible benefit I could have gained from those early experiences in the callous hands of the medical profession was the consequent body-conscious reduction in my electric-light bills! The only reason I'm scribbling away at this page at the unearthly hour of three-o-clock in the morning is because I'm too frightened to go to bed. Night after night my sleep is interrupted by the raw terror of dreams stripped of all human decency. In various states of undress or totally naked I find myself being hounded by the law or lusted after by school-girls and old, gold-toothed men in white suits. Many's the night I've woken in a cold, insecure sweat, only to be pacified by the removal of my stockings and suspenders and the putting on of a greatcoat and Wellington boots. All the blame for this nightmarish activity - devoid of any pleasure on my part, I hasten to add - is laid squarely at the disinfected portals of the National Health Service. If it weren't for the barefaced perversity of those so-called carers I'd have probably been a famous film star of even a cardinal by now, and naturists would no doubt seem as natural to me as do the dirty-Mac and dark-glasses!

Another of our favourite cycling destinations was Canvey-Island. The way we used to get there in those days is now all but unrecognizable. Under the trees, a concrete pathway that connected a number of bungalows to Station Lane on the north side of the railway - ran down to the marshes. From there we cycled along the edge of the grazing meadows, meadows that were still lushly divided from each other by stands of elm and their attendant hedgerows. A crossing gate and some sleepers took us over the railway lines and down to the marshes proper. There it was far more open and reeded with freshwater dykes and fleets and the oozy curves of tidal creeks and saltings. A hard-rutted, unmade-road, led on from there beneath a thorn-thicket, more elms, the occasional oak, and tall breeze-echoing poplars. We crossed the railway lines again and cycled along another unmade-road that wound its way through a long, leafy tunnel. As if characters in a Tunnicliffe drawing we travelled through a swallow-haunted farm and its surrounding outbuildings. The chiaroscuro of sunlight and shadows falling from the trees and rippling over the dappled ground gave all the impression of riding through a watersplash. Cows mooed, sheep baa'd, and doves and

141

pigeons cooed and crooned in the summer heat. Slumbering collies leapt from their farmyard siestas and snapped at our circulating heels. From there, past cemetery corner, and on down through the church-centred tumbling village of Benfleet itself, we eventually came to the bridge that separated Canvey-Island from the mainland. An island, no less, - a Robinson Crusoe world of parakeets and coconut palms, of coral reefs and footprints in the silver sand. Don't we all have our island fantasies? Nature bountiful, fruit and fish in plenty, work restricted to the bare necessities of food and shelter - that South Pacific peacefulness, bubbling white banks of cumulous and the hush, hush of beachcombing wavelets breaking the silence of a blue-green, turtle-delving, tropical ocean. As a child the Essex marshes were all that to me and more. As we cycled off through the Winter gardens, past the willowy, well-fished lake and down towards the Monica, our shirts flapping, square-rigged against the salt-laden air, we felt that anything, but anything was possible. Canvey on its Thames side is the strangest of places. At high tide the sea is many feet above you. The only way you can get a look across to Kent is by climbing the steps cut into the grass-banked flood defenses and peering over the top of the sea wall. From there on a level with the tide you can look back down to the people promenading below and imagine the terror experienced in the 'Great Surge Tide' of 1953 when the sea breached many of the defenses and Canvey Island was flooded to a depth of Twelve feet in places. Many lives were lost in that East-Coast disaster and as a child of seven I remember using a wooden cart to help ferry blankets to Pitsea Primary School which was then being used as an evacuation centre. Another of my memories concerning that dreadful event was that of standing by the level crossing at Pitsea Station and looking out across miles of inland sea, where normally only horses, cattle and sheep sailed through the billowing grasses. But let's get back to the summer in question and to far, far, happier times. Along the promenade there was a cluster of amusement arcades that led on to a permanent fairground. This was the main reason for our frequent visits to the island. If ever we made enough money from Pitsea Market, paper-rounds, or collecting bottles, we knew exactly where to spend it. It had everything a good fairground should have, a ghost-train, a crooked-house, dodgems, a carousel and much, much, more. One of my favourite attractions was the helter-skelter. I can still feel the excitement I felt carrying my coconut-mat up and around the spiralling wooden staircase inside that patriotically painted red, white and blue, conical structure. I used to imagine I was in a windmill. I could hear the sea breeze in the sails and saw sacks of corn hoisted by ropes up into the winnowing, dusty, grain-loft. At every pane-less window I gazed out proprietarily across the widening acres of my wheat-whispering kingdom. As I neared the top my musings on land ownership were overwhelmed by the waves of trepidation that height bestows on the faint-hearted. From the all too open platform beneath the surmounting dome I could look down on the diminutive welter of revelling Lilliputians. Like all who suffer from stomach-churning, head-dizzying, bouts of vertigo my first thoughts were always the same; I wonder what it would be like to jump? It wasn't just a case of daring oneself. Oh no! It was far worse than that. There was that deliciously terrifying urge - desire even - to leap off regardless into space. I often wonder how many supposed suicides were really no more than tragic accidents, the result of sudden spine-shivering impulses, when thoughts in that state of poised equilibrium between life and the for-never-ness of impact, tilted the balance irretrievably. It was during one of those heart-thumping moments that I lay flat on the coconut matting and made a swift, frictionless descent towards the welcoming arms of terra firma and safety. Above me the sky spun giddily and the tapering finger of the tall convolving tower pointed somewhat disconcertingly into the terror-struck realms of breathless infinity. At the bottom of the slide there was a large, polished wooden bowl sunk deeply into the ground, where we would pour out over the chute like tea from a gushing spout into the brown swirling cup. If we hadn't been frightened enough by the helter-skelter there was always the ghost-train. Being a simple dualist at heart, even

143

then, I had an innate belief in the powers of good and evil and recognized that if I were to experience the spiritual satisfactions that courage invests one with, I would have to confront its opposite! Nevertheless, Charlie and I would spend a lot of procrastinating energy shuffling backwards and forwards in front of the ticket-office. "D'yer really wan' a go Merv," questioned Charlie, tentatively. "Cos I do!" I blustered. "Fink I'm scarred or suffink, do yer?" "Nah I don't fink that mate," he said appeasingly. "I jus' fought we might not 'av' enuff money, that's all." This outward expression of inner turmoil would go on for quite some time, until that is, in truth, both of us had summoned up enough of the necessary bravado to see us through the approaching ordeal. To adults, stiff, black, cardboard spiders dangling from the ends of bits of string may not seem very frightening at all, but when accompanied by eerily piped moans, groans and chain-clanking screams the affect was altogether more startling! Whizzing around in the dark on our switchback careering carriages, Charlie and I took turns in ducking down, bobbing up, closing our eyes, opening our eyes, screaming, closing our eyes again, hanging on to each other for safety and laughing loudly and nervously. Red, white and green lights flashed on and off intermittently. Skeletons sprang bone-rattlingly out of unexpected cupboards, tableaux depicting the blood-spattered, racked and headless victims of terrible tortures, strobed on and off in sudden illuminant corners. As a *piece de resistance* we shot through the double-doors of a vampire's mouth into the flesh-shrivelling glare of the decomposing sunlight. And there we stood, a couple of jelly-leggéd heroes, imaginary silver stakes and mallets in our fear-sweaty palms, ready to tackle anything that Transylvania could launch malevolently in our direction. When I think of that fairground it has as much to do with the sounds and smells that come vividly back to mind, as it has to do with anything else. Doughnuts and hot-dogs are imprinted odorously in my twitching nostrils. Candyfloss and the burnt, electric smell of dodgems waft through the mists of my olfactory dreams. The steamless organ of a fifties galloper flutes its shrill and gaudy music into the open ears of my lamented reminiscences. The rattle of pennies shoots through the slots in my memory; springs are sprung, hammers struck, and glossy, silver ball-bearings negotiate the metal pins erratically only to bolt down the hole marked lost, like the receding scut of Peter Rabbit himself!

Chapter 10. 'The Railway Children'.

Since I first met Charlie and introduced him to Eddy we'd gradually formed something of a three-way unholy alliance. During the summer holidays explorations of the surrounding countryside accounted for much of our mischievious leisure time. Although there were still some working farms in the area much of the acreage not taken up by the plotlanders had already been earmarked for future development and left to its own natural devices. For those with a safari-like mentality it was ideal big-game country. Fortified with Cod Liver Oil and Haliborange tablets we could often be seen marching single-file across the savannahas or cutting a swathe through the impenetrable jungles of hawthorn and sloe that rose up hostilely to impede our machete-swung progress. Many of the roads leading into the wilderness - metalled or otherwise - had names commensurate with the wonders of exploration. Two that spring readily to mind should suffice to underline the point: Stanley and Livingstone. Knee-deep in the lilac and purple smokes of vetches, butterflies, like blown embers, flickered warmly in all directions. Browns and fritillaries, blues and coppers, danced their aerial dances or fluttered haphazardly through the shimmering haze. Resplendent peacocks opened and closed their delta wings to astonish with eyes like RAF insignia. Small and large whites convolved in ascending spirals, then broke off from their territorial engagements and plummeted back to earth. Here was the world of the Essex-skipper and the bronze-green, scarlet-spotted, day-flying burnet moth. All was hum and heat and stridulation as a torrent of spring-heeled grasshoppers gushed out before us from the trampled herbage. Hands were cupped and kicking insect legs tickled the captive palms. Likewise, butterflies were chased and snared, their frenetic powdered wings leaving a guilt-smeared residue. Beetles were normally left alone, though the amber-coloured soldier beetles - set like a jewel in the mountings of the white umbellifers - were often encouraged unwillingly to fly. And the ladybirds - probably

146

the most handled of insects - were allowed to run their six-legged scuttling races over our bare untroubled skin. Cranesbill and storksbill, mayweed and meadowsweet, cushioned our sky-watching selves as we lay in the lap of the fragrant Gods. Clover was counted for luck and bird's-foot-trefoil was egg-and-bacon to our ever hungry, ever-feasting eyes. Darts of rye-grass were plucked, aimed and fired into tousled hair, and to the strains of "first a tree, then a bush, now you've got it in your mush!" seeds of sorrel and docks were stripped off their stems between thumbs and fingers and hurled into sneezing faces. Lizards were hunted ruthlessly. Anthills were crept up upon and scoured for a glimpse of their tiny, tongue-flicking, prehistoric snouts. Grabs were made and tails detached to wriggle off in their own uncanny way. Slowworms suffered a similar fate. If we couldn't find any on the anthills we would pick our way methodically over the ground upturning any loose rubble or timber large enough to shelter the slithering prey. Sometimes to our zoological amazement we would unearth one of the rare blue-spotted variety. Those light-coppery-bronze creatures, flecked with azure were breathtakingly beautiful, and even we - iron-hearted, red in tooth and claw savages that we were - could be overcome, temporarily, with compassion. Sadly, aesthetic and spiritual considerations were never long lasting. Adders were our specialty. I can never read D H Lawrence's poem 'The Snake' without feeling the full weight of its attack on our accursed human education in general, and my lily-livered pettiness in particular. Mild natured pantheist that he was he only threw a log at the water trough and watched guiltily as the snake disappeared in an undignified haste down a crack in the wall. We on the other hand, let loose with a formidable and impressive array of bows-and-arrows, air rifles and catapults. Somehow we'd got it into our addlepated skulls that adders were so deadly dangerous that the authorities were prepared to pay as much as half-a-crown a skin for them. Who those authorities were and where you took the carcass in order to claim your bounty we never found out. But that didn't deter us from the incessant unnecessary slaughter. They were easy prey. On cool damp days they were to be found cold-bloodedly sluggish beneath sheets of corrugated iron and the likes. In the heat they could be seen coiled and dozing almost anywhere. Occasionally, in the spurious name of bravery, instead of using our weaponry, we would employ a more direct method. Cleft-sticks were cut from the bushes with our prized Bowie knives and the unfortunate reptiles would be pinned by the neck. Then like members of some loony, Mid-Western religious sect, we would pick them up by the inverted V on the back of their heads and swing them round dangling from the ends of our outstretched arms with all the evangelical fervour of born-again Whirling Dervishes. Afterwards we would hold them vertiginously close to our faces and stare indifferently into their lidless, blood-shot eyes. Then, as one final indignity before dispatching them we would elicit venom from their drawn fangs on the tips of tormenting knives. Paradise was ever thus. The Devil and his writhing symbol being a scapegoat only for the deep unbridled lust and violence that seethes insatiably in the primal pits of our deep unconscious and unruly being. Or as Hereward the Wake is supposed to have said to William the Conqueror on being informed that the Normans were only interested in bringing civilization to the Country: "What then is civilization? It is but a handful of rose-petals, strewn upon a sea of pus!" Well, I don't know about you, but I certainly feel a lot better for that! And I'm sure that most of my white-cowled, black-habited mentors would be duly proud of such high-flown, sin-affirming rhetoric!

We were all railway enthusiasts in those days. Not that we collected engine-numbers or anything sensible like that. No, we were more interested in the fact that access to railway property was prohibited and that there were warning notices to prove it. Trespass and childhood were synonymous even to our illiterate reasoning. Red rags and bulls were as sheep and lambs when compared to our reactions to the dictates of authority. To keep us off of those lines would have required the combined forces of the Railway Police and the Essex

Constabulary to have been permanently on patrol. As it was railway policemen were rare specimens indeed and our local bobby was more concerned with shiny-boots and cycling proficiency-tests - something I could have well gained advantage from, given the right frame of mind - than our felonious trackside activities. Being as Pitsea was a junction we had the good fortune of having two railway lines to choose from. The Tilbury line curved out along the edge of the marshes through Vange and Fobbing, then on through Stanford-le-Hope to Grays and Tilbury-Riverside and the Fenchurch-Street line cut across inland through Laindon, West-Horndon, Upminster and Barking and then onwards into the City itself. In the opposite direction, the two lines having joined again at Pitsea, went on through Benfleet and Leigh-on-Sea and then out through Southend to Shoeburyness and the gull-enchanted five-mile tides. Not that we had to travel any of those distances. All that we needed to keep ourselves dangerously amused could be found very close at hand. Timberlog Lane Bridge took the road from Nevendon to Vange over the railway just prior to the junction of Bull Road. It was a brick-built bridge that carried traffic on one side of a parapet and had a wooden walkway on the other for pedestrians. Between the walkway and the track beneath were a set of iron-railings - sharply spiked by way of a deterrent - and a square riveted metal aqueduct to channel ditchwater from one side of the bridge to the other. I couldn't tell you just how many abortive attempts were made at scaling the defenses in order to wade in the torrential waters, but for once the authorities had defeated us and we had to make do with rattling the bars of our cage and leering at the world beyond with simian, tongue-extended, faces. Some people - against all the laws of right-mindedness - throw stones at trains. That, I'm ashamed to say, wasn't good enough for us. We wanted to drop them straight down the funnel. I don't think we ever managed a direct hit, but in the course of our efforts we certainly made the most of all the available smoke and steam. Trains arriving from the far side of the bridge were the most exciting. Although you could hear them coming you were

149

never quite sure exactly when they would emerge out into the waiting daylight. It was always a shock, a wonderful, earth shuddering clangorous roar of a shock. The drivers being constantly aware of the presence of children would sometimes add to the excitement by giving a full-blast on their whistle as the train went screaming beneath us like a screaming banshee. It would thunder away leaving us wreathed in its billowing effusions. Eyes - and clothes, much to my mother's displeasure - full of smuts, we'd jump up and down screeching like a tree-load of Howler Monkeys, until the air cleared and we could see the receding carriages rocking away under their twin plumes of black and silver. The mixed odours of smoke and steam were to me as the bouquet of a rich Burgundy might be to the wine connoisseur. I had a nose for such things you might say. As much fun as it undoubtedly was the whisper less lull between trains could become very boring indeed and other distractions would have to be found. On one side of the tracks there was an empty bungalow with a decidedly un-empty orchard. Up to our ankles in daisies, buttercups and dandelions we roamed around purposefully shaking the individual trees in order to dislodge their bountiful fruits. The best thing about that particular Paradise was that for once nothing there was forbidden. Plums, apples and pears were all welcomed - ripe or otherwise - despite the perennial recurrence of stomach-cramps and far, far, worse! There was one tree that received a greater share of our attention than all the others, a greengage tree. I don't know whether it's due to nostalgia or whether the taste buds bloom and fade and drop their petals, as we get older, but I've never since tasted greengages as sweet, moist and delicious as those were. Every year after telling myself time and time again that's it's going to be a complete waste of money - I buy some. It has to be said - albeit something of a contradiction in terms - that the flavour of nostalgia's not what it used to be. I sometimes wonder if the new varieties of greengage are the result of saplings being grafted on to rolls of cardboard. Anyway, they certainly taste as if they've been made out of papier mâché. Is this just the natural cynicism of middle age speaking or is there really a conspiracy amongst the retailers and producers of comestibles to create the same sort of uniformity in the realms of nutrition that we already suffer with 'muzak' and designer-footwear! Well, I tell you, I'm sticking to brogues and Raph Vaughan Williams! Whenever I see a lark on the up I want to be wearing shoes that are eminently suitable for the occasion. On the other side of the tracks - there's a maxim there somewhere I think - was the then T junction of Timberlog Lane and Bull Road. There was sited the Old Bull Inn - a fairly recent mock-Tudor building - an omnibus-garage, a row of tumble-down shops, a terrace of brick-built houses and a 17th century white- weather boarded cottage with a red, peg-tiled roof. Opposite those buildings there was a small corner field, which to our delight was occupied a couple of times a year by a travelling-fair. One of the shops that I remember very well was simply called 'The Tuck-Shop'. It was run by the archetypical grey-haired old lady. Either because of not knowing us that well - or more likely being so anciently innocent, and not knowing any better - she used to greet us with such endearing bucolic phrases as: "Hello me dears, what you be wantin'?" We'd oblige by rusticating our cockney patter. "Ooh! Aah! Missus; baint be sure yet, we jus bin looking we does." You'd just catch a hint of disbelief in her saintly, ever-trusting eyes before she shrugged off any doubts she may have had and returned to her rose-coloured 20/20 vision of the world. Whatever the state of her vision was - literally or otherwise - to our eyes, despite the mocking banter, she was something of an alchemist. In the back of her shop - with no more than coloured powder and tap water - she could concoct fruit-flavoured elixirs fit for the Gods. These she sold in those dumpy third of a pint milk-bottles, you don't see very often nowadays, for as little as a ha'penny a go. Refreshed and sherbet dabbing our way back towards the railway lines our wayward orbits were often attracted by the mysterious gravitational pull of that 17th century white-weather boarded cottage. It hadn't been lived in for quite some time and its front and back gardens had become rankly and richly overgrown. Whereas some

151

picturesque cottages are said to be sunk in thatch, that one was drowning in foliage. A many-shaded green sea rose up in rolling leafy waves, crested, fell, and swamped it on all sides. To go into that shadowy sunlit garden was to be as if swimming under water. Great golden pears swung like hurricane lamps from the swaying branches of the shipwrecked trees; and birds - like fishes - rowed through the currents of the rollicking air. When we peered into the sub aqueous windows it was Neptune and his entourage we were looking for, even mermaids were possible, and as an initiate in the piscatorial arts I was beginning to fancy my chances. We could never resist the pluck on our lines whenever we passed that cottage, but of course, it was always us who were hooked and caught. It drew us in to its deep, sea-weeded secrets over and over again. We were willing victims to its goose-grassed, coiling tentacles, and the administered priest of its knockout, wind fallen pears.

Back at the railway line we scaled the six-foot wire-mesh fencing, dropped to the ground in the regulation paratroop rolling manner, and then slipped and tumbled down the steep embankment. The ox-eyed daisies eyed us suspiciously as we scuttled along the rust-coloured stone chips beside the track. The yellow-headed ragwort - living up to its Latin tag; senico squalidus (squalid old man) - had jumped train in its hobo-hobbling multitudes and uncharacteristically taken root. Rosebay willow herb - that colonizer of the burnt and battered land of the London bombsites - had made the most of post-war seaside excursions and wended its fire-weeded way in great smouldering swathes. There it was that our games of do-and-dare were about to be enacted in earnest. Senseless beyond the bounds of all possible human reasoning, we would lay our heads against the shiny polished rails and listen for the wheel-resonant rumble of oncoming trains! "Can yer 'ear any fink yet," I asked, expectantly. "Not a fing," replied Charlie from his suicidally prostrate vantage. "Me niver," added Eddy, somewhat disappointedly. As if that wasn't bad enough, when we did spot a train coming - If you'll excuse the unwarranted hobbyism - we would place a penny on the line and dare each other to stand for as long as possible in front of the disastrously looming express. The extent of our incredible stupidity never ceases to astonish me. Our judgment in matters concerning speed and distance was about as sound as that displayed in the operation of our five-fingered arithmetical incompetence. Many were the instances of last-minute, heart-stopping escapes. Stranded in mid-air between train and undergrowth, the buffeting blast of the slipstream augmented the pitch of our raised hysterical voices. "Bloody 'ell! Bloody effin' 'ell! Stuff me!" There was nothing quite like a steam train. That they polluted the atmosphere with soot and smoke, set off uncontrollable bush-fires in the summer, and filled the air with screaming, diabolical decibels, didn't seem to matter. Diesel and electric seem somehow feebly inanimate in comparison. Perhaps it has something to do with the fact that the power of those great lumbering beasts was in part externalized. You could see the breath exploding from the funnels and the mechanics of their iron metabolisms were there for all to see in the shape of pummelling pistons and con-rods. They weren't subservient to the push-button computerized tyranny that we've all become so willingly enslaved by. They were individuals. They needed coaxing. Like the farm-horse they had to be fed, pampered and persuaded. Cruelty undoubtedly existed but it was as counter-productive as was the ill treatment of pit ponies. You might be able to keep the drivers and firemen going at the brink of starvation wages, but if you wanted to get the economic maximum out of your engines, then their steamy, industrious whims, would have to be pandered to. Their arrivals and departures throughout our young lives were heralded both firstly and lastly by the arcane workings of the signalling system. A network of silver wires wound its way - gossamer-like - through a seemingly endless succession of rings and pulleys. Signal trees, both singular and branched, hoisted the whispering threads up into their spidery gantries, where deft, colourful arms were raised and lowered in clattering obedience to far off invisible commands. Naturally for us -

153

with hands wrapped in old rags - we assaulted the wires and tried to operate the signals manually. Fortunately for us - and for the safety of the passengers - we never actually succeeded in our efforts. I often wonder whether Dickensian minded signalmen sat petrified in their boxes as the ghostly levers rocked backwards and forwards unaccountably. What we did manage to do however was to climb the ladders of any of the gantries so conveniently equipped. I'm still haunted by that Ealing-Comedy - The Lady-killers, I think - where both film and Alistair Sims, met their concussive end at the hands of a down-crashing signal. Many an empty good's wagon since has been impressed by the spread-eagled thought of my imaginary self, being freighted - habeas corpus-wise - towards oblivion.

The next bridge down the line was at the junction of Sandon Road and 'Pitsea High Street'. Whereas Timberlog Lane Bridge carried the road over the railway, this one did exactly the opposite. The obvious benefit in this for us children was that instead of looking down on our esteemed engines, once we'd scaled the sloping embankment, we found ourselves on a wondrous level with them. The bridge was constructed in such a way as to leave a gap between the brick piers and the ironwork that was just large enough for a child to squeeze through. This - as you may have already guessed - we took full advantage of. To start with we just took it in turns to stand in the gap as the trains went thundering by, but as you can imagine we soon got tired of such a relatively innocent prank. Dividing the up and down lines along the length of the bridge was a three foot high, flanged and riveted metal partition. Once the possibility had occurred to us of concealing ourselves inside the flanges on one side of that partition as the trains passed by on the other, then a greater share of the world's excitement was assured. A cursory glance from left to right, and a quick dash across the lines, found us ensconced and ready for action. It wasn't particularly dangerous but to be that close to a steam engine as its reverberant tonnage pounded across the bridge was an unforgettable experience. In fact we were so loathe of ever forgetting it, that we made a point of doing it as often as we could. Once, unfortunately, I was caught out by the unthought of and unthinkable realities of railway timetabling, i.e., two trains being scheduled to pass the metal partition in opposite directions at precisely the same instant! Whilst I was crouched expectantly, waiting for the ear-shattering thrill of a non-stop express - from which I would be amply separated by the intervening cast-iron - Charlie gave me some disturbing news. "Look out Merv, there's one coming on your side!" he clarioned. Who was it who said that 'no news is good news?" Whoever it was, at that very fear-inducing moment I knew exactly what they meant! I did something on that occasion that I'd never done before. I pressed my feet and shoulders against the metal flanges and eased myself a foot or so off the ground. That involuntary action proved to be my salvation. As the two trains came stampeding by - whistling in unison like a pair of contending elephants - steam and scolding water, gushed and spurted into the space beneath me. I've always liked railway engines but to be that close to one in full rampaging fury, is perhaps not the best way to develop one's appreciative skills! You could say that it was even more of a blur to me then than it is now. What with the noise, the speed, the explosive air and the flying dust I could scarcely see or think. When the trains had finally passed my heart and ears drummed their accompaniment to the rhythms of the bridge in repercussion. "Bloody 'ell Charlie!" I understated. "I was nearly a gonna there!" We were all nearly gonna's nearly all of the time. Boys, it seems, have always had a potentially fatal attraction for railways. Girls are fond of them in their own way admittedly, but this usually consists of standing demurely at discrete distances and waving their scarves or handkerchiefs politely to equally polite and responsive passengers. That was never good enough for us. The only reactions we ever expected - and received - from passengers, were the results of thumbed noses and protruding rasberried tongues. If we wanted to avoid the prying eyes of passengers altogether we would wait for Sundays and make our way to the sidings down by the Tilbury Line. There it was that we could play at being real railway men. Lines of empty goods-wagons with their attendant brake-vans awaited the undivided attention of prospective shunters and guards - the track - ditto - for navvies and platelayers. I was never very fond of shovels and sledgehammers. If there was any dignity to be found in labour, then I for one had yet to come across it! Personally, I preferred the responsibility attached to the position of guard. In spite of all the propaganda to the contrary, I've found that the closer you get to the seat of power, the further removed you are from the sweat of your brow. Against my already prematurely engrained habit of a lifetime, I would usually volunteer for a spell in the caboose. There - as was my sovereign duty - I could take charge of the proceedings. Out of the slit-eyed windows I could see the rest of the crew hard at work. Charlie was shovelling loose chips and ramming them under the sleepers. Eddy, equipped with a sledgehammer, nearly as tall and heavy as he was, was checking the resounding wheels with a swinging belligerent grimace. Thinking that they might slacken unless I kept them on their working-class toes, noblesse oblige, determined that I should shake them up a bit. In the brake-van there was a large, spoked horizontal wheel, from whence the legendary vehicle got its name. Loosen its ratchet-lock and give it a couple of turns anticlockwise, and something miraculous would happen. The braking mechanism disengaged and a bumper-to-bumper clank and clatter rumbled shockingly along the entire length of the train. Workmen - normally fearless - have been known to whiten perceptibly in the face of such an unexpected occurrence. So as you can probably imagine the effect it had on mere boys was a delight to behold. Charlie's shovel was, I think, the first of its kind to go into orbit! Evidently, Eddy couldn't manage such a levitatory feat with the sledgehammer and had to content himself with bruised toes and bouts of hopping-madness! Why the pair of them should have taken such a harmless little joke as that to heart, I'll never know. Not that I minded marmalisation as such, I was quite used to it by then. It just seemed petty on their part, in an over-reactionary sort of way. "Yer pissin' good fer nuffin basstard," yelled Charlie as he scrambled expletively up into the guard's van. Eddy, meanwhile, was still too engrossed with his sissified game of hopscotch to join in with the affray. What's a matta wiv yer," I said inquisitively, while all the time keeping the protective brake-wheel between the demented platelayer and myself. "Can't yer take a joke?" "I don't fink it's bleedin' funny!" came the considered, poe-faced response. "When I get 'old of yer, I'm gonna bash yer bleedin' face in!" Well, I'd never read the NUR rulebook as it pertained to industrial disputes, but I'd heard of such things as arbitration and cooling off periods and decided to put my paid-up knowledge to good use. At the first available chance I leapt out of the caboose and made off like a through-train to Milksop Junction. Negotiations would have to wait!

There are a couple of things concerning the railway and its environs that still cause me problems to this very day when trying to talk about them with newcomers and plotlanders alike. One I can verify from source material dedicated to the etymology of road and place-names, but the other - and the more I think about it the less likely it seems - may well turn out to be another figment of my hyperbolic imagination. Where Basildon Town Centre stands now, there was once nothing but the ubiquitous scrubland and smallholdings. An ruddy, brick-bridge arched across an unmade road that wound its winding way - from Old Basilidon to who knows where - under the Fenchurch Street line. This road was somewhat romantically called 'Honeypot Lane'! Bees there were in plenty at the time, but hives and honeycombs were something of a rarity as far as I can remember. At the risk of dispelling the cherished beliefs of many a local poetaster I'm afraid that it has to be said that the Honeypot in question had nothing to do with our pollen-laden, nectar-supping, industrious little friends. Once again it was the notorious London Clay that was culpable. In heavy weather that claggy, impassable sludge, had in days of yore been ironically referred to as being as sticky as a honeypot. Having walked that lane myself through many a rain-sodden winter's day, I can vouch for the sole-

157

squelching authenticity of the said derivation. In summer on the other hand - assuming it to have been one of the long, hot, dry and nostalgic variety - things were very different in a bee-buzzy, blue-skied, rock-hard and balmy-breezed sort of way. This brings me to the second of the questions that concern me. 'Come to sunny Pitsea by the sea!!!' I'm convinced that there was a billboard to that effect propped up by the railway lines somewhere near the Honeypot Lane Bridge? Does this make me as sentimentally inclined as those budding romantic poets and apiarists I've already so rudely implicated, with regards to their IQ, or am I just barking mad? By no stretch of the imagination could Pitsea Creek - the sea in the place name Pitsea means island incidentally - be considered in any size, shape or form whatsoever, as a part of the seaside. Wet, once or twice a day it may have been. Boats in a leaky, loose-boarded, grass-decked fashion, it may have had. But bucket and spade territory it definitely was not! So why is that sun-shiny billboard so obsessively engrained in my mind? Could it be just wish fulfillment on my part? Maybe, maybe not. If it did ever exist I suspect it had more to do with the wish fulfillment on the part of property-speculators, who tried to sell off as much derelict farmland as possible to gullible, land-hungry Londoners, from the turn of the twentieth century onwards. Some of the bumph I've read from the time leads me to suspect that this explanation could be one of distinct possibility: From a page of the sale catalogue of The Land Company, Cheapside, London, circa 1906. 'Popular, prosperous, picturesque'. 'Within easy reach of London'. 'Improving train services'! 'One of the healthiest localities in the South of England'. They forgot to mention that at about the same time, an unfortunate couple, Mr. and Mrs. Watson of Honeypot Lane were shot dead at point-blank range by a local landowner for daring to draw a bucket full of water from his pond during a period of prolonged drought! Very healthy! Wouldn't you say? As for all the chitchat about ease and accessibility, here's a quote from one of the newspapers referring to that tragic event. 'The district is such a remote one that a motor car is a real necessity and the tragedy suggests

158

the desirability of the Chief-Constable being supplied with such a means of progression so as to be ready and well equipped for any future emergency'! Even so, from my memories of driving clapped-out old jalopies over the rut-hardened roads of that isolated area, they'd have been better off sticking to the Bow Street Runners! The Estate Agents would have done better to extol the virtues of the real seaside just ten short miles up the line - Southend-on-Sea, butt of so many kiss-me-quick, stuck-in-the-mud, cockle and whelk type jokes. Estuary or not, to us it was the coast proper and we always looked forward to our regular summer excursions. Naturally enough we caught the train from Pitsea and even though it was quite a busy junction, it was still very much a country station in those days. The side below St Michael's Church was flanked by sloe, hawthorn and a row of elms. On the other side of the tracks there was more scrub and rough-pasture and beyond that the marshes stretched their five mile way out towards the Thames and its estuary. As you came up to the old Victorian ticket-office - attached to the Station Master's house - you passed a terrace of brick-built railway worker's cottages. Behind then were some sidings and a coal-depot and directly opposite on the other side of Station Approach there stood a dilapidated wooden shed that served as a cafeteria. I think at the time the return fare to Southend was about half-a-crown and to my mind it was worth every penny. Express trains would rattle through in the direction of London at an ear-shattering, seventy miles an hour and the mix of fear and pleasure they induced was exhilarating indeed. Initially, movement in the other direction was a far tardier affair. We boarded the train, sat down, and waited expectantly for the guard's pea-rattling whistle. When it came, steam in slow loud bursts, was the prelude to the shuddering of carriages. We were off! The pulse of hissing steam became more and more frequent. Wheels spun mechanically, gained friction, took up the slack, and the train drew ponderously out of the station. As both the train and we gathered momentum, from out of the windows on the landward side you could see the undulating hills of Howard's Farm, as a plume of black

159

smoke trailed out, expanded, and then dispersed into the receding distance. A notice above the carriage said - in red cautionary letters - 'Danger Do Not Lean Out Of The Window'. An obvious invitation to the recalcitrant amongst us! But as always the Great Steam Maker in the sky had tried and tested methods for dealing with the disobedient. As a result of unexpected curves in the track the train would often find itself ploughing through its own belching smoke and a punitive cloud of soot and smuts would envelope the excitable miscreants. With spluttering, black, tear-stained faces we'd rush to the window on the other side of the carriage and nearly have our blocks knocked off by a thundering London bound express. Sometimes progress was impeded by the need to replenish the engine's water supply. In fact, seeing as the water tank was no more than about a mile out of Pitsea Station itself, progress wasn't so much impeded as being virtually non-existent. This, as you can no doubt imagine, caused much consternation amongst the prospective seaside revellers. 'Ten green bottles' would invariably be changed for another old favourite, ' why are we waiting'.' Time and tide', being the maxim of the day. But an engine and its thirst is something that just cannot be rushed. The fireman would climb the ladder up the side of the tank, push across the swivelling arm with a leather hose attached, and leave gravity to do the rest. I don't remember just how long it took to complete the job, but to us it seemed to take an eternity. As far as I know the railway followed the natural spring-lines and obtained its water where sand and gravel and brick earth met the near impervious London Clay. Nature's way of doing things may well have been sufficient in the winter months, but although I never thought about it at the time, being as Essex is one of the driest counties in the country, it must have been touch and go during many of the summer droughts I remember. But stocks they always seemed to have in reserve and Southend with its funfairs and boat-trips was never denied our company.

Some of the most enduring hot summers are prone to end with

the suddenness of thunder. One of the most violent storms I've ever experienced started on a warm September's evening and rumbled on throughout the rest of the night. The incidence of sheet and fork lightning was of a frequency that I'd never seen before and have never seen since. Flash after flash illuminated the night sky with an intensity that left trees and houses silhouetted against the glare, like backlit daguerreotypes. The electrifying severity of the storm was matched by the air-splitting amplitude of each succeeding after-shock, and the down-hurtling drench of rain and sporadic hailstones. Even though we lived on the top of a low hill we were not to be spared from the inevitable flooding. My father was out in the back garden clearing the drains as quickly as he possibly could, but the accumulated soggy weight of starling and house sparrow nests finally defeated him. We opened the back and the front doors and watched helplessly as the clay-coloured, swirling floodwater carried its debris from one side of the house and out through the other. It all happened so fast that there was no time to take up the carpets or carry the furniture upstairs. We just stood and looked on disbelievingly as our parched summer castle suffered its one and only inundation. As a final indignity a can of worms - freshly dug for fishing by my elder brother - sailed through the living room on their wriggling way to a premature ducking in the river that was once a road! They did at least lighten the mood a little. The irony of it all wasn't lost on anyone and even the dourest faces have been known to crack in adversity. For me, I have the sneaking suspicion that I was probably enjoying myself far more than should have been allowable on such an inauspicious occasion. The biblical story of Noah and his Ark was taking on anew relevance and my two by two account of fantastical beasts was moving on apace. The added advantage of that nocturnal inclemency was that the count didn't have to include sheep and the dreaded sandman had for once in his somnambulant life found himself redundant. To stay up all night was worth any amount of silt across the floors and tidemarks up the walls. Especially as I didn't have to fork-out for any of the refurbishments! Of course, I didn't consider my attitude to be selfish in any way whatsoever; it was just the natural consequence of child-like innocence. If we were expected to be seen and not heard and to do as we were told at all times, then there was no reason why we should aspire to adulthood and take on any of life's more irksome responsibilities. After all we didn't ask to be born, did we, as the scratched record of my grating voice was so often fond of reproducing. Bleary eyed or not the next yawn provoking day found my conscientious parents engaged in the mopping-up process. Despite all inducements to take an active part in the proceedings - and even in the face of hand-swiping threats of physical violence if I didn't - something had happened that previous night that made it an imperative that by fair means or foul I had to get to the railway line, *toute de suite*! The jungle tom-toms had been pounding away since the crack of dawn and rumours of a landslip on the Fenchurch Street Line were encouragingly rife. So to the sound of harsh berating voices promising all sorts of pummelling retribution for the sin of personal omission, I ran zig-zaggedly away to call for the two other notorious runagates of my acquaintance, Charlie and Eddy. When we got to the trackside we found that our earlier hopes had been realized to the full. A great section of the embankment had dislodged itself during the night and had slithered downwards to cover the down line with a few feet of clay and its accompanying herbage. More importantly for us the other side of the track was chock-a-block with an array of railway equipment as yet undreamt of in our short steam-filled lives. Apart from the tank-engines and attendant trucks used for the removal of loose earth. There were steam-powered draglines swinging their jibs and biting into the underbelly of the sub-soil with their metal-toothed, plummeting buckets. This was even more than we'd hoped for. Calamities were our specialty and this was one of stupendous proportions! We climbed over the fence under the cover of a clump of bushes and made our way - surreptitiously - towards the newly exposed precipice. There we crouched down into the summer-high grasses and settled back to observe the unfolding spectacle. It was a day of summer renewed. Unusually the storm hadn't cleared the air and it was still, hot, calm and muggy. Convolvulus, pink and white-starred sprawled waywardly over the ground. Its, Jack-pop-out-of-bed, pure white cousins hung their Gabriel's Horns from the surrounding hedgerows and fences, and bees - like the lost chords of the saintly arch-angelic messenger - bumbled in and out on divine improbable wings. Straggling sprays of musky, sweet-scented buddleia, plucked butterflies from the air with purple gathering fingers, and teasels tinged with amethyst wore eighteen-carat gold glistening finches on their prickly bonnets. Orache, fat-hen and good king Henry, spread both their abundant seeds and their quaint folklore-ish names greenly abroad and the red-recoiling limbs of brambles buckled under the succulent weight of sun-ripened blackberries. Oblivious in Eden, we were taken unawares by a voice rising sharply up from the workings down below. "Oi, you lads!" came the unexpected summons. "Come down 'ere a minute!" "Shit!" said Charlie, instinctively. "We've bin spotted!" Our first reaction was to run, but the voice came reassuringly back. "Aint nuffin to worry about lads, I've got a job fer yers, that's all." Our future employer was standing on the footplate of the engine in his charge looking for all the world the spitting image of Casey Jones in his greasy BR issue dungarees and his slick, deep-sooted, peaked-cap. "Christ!" intoned Eddy, somewhat irreverently. "We're gonna get t' meet a train driver, a real blimmin' train driver!" Could it be true? Had that Great Steam-Maker in the sky relented at last and decided that we were ready to be ordained into the huffing, puffing, priesthood of nutty-slack and pressure valves? We proceeded down what was left of the embankment with all the single-filed solemnity that the occasion demanded and made our ritualistic way towards the black-hatted bishop. "Would you lads mind runnin' some errands fer us?" he said. "We'll giv' yer somefink fer goin'." "Course we will mista," I replied, keenly. "We'll get yer anyfink yer want." This was extraordinary, not only for the first time in our lives had we been given tacit permission to wander at will over railway property, but also – unbelievably

163

- we were going to be paid for the privilege. As red-lettered days go that one was even more illuminant than most. Apart from earning some welcome and unexpected pocket-money, we were to be given that once in a lifetime opportunity, that most young boys can only dream of. We were to be allowed to stand on the footplate with the driver and fireman, no less, and to help - or hinder, depending on which way you care to look at it - with the driving of the very engine itself. We may have only been going to shunt some trucks of earth backwards and forwards along the track, but to us it seemed as glorious as taking to the main line on an A4 Pacific. What had the Mallard got that these little tank-engines didn't possess? I think at the time they may have already lost their individual names to the bureaucratic numeral mindedness of early rationalizers. But to us staunch individualists they remained firmly in our memories: 'Vange', 'Pitsea' and 'Benfleet', may not seem to be names of quite the same exotic calibre as 'The Coronation Scot' or 'The Golden Arrow', but in a home-spun, familiar sort of way they were more than good enough for us. When we finally boarded the engine the excitement was almost palpable. There was no need for the imitatory chuff chuffing of our former pedestrian selves, or for the obligatory woo-wooing - through pursed lips. This was the real thing and we were going to make the most of it. I couldn't tell you what all the little metal wheels, levers and dials were intended for, but it goes without saying that they were all pulled, tapped and twisted with vigorous inquisition in order to fathom the depths of their locomotive mysteries. Charlie - at home again with the shovel - was busily stoking the firebox. Eddy - on tiptoe - leaned with his elbow out of the cab-window - with all aplomb of a seasoned railway man. I - on the other hand - released a lever and turned a tiny wheel. Brakes slackened and steam miraculously found its way into the pistons. Our soot-happy, impish faces, beamed in the glow of the cavernous firelight as the mighty engine got underway. "Smashin'!" "Great!" "Whoopee!" I pulled a handle at the end of a down-reaching metal- rod. Steam hissed, venomously, and the whistle shrieked as the serpent struck with its fangs.

That unbelievable day takes pride of place in the rolling, stock-in-trade of my earliest memories. In the runaway train of my diminishing downhill life it is often the gradients of the past that slow me down enough to appreciate the things I see in the present. To shuffle off down the sidings of my lost youth and to look again at the world through eyes made paradoxically wider by the very narrowness of their restricted view: to see, to feel, to experience and accept. Let the words be seen for what they really are. A drawing us out, always, from the very things we long to be an integral part of. Se pa ra tion, a li en a tion - se pa ra tion, a li en a tion - sep a ration, a lien ation - separation, alienation, separation, alienation, woo, woo, wooooooo..........!

Chapter 11. Factory Fodder.

Another summer pastime much favoured by those of a sporting disposition was that of cricket. Personally, I've never had much of a liking for sport of any kind - unless you're prepared to include such civilized things as darts and fishing - and have always had a proclivity towards more contemplative activities. Or perhaps I should say, inactivities! Nevertheless, not wishing to appear antisocial, I would often watch the sweaty proceedings with a certain amount of feigned interest. Bordering onto the street next to mine there was a triangular area of pebbles and tufted grass that used to serve as a pitch. For those of you toothed long enough to recall the theorem of Pythagoras, it's sufficient to say that the sum of the squares of the two angles equaling the square on the hypotenuse were formed by the abstruse juxtaposition of two geometrically similar rows of terraced housing! Simple, isn't it? I remember on one warm summer's evening sitting on a low brick wall - Flemish-bond I suspect - thinking of nothing in particular whilst pretending to watch the action, when something untoward occurred. A budding W G Grace lashed heroically into a full toss, only to thick-edge the ball and send it hurtling through a nearby window. For those of you who don't believe in the supernatural I can only instance the speed of the disappearing-act. No abracadabra, no waving of wands; nothing! One second they were all there; two full teams, plus spectators, and the next, hey presto! They were gone. By the time I'd collected my thoughts and returned from my far away musings, not only was the crease deserted but doors and windows had already begun to open and adults were ranting and raving at each other as only adults know how. Coming from a religious background I decided to follow the advice of my spiritual mentors and to profess my innocence. After all, wasn't it they who had told me time and time again that honesty was the best policy? For once in my life I'd done nothing wrong and as far as I was concerned the natural follow on from that was that as long as I told the truth I should have nothing to fear. There are times in this life that I despair at the injustices of the world. "Yer brazen little tike!" spake the neighbourly investigator of the parish. "Break me bleedin' winda would yer, and then bleedin' well sit there as if nuffink 'ad 'appened!" "I didn't do it mista, 'onest I didn't," I said with sacred conviction. "I was jus' sittin' 'ere watching, that's all." "I don't giv' a shit wat yer was doin'," he reflected. "I know yer muvver an' farver, an' I'm goin' righ' round there t' get me money fer the broken winnda, an' your comin' wiv me!" he continued. Well, there are limits to anyone's adherence to a false creed and by that time I'd well and truly reached mine! The virtue of honesty had been sorely tested. "Yer gotta be effin' joking," I ejaculated in transit. "You'll never catch me, never!" I was as quick on my feet in those days as anyone and before you could say 'people in glass houses.......' dust was streaming out behind me as I beat a hasty path across the neighbouring fields. Running away was the easy part of course. What to do next, that, was the problem. It was already nearing dusk and I wasn't dressed for a night *en plein air*. Apart from that, the prospect of drowning in the coming darkness - so to speak, somewhat pretentiously - with nothing for company, excepting the hoot of owls and the otherworldly scuffle of foraging hedgehogs, wasn't a prospect to instill one with much in the way of confidence! I made my way cautiously through a clump of blackberry bushes. Sadly, caution and blackberry bushes have never really hit it off and before long my clawed legs and arms were smeared from top to bottom with blood and blackberry-juice. To add insult to injury, nettles sprang out of the shadows like a tribe of spear-wielding pygmies and added their *coup de grace* to the thorns' combative preliminaries. I found a grassy clearing and sat down to lick my wounds and assess the worsening situation. As so often in my life I found the problems irresolvable. Either I stayed where I was to shiver through the night with fear and trembling, or I went home to confront my father, whose fist would have become heavier in equal and opposite reaction to the enforced lightening of his pocket. Physics, you understand, being heir to the only absolutes I trust in! Still, dithering and indecisiveness were also part of my make-up, so at least I had my procrastinating self to share the trauma with! I don't know if you've ever noticed just how dark darkness can be? But when you're on your own and terror-struck, it can deepen into the depths of a black, despairing magnitude Indeed. And the silence! God! The vacuous galactic silence! My heart sounded as though it were auditioning for the major percussive part in the 1812 Overture. All of that, all that pain and fear and suffering, all in the pusillanimous name of truth. Truth! What had those five letters ever suffered in comparison with the predicament I now found myself in? It stands there like a great wagging finger-post at the lyrical edge of every poetic utterance. TRUTH! Write on if you dare, it says, but know me as your goal, your duty. Stuff it! That's what I say. If I'd been less concerned with truth and all its spurious ramifications, I'd have already been tucked-up in bed experiencing it, snuggly and comfortably, through the blessings and beauty of my juvenile dreams. No, lies I was good at, and lies I should have stuck to. Why outreach oneself? To find oneself clutching at notions beyond the grasp of one's natural talents is to suffer the pit-falls of vertiginous abstractions! That being said, the objective correlative that followed, didn't exactly turn me into a fan of Apollinaire overnight! "Where yer 'idin', yer little cowson!" came the voice of parental concern. "Yer muvver's in a righ' state, worried sick she is!" Dithering and deliberation would have to cease. A decision had to be made, a night beneath the shooting stars, or a night beneath the showering, meteoric rain of my father's fists. Either way, I was assured the effects of sidereal vision! "I'm ova 'ere," I whispered, in my best fist-deflecting voice. "Well come out 'ere where I can see yer," said the spider to the fly. I remember little of the journey home. What with the fist, the slap, and the boot, I felt like a stand-in for the third maltreated order of The Three down-pecking Stooges! When we finally arrived home my mother was in such a worried state, that in order to displace her anxieties, she too joined in with the general lambasting. "But I didn't do it, I tell yers!" I snivelled.

168

"Won't nobody believe me?" I don't care wevver yer did it or not," my father confided. "All I know is I've 'ad t' pay fer the winnda!" "That's righ'," rallied mother. "I spose yer fink money grows on trees!" Well, I might have been born under a gooseberry-bush, but I wasn't that stupid.

After all, why go to the Klondyke when the woods are full of Humus - If you get my deciduous drift? "But I didn't do it!" I repeated, pleadingly. "We don't care, you're not gettin' no pocket-money 'til that winnda's paid for," came the sentence. "And that's final," they added as they threw away the key. Bed without any supper and threats of restricted privileges were all I had by way of offerings for the sandman that night. As I lay there catacombed in grief and shrouded by my troubles I reflected again on the subject of honesty. "Never, ever, not in a million, trillion, billion years," I exaggerated to myself. "Will I ever tell the troof again?" For those of you who have persevered thus far, it should be said in passing, that anything I have said or may yet say, should be seen in the light of my cricketing experiences and the moral dilemma they created. If you're looking for the truth may I respectfully suggest that you make a study of the Grail Legends or else go for a weekend retreat with 'The Cloud of Unknowing' stuffed reverently into your almost certainly empty pockets. I'm more than happy to make things up as I go along and if I accidentally stumble into a crock of gold on the way, then you can rest assured that my fingers will be sticky enough to cope with it! If anyone is audacious enough as to inquire how I came by my ill-gotten gains, I shall be able to say in all spectral honesty, through the knowledge acquired when watching a game of formative cricket. And if that doesn't make a silly-point, then nothing will!

In the interests of balance it should be stated that guiltlessness was not a condition that I could normally have been accused of. One summer pursuit in particular took the full culpable weight of my light-fingered-ness: scrumping! What a delicious word that is - scrumping! So sumptuous in fact that just the recollection of it sent me straight to my dictionary of word origins. And what did I find therein? Nothing, absolutely nothing. Not one single reference to one of the juiciest words in the whole of my mouth-watering vocabulary. Well, I couldn't leave it there, could I? So I went to the shelves, took down the Shorter Oxford, opened its copious bulk at the relevant page, and laid it across my expectant lap. What did I find in that august tome? Likewise - the word it seems does not exist! I wouldn't have minded had it been there in the addenda, even if it had been written of pejoratively in terms of it being a slang expression – but alas, no mention whatsoever. I felt as though my entire childhood had been slighted. Until, that is, I eventually found it in the most unexpected of places: the Collins/Robert, French/English Dictionary! It was marked down as slang, right enough, along with its more formal derivative cousin, scrumptious. And yet, funnily enough, scrumpy - which one feels must be related in some colloquial way - was given full recognition as a valid translation of cider. That was where my researches stopped. I was both fuming and fermenting mad, as far as I can see this is some sort of conspiracy perpetuated by the establishment - and the lexicographers in their pocket - to deprive me, and the rest of you, the full illicit benefits of our nefarious collective past. If nostalgia's good enough for the French - and they've taken as big a bite of the apple as anyone - then it's good enough for me! And that's my final word on the subject - *peut-être*....... At intervals along its entire length the bridle path passed through orchards belonging to the plotlanders. At least, that's what they thought! We of course had other ideas concerning ownership. Like the mirror image of the three wise monkeys, Charlie, Eddy, and yours truly, set off to sample the First Fruits of the season. The difficulty was in knowing exactly where to start. Immediately on entering the alley we were flanked on both sides by a bewildering array of sweetly laden fruit trees. Choice overwhelmed us. One of the orchards belonged to an old grey-haired lady we knew as Nan. She was such a nice lady that she would often invite us in to help ourselves to the windfalls or to sample some of her homemade ginger beer. This was far to tame for louts of our calibre. Fruit just didn't taste the same if it was freely given. In retrospect I think it was probably a clever ploy on her part just to keep us away from the better share of the harvest still suspended, temptingly, form her overburdened branches. If it was a ploy, then it was certainly a good one. Against our worst natures we usually left her property alone and made our way towards that of more challenging landowners. One orchard especially attracted us. Sometimes I wonder how fruit ever grew there. It was completely surrounded by oak and elm and hawthorn thickets, and even in high summer it seemed to drown in its own enveloping shadows. I think that it was probably the otherworldly darkness of that mysterious orchard that helped to make the place so irresistible. The contrasts made by the striated diagonals of penetrating light were spectacular. Apples and pears and plums hung - lime-lighted - in mid air. Golds, blushed pinks, and glint metallic purples glittered like trove in that diaphanous fairyland. Victoria plums - as big as a baby's fist - glowed in their clenched hoards. Conference pears glimmered greenly, like light through bottle-glass, and apples - with or without the flush of farmer's faces - exerted their ruddy influence. Unhappily for us though, one of the local roughnecks lived in the house next-door and thought absolutely nothing of letting rip in our direction with catapult or air rifle. Making a sortie into the fermented stillness of that bountiful place was often interrupted by the stinging thud of a ball bearing or the ear-screeching whistle of lead pellets. Although we felt that danger added a certain spice to our activities we not unnaturally concluded that scrumping and ballistics were not exactly compatible and that our larcenous trajectories would have to rocket us off elsewhere. In one of the properties bordering the bridle-path there lived one of the tallest, thinnest men that I've ever seen in my entire life and as children we often thought of him as having the perfect physique for a fruit growing horticulturist. There was definitely no need for ladders in that man's orchard. He could just wander around Gulliver-like picking the fruits of his labours at will. The one thing we didn't connect with his wiry stature - disastrously for us, as it turned out on a number of occasions - was speed! That man could have covered a hundred yards in four gargantuan bounds. He was as near to being a gazelle, as Darwin's originating theories would allow. With jumpers tucked into our trousers, ready to accommodate the booty, we made our way one at a time through a hole in his hedge. "I'll stand 'ere as lookout," I said, in my best military whisper. "An' when yer'v filled yer jumpers it'll be my turn." At first everything went according to plan. Charlie and Eddy loaded up with fruit then came back to the lookout-post. "Righ' o Merv," they murmured in plunderous unison. "It's your turn nah." Stealthily I crept on hands and knees through the orchard grasses. In no time at all I was Cramming my jumper full to the brim with the choicest windfalls. Just as part of my bulging crop was beginning to spill from its confines out of the sleeves and over the top of my V-neck Fairisle, Charlie blurted out the pertinent warning. " 'E's spotted us Merv, quick run fer yer life!" By the time I got to the hole in the hedge my two loyal associates were already some five hundred craven yards ahead of me. The path was a mine-field of dropped fruit. Split and bruised apples and pears were strewn across the surface of my slippery escape route. I looked behind and saw the loping man of the house gaining on me with every contending stride. My perilous cargo was jumping up and down with such force against the flow of my youthful athleticism that it had to be jettisoned. Run I could in those days, but not against a springbok! I had no chance. Whilst catching up with my friends with every step, I was nevertheless gradually losing out to the scissoring legs of my inhuman pursuer. He caught up with me as I was banking into a bend like an odds-on White-City greyhound. "Yer thieving little git!" he stammered breathlessly, as he held me dangling like a broken marionette from the scruff of my neck. "Nick my bleedin' fruit would yer!" he continued, accusingly. "Well I'll show yer!" Whack! Whack! My ears have begun to ring just thinking about it. Those were lawless times and plotlanders were their own judges, juries and hangmen

172

whenever crimes against their person or property were committed. My only consolation was that I didn't have to suffer the double indignity of having my father told about my evil doings. If anything the consequent chastisement would have been even worse. On top of that my share of the stolen goods had been lost in heart-pounding transit so the chances of an excruciating sour-faced stomachache had been reduced to zero. If nothing else, I could at least look forward to the green, cramp-contorted features of Charlie and Eddy as they paid the gluttonous penalty for their
cowardice in the face of the enemy.

The end of summer, was then, and still is to a great extent, associated in my mind with the marshes. Marshes are not everybody's favourite landscape. Most people it seems are far happier with fanciful artistic representations of the natural world. Misty atmospheric scenes of mountains and waterfalls are much admired, along with the ubiquitous chocolate-box thatch and cottage gardens. Saltings and reed-beds just can't compete with these pictorially. If you're looking for the picturesque then perhaps the Thames delta is best avoided. But if it's the sky you want to see in all its resplendent glory; a horizon-to-horizon great vaulted voluminous sky, then this is the place for you. You can watch the moisture forming into billowing and showery, glacial cloudscapes, a score of miles away, or more. You don't only know where the weather is, but you know where it's been and where it's going. It's like living in a glass dome. Salt winds carry their freight of sunlight and shadows, sometimes diffuse and misted, sometimes clear-cut and definitive across the endless sibilating vistas. At the cusp of August and September a powdery wash of salt marsh lavender blends with the yellow disks and purple rays of blossoming asters. Purslane in a sea green, blue-grey mass, sprawls across the salacious saltings and the bleach-blond reeds seduce on the airwaves with their husky voices. What child well along the road to puberty could not be enticed by these alluvial charms? I for one can name three who couldn't resist the allure. One blowy September Sunday in the sun Charlie and Eddy and I decided to walk the five sky-racing miles to the refineries and the sea beyond. That I was supposed to be back in time for Sunday-lunch and an afternoon trip to my grandparents in London did nothing to deflect me from my outlandish purpose. The jaunt would have been an impossibility given twice the allotted time, but when you take into account - which we didn't - the dykes to be crossed and the creeks forded - time and tide permitting - then our optimism rambled off into the ridiculous. For Charlie everything was possible. When he set his mind on something and gritted his teeth to match all you could do was follow in his determined wake. "Come on yer stupid slow-coaches," he encouraged. "You'll be there for yer know it." Eddy didn't seem convinced and muttered something untranslatable. "You're sure I'll be back in time fer me dinna," I interjected, hopefully. "Cause yer will," Charlie reassured. "Yer can rely on me." Well, I knew I could rely on Charlie, sort of, but we'd been walking for a hell of a time and were now to be confronted by our first major obstacle. " 'Ow we sposed ter git across that friggin' dyke," asked Eddy, with more than a hint of defeatism in his voice. "It's as wide as the bleedin' Zambezi!" "Don't exaggermerate," countered Charlie, ungrammatically. "You've seen 'ow they does it in the jungle, we'll take out cloves off, 'old 'em above our 'eads, an' wade across, it's simple!" Put like that it did indeed sound simple, but unfortunately words and reality are never quite the same thing exactly! This was September after all. The sun may have been shining but it was low in the sky and sucking the wind towards it from a point somewhere north on the compass. It was definitely not the season for skinny-dipping! I don't know about you but whenever I'm up to my neck in water the first thing to come to my mind are sharks and crocodiles. I blame Tarzan and Jacques Cousteau for this; I just can't help it. Even after convincing myself of the unlikelihood of ever finding such warm water creatures in temperate latitudes, they're still there, lurking in the depths of my tormented imagination. Fears don't have to be of the exotic variety though. The thought of a three-foot slippery eel having its intravenous way with one is just as mortifying, I'd say! And what about a rubbery-lipped mullet nibbling away at bodily encrustations and protuberances! It doesn't bear thinking about does it? Anyway, like three spooked porters on safari, we waded our way in single-filed trepidation across the dyke with our clothes in bundles on our heads. Charlie was the first out and in a brisk Teutonic manner he ran up and down on the bracing spot and threw in a few knee-bends and arm-raisings for good measure. Eddy and myself, purple and teeth-chattery, were not amused, and nor it seems were a pair of irate swans flapping frantically in our direction. "I 'ope it bites yer cock off," said Eddy to Charlie, somewhat unkindly I thought. Charlie, wishing to maintain his rightful place in the pecking order, pushed Eddy backwards into the dyke and into the path of the marauding swans. Well I've seen the difficulty swans have when it comes to taking-off from the water's surface, and I tell you now, Eddy would have been able to give them a lesson or two at that particular moment. He was back up on the bank and at Charlie's throat as if someone had reversed the film in life's bathetic camera. "Yer stupid pratt, I could have been drowned or pecked to bleedin' deaf even," he bellowed, rather dramatically one feels. Charlie, not into boxing in the buff, ducked down, picked up his bundle of clothes and ran bare-arsed out across the marshes, closely followed by two equally nude and equally nasty sons of the squelching soil. We were in and out of our clothes that day more often than Gypsy Rose Lee, although, with more strip than tease, it has to be admitted. Prior to that day whenever my bare flesh had come into contact with fresh air I'd felt certain unnamable - not to say unmentionable - stirrings in the erogenous depths of my very being. Part of my infantile anatomy would swell so inexplicably that it demanded immediate attention from my jiggling exploratory fingers. Could it be that that very day was to see the first and irreversible shift in my sex-drive? Was I moving inexorably towards neutral? I felt nothing. There was nothing to feel! I was just cold and wet and fed-up. I may have even had a headache, I can't remember now. If the swans could find my ever-shrinking member then they could have it as far as I was concerned. I'd had enough. I couldn't tell you just how many dykes and ditches we forded but by the time we came to East Haven Creek - the final and insurmountable high-watered hurdle - Sunday-lunch had been well and truly frizzled! Even the redoubtable Charlie was showing signs of faintheartedness. "Praps we should start back nah," he muttered, indecisively for once. "It'll be dark soon." The sudden realization of my broken familial promises and the predicament that I now found myself in made me feel more wretched than ever. The thought of long-distance stripping all the watery way back to dry land was too much to <u>bear</u> in all the different spellings and senses of the word. "I'm not takin' me cloves off again fer no-one," I said, prudishly. "I'm goin' ter git a good hidin' any 'ow," I added. "So what's the point?" Though not scholars by any means, Charlie and Eddy were astute enough in adversity to see the logic of my statement. The three of us - a touch more sedulous that at the outset - made our simian way back across the marshes. The hook of a harvestless moon lit our lingering way beneath the stars. A short-eared owl pampered the air on hushed wings and a train's receding whistle followed the lights of its sea-bound carriages. We climbed the hill of Station Lane like creatures emerging from the deeps. Sopping wet and covered in pond and duckweed we oozed and stank by dejected turns. When I reached my home Charlie and Eddy had scarcely the strength to wave as they shuffled silently off towards the thumbscrews and the rack. I had my own inquisitors to face, but for the present I was safe. It seemed they'd given up on me and had gone off to London after lunch as planned. So for the time being it was just the doorstep and my thoughts. My empty stomach was rumbling with all the sonority of an idling outboard motor. I hadn't eaten anything since breakfast and I was famished. No doubt the dogs had already polished off what was left of my Sunday roast to the military sounds of 'Forces Favourites' and cockle-teas and Madeira cake in London would have been digested long, long ago in the company of 'The Glums' and 'Sing Something Simple'. There was nothing left to do. I lay my tired and soaking self back against the door and drifted in and out of sleep, dreaming all the while of my imminent Armageddon!

All those nostalgically long, hot summers are by now so mixed up in my memory that I scarcely remember which of them came before and which of them came after the commencement of my secondary education. But it doesn't matter really, does it? After all this is poetry we're talking about and we shall have to leave sequence, logic and pretences to realism to those authors who wish to share some sort of mutual rationality with their readership. For myself - as my desultory mind ranges backwards and forwards throughout my confused life - so in the best possible post-modernist tradition, do my words. It has to be remembered that while you're reading - and hopefully enjoying - this momentous work, every word you see before you was at one time no more than a blank and uninspiring space beneath my poised - not to say artistically inclined - pen. The creative effort involved has been immense and personally I think that a vote of thanks for the author is now well overdue. Proposed? Seconded? Motion carried? Was that a yes I heard? Good! Then I thank you all warmly for your vote of confidence and shall endeavour to continue with my scholarly task. If perchance you happen to think that all this sub-literary waffle has something to do with disguising the fact that after having written one draft longhand and whilst typing out the second I have discovered some inconsistencies in the text and don't wish to write the whole damn book over again. Then apart from just having read one of the longest sentences in the English language, you may also have some little reason on your side. So, by the way of this *Deus ex machina*, while the text is busily deconstructing itself, along with my memory, I will in the time-honoured writerly fashion try to wrest some form of coherent meaning from the events surrounding the month of September 1957 when Timberlog Secondary Modern School *à la* Basildon became my second rate alma

177

mater.

As Secondary Moderns go, this one was very modern indeed. In fact, when I arrived at its learned portals, I found myself a part of what was only its second intake. It was to be a couple of years before the school was to become full to overflowing with semi-illiterates in dire need of edification. What I liked about the school immediately was its Protestantism. There was a perfunctory nod towards Christianity at assembly and during RE lessons, but apart from that so long as one wasn't too heretical religion could be safely left between the covers of The Big Black Book to look after itself. After years of enforced devotion this came as a merciful release. Instead of worrying about my sins all the time I could start enjoying them! Although I was to make a number of new friends at that school most of them could only be considered as on the acquaintanceship level. My two major partners in crime - Charlie and Eddy - had been enrolled along with me and therefore the evil threesome would be allowed the privilege of travelling the road of puberty together. If anything we grew even closer as we moved into our teenage years and suffered all the traumas of spots, bum-fluff and masturbation. Loud bangs heard over Basildon in the late fifties were not - as people supposed - the effects of military aircraft reaching mach 7 but were the result of the headlong pustulant threesome assaulting the barriers of adolescence. Being a new school in a new town with all the weight of post-war optimism behind it, it was as you might expect, extremely well equipped. That much of the equipment was there to point the majority of us in the direction of the factory or the building-site wasn't fully explained to me at the time. That it needed explaining at all in the face of such soul-destroying menial activities on the timetable as woodwork, metalwork and gardening probably speaks for itself. Teachers on the whole were Welsh as far as I can remember with a touch of Owen Glendower to the backs of their hands where the English were concerned. I should think we had more teachers from the west of the Marches than there were taffies down the mines! God knows what the situation's like now that the Government and British Coal have conspired between them to close down Wales altogether. I dare say that the literature syllabus probably contains Daffyd ap Guillam as well as Dylan Thomas - nothing wrong with that though. One feels that a large dose of compulsory Mabinogion would do the heathen Anglo-Saxons the world of good! Assembly was the start of our school day as ever and ever amen! Usually some pale-faced, four-eyed, goody goody would begin the proceeding by scraping discordantly at catgut or by tinkling the devotional ivories. The rest of us between singing hymns, farting through the school anthem and being thrown out for giggling, tried our level best to lower the moral tone of things. Our headmaster had the unfortunate Christian name of Vivian and most of us children of course thought that this was highly amusing. But in reality - like 'The Boy named Sue' - he'd compensated for the misnomer by developing an exterior as hard and all-knowingly brilliant as diamond. He was without doubt a good man. He devoted a lot of his energies towards the preservation of wildlife and would lecture us endlessly on the subject. That it was all wasted on the savages in his charge doesn't diminish either the effort or intent. The fact that I'm now the classic hunter turned conservationist is I think in no small part due to those early encouragements. But savages we were and he treated us accordingly. Most of us were terrified of the man. To see him in full Transylvanian flight along the corridors - black gown flapping in his wake - was petrifying. One had a spontaneous empathy for whomever it was who was about to have the life-blood sucked out of them. One of the ways he maintained his reign of terror was to administer corporal punishment on stage in front of the whole school at assembly. Like a crowd of callow and callous tricoteuses we watched as the doomed were paraded before him. Thankful in the knowledge that on this occasion at least we were to be spared the rod and allowed to spoil for a little longer. Beatings I had in plenty, but never on stage. As far as I was concerned that was taking histrionics to extremes. Once a boy had been in the punishing limelight it was as if he'd mentioned that unmentionable name feared by all thespians. He was branded. In the eyes of both staff and pupils he would thenceforth be treated with suspicion. Teachers would see him as a potential troublemaker in class and be on his back at every available opportunity and most of the pupils would see only his criminal reputation and avoid him because of their own irrational fears. Smoking at that school was frowned upon with as much prohibitive fervour as was reserved for blasphemy elsewhere in my educational journey. Did the interdiction stop us? Did it hell! Before assembly every morning the cycle-sheds had something of the appearance of an opium-den! In the middle of a nicotine haze dozens of boys would be busily stunting their growth on Woodbines, Weights and Turf Airman. There was always a lookout so the chances of being caught were minimal; or so we thought! On one occasion the lookout alerted us. " 'Ere comes ol' boyo, put yer fags aht!" Ol' Boyo was our gym teacher and as you've probably gathered by now was another refugee from the Valleys. Most of the boys scattered like shrapnel. I on the other hand just walked out as calm as you like thinking that as I didn't have any smoker's requisites about my person I'd have nothing to fear. "Linford, come over here!" he demanded. "Have you been smoking boy?" "No sir," I lied. "I've just bin lockin' me bike up, that's all, honest!" "Open your mouth and breathe out," he persisted. "We'll soon see!" That was the first of my many trips to the headmaster's study; or death row, as we'd fearfully christened it. Standing outside that door was almost worse than the inevitable beating to follow. I've no doubt that it was all part of the master plan. Let them stew for a bit first. Let them taste their fear for a while. When the summons finally came the bottom fell out of your stomach and your legs became decidedly rubbery. All that books down the seat of your pants; "Oh crikey! Oh golly! Billy Bunter nonsense was a million miles away from the tear-inducing, excruciating reality of what was about to happen. It was all done by the book. After the statutory lecture on the errors of your misbegotten ways, a thin, hooked bamboo-cane would be held horizontally at arms length. How he managed to get

180

so much force into the stroke over such a short distance was mystifying. A magic wand indeed! But force there was, and pain, and the welts to prove it. You held your breath; you didn't cry out, you tried to be brave. When you left his study the tears were already brimming in your eyes. By the time you got to the toilet you were beginning to sob uncontrollably. Locked inside a cubicle with your trousers down around your ankles and your arse on fire you reflected on authority while the seeds of incalculable hatred were sown and beginning to germinate. One of the problems with authority and its consequent laws is that these laws are administered by people with different principals and approaches when it comes to their implementation. Dual signals are often given and the inevitable ambiguities arise. Our Rural Science teacher - gardening to the non-agrarian amongst you - was also a man from the Valleys. But contrary to all perceptions of the rule, he seemed to genuinely like children, and even it appeared, East End children! He never actually gave us permission to smoke but he knew we did and left us to get on with it in the potting shed. Whenever I hear somebody talking about crop rotation I begin to cough involuntarily. How were we ever to reap the benefits of role models when there was so much Jekyll and Hydism involved? That very same teacher caught us smoking in a hedge one day on the borders of the school playing-fields and did no more than wag a perfunctory finger at us before confiscating all our fags. Within days his usually green fingers had turned decidedly yellow! Perhaps we'd learnt some sort of lesson after all! One of my early form teachers was from the hard-but-fair school of educators. He wasn't Welsh but there was more than a smouldering of Celtic fire about his person. Being as he was a science teacher instead of sitting at the normal desks we had benches with taps, sinks and Bunsen-burners to amuse ourselves with. Not conducive to serious study perhaps but enjoyable nevertheless. Our constant fiddling with the apparatus naturally enough irritated our form master who would glower at offending individuals with his dark, Frankenstinian eyes. I never once saw him lash out at anyone. He didn't need to; one look was enough. I don't know how he managed to keep such tight control without the use of physical force, but manage it he did, and with consummate ease. I'm sure that many a young teacher would give their right erasing arm for just a glimmer of that crazed professorial power. Faustian legends are made of such dreams! Maybe he learnt all he needed to know about order and control from his extra-curricular obsession. He was a dedicated apiarist and in conformity with all obsessed and dedicated people he felt that the rest of the world was missing out on something extremely important and would evangelize on behalf of our busy little insect friends at every available opportunity. For myself this was very providential. Not knowing the difference between H20 and CH3 OH (methyl alcohol) - a staggering lack of knowledge on my part, I may add - I much preferred bee-talk to test tubes and litmus paper. To help us with our studies of head, thorax and abdomen - what a memory - this ardent gatherer of nature's sweetest bounty had installed an observation-hive in the classroom. Being as we overlooked the school garden the mutually beneficial exchange of pollen and nectar were assured. That the occasional swarm would envelope and terrify the serfs working at the unpaid behest of their feudal overlords, was purely incidental. The occasional sting was brushed nonchalantly aside by some of the children as if it was a mere bagatelle, whereas I personally thought that it was more like a painful bag of pus than anything else and far removed from the realms of nonchalance. Still, if the Gods want to keep a special drink just for themselves, then needs must I supposed. Aye, there's the sting! At that school there were three types of scholar. At one end of the spectrum there were the manipulators of the ABC and the abacus, still struggling with Janet and John book one. What they lacked with regards to intellectual skills they more than made up for in other departments. They all had the look of mug shots from Dragnet, big-fisted, square jowled and heavy-eye-browed. And some of the boys were even more frightening! Those apparitions of atavistic proportions were avoided like the plague. They were the untouchables of our educational caste

182

system. The intervening years have enabled me to see things in a more rational light however. I now realize that a complex of socio-political factors that can be appraised by the simplest of dialectical methods are responsible for their material and psychological deprivations. (You can't be too careful since the advent of adult-literacy classes, can you?) Those unfortunate souls were exploited even further by the system by being obliged to take on any task to demanding for the caretakers. Desks and cupboards would seem to levitate along the corridors when handled by those magicians of manual labour. They could be seen day in and day out slaving away in the school garden like a tribe of dispossessed scarecrows. Such scandalous treatment obviously had a detrimental affect on them. Understandably they regarded the rest of us as some sort of privileged citizens. In their eyes we were no less than the freemen-journeymen of our day and were despised because of it. In the manner of the Dark-Ages their laws were unwritten but nevertheless tacitly understood. They seemed to be constantly on feud-alert. Budding esquires continually ran the gauntlet of their collective unrest and were often subject to disgruntled ambuscades in lonely corridors. If there was ever a fight in the playground you had no need to claw your way through the assembled multitudes to discover who were the contending parties. One look at the C stream register would be enough. It would almost certainly be two of the residual malingerers who were not having a granny buried on that particular day! At the other end of the scholarly spectrum were both the swots and the self-appointed leaders of humankind, all potential head-boys, or girls, to be chosen from among a conclave of monitors. These were the white knights and favoured virgins of that edifice of knowledge and were equally pernicious in their own way. If anything their forms of brutality were even worse. They took the moral high ground and anything they did or said to the rest of us was sanctioned by higher authority. If anyone's going to give me a hard time either physically or psychologically I'd prefer him or her to be downright evil. There's nothing worse than to be feeling wretched at the wrong end of someone's fist or tongue

183

only to be told that the assault had been committed for your own benefit. Smug bastards! They mimicked their masters and mistresses and made our lives a misery at the slightest pretext. They were invincible - or almost. Only once did I ever see a monitor lose a fight. Normally, like young Sir Galahads, they snarled through their pebbled visors and trounced the black knight at a blow. Good had once again triumphed over evil and all was right with the world. But as I said, once, just once, against all rectitudinal odds the villain came out on top. I can remember the suppressed cheer even now. Whenever I get a brown official looking envelope through the letterbox nowadays I think of that occasion and the possibilities of proletarian ascendancy it presented to my formative mind. There's always hope for the underdog I think, as I sit here dutifully crossing another cheque. Some hope! As for the third group, well, the only reason that extremes exist is so that the average can be determined. Myself, the bulk of the school, and probably most of my readers come into the latter category. It's a sad fact I know but proportionally unavoidable! My whole life's been pretty average really but this in itself has had its advantages. Averages are assessed statistically and statistics are as good a place as any for hiding things. *Cache a cache* from life has at times seemed like my sole *raison d'etre.* If I learnt anything at that school it was how to merge in with my human surroundings. As Confucius say: man with sore tongue needs plenty of bandages. Well, if you start with a poor joke you've got to stick it out! Haven't you? No, over the years I've cultivated a somewhat multifarious personality. I'm a social chameleon and can change the colour of my language or opinions to suit any cultural habitat. I've pretended to support every cause, lobby, religious and political ideal known to mankind in order to affect the necessary protective camouflage. Possibly the greatest lesson I learnt at that school was that of how to appear to be on all sides of an argument at one and the same time. Bluff and double bluff that's the answer. Straight-facing it time and time and time again with fingers and toes well and truly crossed. Those who crave for fame or wealth or glory will have to suffer the consequences of their sybaritic desires. Famous or infamous alike the sights of every sniping socialite or paparazzo will be pointed conspiratorially in their direction. If school was to be survived, as well as endured, then anonymity was to be of the essence. Unhappily, tests, exams, streaming and the likes are not amenable to wishes of blissful anonymity! Like it or not in a graduated system one has to be allocated a slot and this in itself has the obvious disadvantage of separating one out from the crowd. The model in our school seemed to be somewhat pyramidical in nature. At and towards the apex there were the genii, whilst conversely; the base was made up of an indistinguishable mass of congenital idiots. As a consequence of this incontrovertible fact if I were serious in my quest for anonymity then, naturally I would have to do badly in exams. To this end I devoted my utmost disattention. My ennui was impeccable. For some reason, known only to the designers of neurological circuits, no matter how hard I tried not to try hard whilst a pupil in 1A, I still found myself enrolled in 2A's register the following year. Drastic action needed to be taken. I was in serious danger of being regarded as having swot potential. Bad karma indeed! My year in 2a could thus be defined as nothing more or less vacuous than an intellectual void. I wasn't so much absent-minded as minded towards absence. The windows on my curriculum chart may as well have been just as transparent as the actual ones in the classrooms that I found myself endlessly staring through. It was such a wonderfully wasted year that I even found myself rewarded with my worst ever exam result - 9 out of a 100 in French! *C'est un miracle n'est ce pas!* I'd done marginally better in most of the other papers but was nevertheless convinced that I was at last destined for the B stream and all the rights to street credibility that that entailed. Exactly why systems have always conspired to work against me in my life is difficult to account for. I thought that my marks would have at last been low enough for me to be awarded the Janet and John prize for advanced cretinism! But instead the authorities in their bureaucratic wisdom had decided to shift the

185

scholastic goal posts. They'd - somewhat audaciously I thought - invented another category: lower 3A. So there it was, even when I tried to do badly I did badly at it, and found myself going both down and up at the same time! If there had been prizes for the illogical, perhaps, I would have fared much better. I did, after all it seems, have an existential proclivity towards the contradiction in terms. I decided in my naivety that if my mentors could be so inconsiderate as to change the rules - mid-stream, so to speak - then so could I. If I were to be fated to join the educationally aspiring ranks of lower 3A then I would nail my colours to the proverbial mast, and as they so quaintly put it across the pond; go for it! Diligence in study was to become second nature to me. The Beano and the Dandy were trashed in favour of more erudite works of literature from the school library and the once detested textbooks were treated in accordance with my newfound esoteric reverence. At the appointed day and hour I was summoned by the invigilator to take my place in the examination-hall. This was the 13+, the big one! I'd failed the 11+ dismally but felt that I was now ready to exploit my erudition and take my rightful place in the realms of academia. As exams go it was a cinch. My meticulous revision was beginning to pay dividends. Question after question leapt familiarly from the pages. Mind and pen flowed together and in no time at all I found myself confidently at the end of my intellectual labours. I don't remember exactly how long it was before the results came through but I wasn't worried in the slightest. You know when you've done well and it was just the degree of success that I was interested in. Eventually an interview was arranged with my form-master and the good news conveyed. I'd passed. I knew it. Not quite as well as I'd expected admittedly, but a pass nevertheless. This was to be a new start. The grammar-tech had probably already ordered the bunting and the Latin-master was no doubt busily conjugating my imminent arrival. "It's a pass," my teacher admitted grudgingly. "But not a very good one I'm afraid; I don't think it would be fair to send you to the grammar school now," he added, dispiritingly. "You'd never be able to catch up with the work." "But! But! But!" I stuttered, hopelessly. "I will, I'll try, honest I will!" It was all to no avail, the decision had already been made and there was nothing I could say that was going to alter that fact. I left that room in a blind, tearful rage. I'd been angry before, many times, but this was different. Never before in my life had I devoted so much time and energy to anything considered so laudable in the eyes of the righteous. Turning points there had been in plenty but none as momentous as that one. I decided there and then that the only relationship likely to develop between Timberlog County Secondary Modern and myself would be one of mutual indifference. They didn't care about me apparently and I certainly wasn't going to give a damn about them. I somehow managed to remain in the A stream for the rest of my time at school, but because of that event gravitated more and more towards such undemanding tasks as gardening and the milk-round. My real education would now have to take place in the age-old university of life, the way being longer but the rewards far sweeter. And anyway the immediate future had needs more pressing than those addressed by the Three R's. Pigeons, pimples and puberty for instance.

Chapter 12. Pigeons, Sex, and other Spectral Events.

When I left London I thought that I'd also left the world of
pigeons and their offspring - pigeon fanciers - far behind me.
But as is so often the case in this tribal society that we live in,
emigrations have as much to do with culture as they do with
populations. Demographic charts of Basildon would
undoubtedly show that such strange species of columbiformes
as mealies, checkers and tumblers, had followed the
movements of the tribe and still polluted the minds of their
possessors as well as their homes and gardens! I've never
really been a fan of the pigeon as such, especially as I was
once sent to collect a gallon of their spurious milk one April
Fools Day by a group of soon to be guffawing infantile adults.
I've always thought them to have something of a dumb
appearance countenance-wise. Although, having read the last
sentence but one you may well consider it a case of the P
calling the K, B! That pigeons did produce 'milk' of sorts was
something that I wasn't cognizant of at the time of my
initiation into the adult world of practical joking. If I had have
been aware of the fact my embarrassment may well have been
tempered by the apposite regurgitation of such useless
information. Certain 'friends' of my earlier acquaintance - not
I stress, the eminently sensible duo, Charlie and Eddy - along
with their demented brothers and fathers, were obsessed by
those feathered inadequates. Perhaps there was some sort of
symbiotic affinity between them that I was as yet too dense to
comprehend. Who knows? Anyway, much against my better
judgment I often found myself in the spellbinding company of
those avid aviculturalists. On days when I had nothing better
to do, I could be found from dawn to dusk in the grip of
pigeon fever! Yawn........ My knowledgeable hosts - between
bouts of rattling maize in tin-cans and making strange
clucking noises through their beckoning mouths - would
lecture me on the finer points of their - to my ears at least -
unfathomable art. Sleek long-distance birds would be
retrieved as soon as they re-entered the lofts. Rings would be

removed from their legs, introduced into a weird one-handled clock and punched frenetically. Although I'd been told time and time again of the reasoning behind that hermetic activity I never really grasped its fully calibrated significance. That it had something to do with racing the damn things I understood well enough. But that anybody could become so painstakingly involved in the nuances of such feather-brained inconsequentialities was as mystifying to me as the homing instinct itself! Nevertheless, I persevered in my attempts at some sort of understanding and if nothing else I learnt as much from my observations of human nature as I did from my from the crop-full, billing and cooing eccentricities of my avian mentors. First on the list of revelations was the callous indifference shown towards other creatures by those with a genetic frame of mind. Okay, I've affected my share of havoc on the natural world, but at least it had been done honestly for fun or sport and not in the euphemistic name of science. Those budding geneticists were ruthless. To listen to them talking about their feathered friends, you would think them to be consumed by the very emotion that so redolently rhymes with the white-plumed pacific cousins of their own dumb charges. Not a bit of it! "If they aint jus' right, we nut 'em," I was informed, conscientiously. "What d'yer mean," I inquired, for the sake of science. "We ring their bleedin' necks don't we, yer stupid git," my education continued. "If we don't fink they'll be good racers, we gets rid of 'em don't we, understand?" I understood all right, but even from my already savage perspective where life and death were concerned, this seemed a mite unreasonable. How unnatural could selection be I thought to myself? Wasn't it bad enough that nature was sufficiently red in tooth and claw of its own accord without this form of selective massacre adding to its incomprehensible slaughter? If I'd have been privy to a copy of 'The Origin of the Species' in those uneducated days I'd have probably subjected its inflammatory pages to some sort of ritual cremation and have become the immediate and inauguratory member of a sect of holier than thou creationists! Fortunately, for my sanity, that of my peers and my future readership,

189

congenital illiteracy dissuaded me from taking the seven-fold path of born-again mathematical inexactitude and I have as a consequence been able to develop methods of systematic bigotry along lines very much of my own making. No, pimples and puberty I couldn't avoid, but pigeons and their megalomaniacal enthusiasts I could and would whenever possible. If they wanted to puff out their chests and have inflated swaggering opinions of both themselves and their supersonic pies without a crust to think with then that was their business. For me the whiff of the local orchards was as alluring as ever and the scent, as I remember, was decidedly fruity!

'Pamela' now there's a name to conjure with. It's a name that's been one of the magical ingredients of my dreams throughout half a lifetime. Our meetings within the illicit bounds of other people's orchards may not have been of sexually titanic proportions admittedly, but they were in my mind at least, days to remember! She was the cousin of another of our local beauties and quite often came to stay for a few days or if I was lucky even a week or more. Those times suffered from all the vicissitudes of thought and emotion that could be impressed upon an unsuspecting world by the dizzying projections of a young and lustful love. I was as infatuated as any of the hormonally tormented pigeons in the strutting lofts of my egg-centred neighbourhood. My normal preoccupations with food and mischief had been rent asunder by the ductless hands of my prepubescent metabolism. One minute I had wings and would soar at the merest glance from her coy, yet concupiscent eyes. And the next, at the slightest hint or suspicion of disinterestedness or coldness on her part, I would crash to the ground in concrete, loveless boots. I followed her everywhere. It was like a re-run of the old familiar story about Mary and the woolliest of all here adherents. Wherever! Wherever! Oh wherever.......! She was a couple of years older than me and when one considers the difference in age - both real and relative where the sexual maturity of the sexes is concerned - it put her - like all the ripest fruit it seems - just

190

tantalizingly out of reach. But that didn't put me off one bit. Like a pencil in the hands of a student of anatomy I followed her curves in an artistic and tenacious manner. Wherever she was my thumb could be found held up appreciatively at the end of a loving and outstretched arm. I measured her every step, her every voluptuous movement. Still life would never, ever again, be sufficient. I had enrolled with the life-class and my perspectives had altered irrevocably. Even at that infatuated time I was heart-rendingly aware that she was only playing with my affections. Not viciously but in the time-honoured way of young women everywhere, who are as yet unsure of their feminine powers and persuasions. A way would have to be found of getting closer to this temptress. Could I from the soundless depths of my unconscious come up with any plan as intricately woven as Poseidon's nets and entrap this emergent Venus? Of course not! Simpler means would have to be employed. It's a well-known fact - to us pre-feminists at least - that girl's legs are better for looking at than they are for climbing trees. This, I'm convinced, is God's way of giving the boys a fighting chance. When Eve bit into the forbidden fruit, you can be certain that it was Adam who climbed the tree. Late one summer, when the greengages were at their best, their most mouth-wateringly delicious, Archimedes dropped in for a bath. Eureka! May or may not be an apt verbal ejaculation for someone who's struggling with his loofah, but as it turned out it did enable yours truly to come up smelling of roses for once. There she stood with her floral dress raised just one delectable inch above her bronzed and downy knees fixing me wantonly with a stare. "D'yer like greengages," I croaked, through intermittent bass and falsetto. "I know where there are some real whoppers." If you're thinking what I think you are; then don't! This is supposed to be a romantic passage, however purple! "Yes, I just LOVE greengages," she aspirated. "Are you going to pluck me some?" Red-faced with steam erupting from the ears and wobbly with involuntary muscle spasms may not have been the modus operandi of your average aspirant to the discipleship of Rudolph Valentino, but it was the best I could

191

manage at the time. "Come on then," I flustered, bashfully. "Follow me." The bridle path was transformed. Light was different, diffuse and lyrical. The bark of every tree was as a stretched canvas and over time each in turn would have to bear the representations of our entwined hearts and cupidian arrows. Thankfully the cuckoo had already flown away and left the once derisory airwaves to the more appropriate croonings of the turtledoves. I looked behind and was immediately mesmerized by the swish of her dress and the sun-shot tumbledown hair about her kissable shoulders. Could this be true? Pamela and I alone at last? Sunlight slanting through the trees, warm skin, warm breath, and passion enough to have scolded the noses of a tribe of lovelorn Eskimos. Like two shimmering apparitions we walked through the shifting veils of a gold-pervasive dream. And willingly there I drowned, drowned deep in the first up-welling waves of a new and irrepressible surge of youthful emotion. That wondrous summer afternoon flows from the pen like May-Dew from a maiden's hopeful palms or nectar from the inviolable, honey-suckled seductions of scent and sensuality. The day was not to be profaned. It wasn't then and hopefully it won't be now. Around the borders of a deserted shack - where once the one-eyed man frightened me as an infant - stood the forbidden trees of a paradise soon to be gained. On this occasion even his one good eye would have been unbearable to me. Shadows and seclusion and Pamela were all that I needed to make my life complete and fortunately for me they were exactly what I had. The scuffing of knees was all part and parcel of such manly exploits even if short-trousers somewhat limited the attempts at machismo! A drop or two of blood trickling down the legs not only added to the effect but also had the supplementary advantage of soliciting concern from the receiver of suit. "Oh dear! Mervyn, what have you done to yourself?" she quizzed in a caring fashion as she licked the corner of her handkerchief lusciously. "Let me have a look and I'll make it better for you." And she would, she would, better than the best of the betterest! There was absolutely no doubt about that

192

comparatively speaking. "If yer would just give us a kiss," I said in as dominant a voice as a short-trousered unphilanthropical oik could muster. "I'd never agin be worse!" "I'll give you a kiss for every greengage," she promised, alluringly. I was for all the world like a scurrilous monkey on heat. I shot up the tree like mercury in a fevered thermometer. Both the tree and Pamela were in my lustful imagination, to be equally denuded. The labours of Hercules wouldn't have kept me from the job at hand, excepting perhaps the acquisition of the girdle of Hyppolyta, Queen of the Amazons! A gargantuan task that would need savouring to the full I should imagine! The golden apples of Hesperides were already mine. The fruit was well and truly plucked and all that was left was the tasting. No matter how many words are used by way of definition, the moist, pouted lips, at the other end of one's first real attempt at a passionate kiss, can only be described on the abstract level of wordlessly experienced emotion. It could have been the source of all electricity for all I knew. At the instant our circuits touched I had the longest crew cut in the universe. Stars and sparks commingled in continuum. The second law of thermodynamics was a lie, the heat death a fallacy. Creativity was all. Form would always be wrested from the void and love was its eternal agency. I stepped back drunkenly from the encounter and watched in alienated silence as she put a fortunate greengage into her mouth. Amazingly, it seemed to me, whenever my teachers had asked me what I wanted to be when I grew up, I'd never once replied; a greengage! But that's precisely what I wanted to be, more than anything else from Alpha to Omega. As her white, galactic teeth sunk milkily into its flesh I groaned ecstatically. When her fully rounded prehensile lips sucked at its cosmic juices, I was a crouton in the soup of my desires, soggy and yet insatiate. In timeless oblivion I collected my labial rewards. Life at last was all crosses and no noughts. One after another the kisses came and kept coming. Tight-lipped childlike kisses they may have been but they were nonetheless ravishing for that. My first real taste of the forbidden fruit had whetted my widening appetites and French

193

lessons from that point onwards would take on a whole new significance. The diction of romance had entered my growing vocabulary and all I could say to the traductions of my heart was: *vive la difference!*

Throughout all of my scuffed arboreal years it had never occurred to me that trees could be put to sexual advantage. Fair enough, I'd done more than my share of showing off from their lofty if somewhat bifurcated hustings. But neither the sex nor the co-related habits of my juvenile audience had concerned me very much. Boys or girls it didn't really matter. It was enough to flutter bird-like through the branches and to receive the appreciative gasps that wafted in the direction of one's aerial agility. But suddenly their foliate potential for the ritual spoony pose had become deciduously obvious. My reasoning may have been of the recently acquired pragmatic variety, but intuition and instant dialectical syntheses had never really been strong points of mine, and anyway, lips-on relative positivism was the only existential proof I craved at the time. If Pamela + trees = bliss and kisses, then who was I to start philosophizing at this stage in my experimental success? The time of the chestnut was nigh, divided as ever into two delightful categories: horse, or conker, for the colloquial amongst you; and Spanish, or sweet, to those roasting in the coals of Dickensian sentimentality. I'm not usually one for homologous description but it should be noticed at the outset that the fruits of both these types of chestnut tree are not only brown on the inside but also green and prickly on the outer. The horse chestnut has hard, knobbly mace-like spikes, whereas the sweet one may look smooth and sylvan-locked, but is in effect by far the sharper of the two. Now, you can call me a bald Frenchman if you like, but this strikes me as rather analogous to the sexes themselves. Boys may be hard-baked and vinegar-tongued but they know when to call a conker a conker. Girls on the other hand are as sweet as a silver-Joey at Christmas, as long as whatever they say, that is, isn't swallowed with the same loonicidal frequency! You may think this diversion to be somewhat uncharitable, especially if by way of gender you've ever suffered the patriarchal whims of the 'Equal Opportunities Commission'. But in my defense I can only say that my earliest experiences at the hands, feet, finger-nails and tongues of the 'gentler sex' has in one way or another managed to colour my later opinions. I lost more fights and arguments; physically, emotionally and intellectually, with the objects - grammar that is, not chattels - of my adolescent desires, than I ever did when subjected to the taunts and tantrums of my male-contending peer groups. Nevertheless the season of niners and spiting coal-shovels had come round again and girls for the first time had found themselves included in the harvest. I would have to climb higher, leap further, and shake the branches more vigorously than ever before if I were to have any chance of filling my basket up to its full, virile brim! The problem was of course that girls just weren't interested in conkers and as a consequence of that fact most of our tree-borne bravado was reserved for masculine eyes only. Sweet-chestnuts on the other hand were very acceptable to the feminine palm, and though they were capable of picking them up from the ground themselves, they were more than happy to exercise their prerogatives and leave us to do the running around in love-struck, woebegone circles. Lacking the opportunity to prove my masculinity through feats of aerial gymnastics, I soon tired of the Spanish-chestnut season and returned to the more celibate world of conkers. I had two favourite conkering locations in those days. One was on the land that probably once belonged to Vange Hall and that is now part of Basildon municipal golf course - where a couple of lonely spreading survivors offer their ancient shade to swung-out exhausted handicaps - and the other was outside the church of Holy Cross where even now the selfsame trees continue to add to their girth religiously under the protective eyes of the church commissioners. Both of those places, and without exception, all of the trees have seen me at my Icarian best. Whether or not I really thought that I was the owner of a set of handcrafted wings waxed by Daedalus is both literally and metaphorically immaterial. I wasn't! Why the ground

195

insisted on turning its gravity against me time and bone breaking, breath-expelling time again, I never fully understood. If Newton's head had been in the clouds instead of far too firmly on his mechanistic shoulders, the rest of us vacuous flat-earthers would have had a much greater chance of aiming for the stars! Still, that's another set of equations, as the de-waxing moon said to the sun gibbously. Fall; as I did frequently, was more to do with flying too close to my ego than anything of more solar proportions. There were always conkers on the ground and they were riper and more accessible by virtue of their earth-shattering descent. But were they good enough for me? Were they heck! 'The further you're off from England, the closer you are to the stars' was my favourite if somewhat plagiarized pastiche. And the stars referred to - immaterial as they were - could be seen just as well during the daytime as they could at night. If there was just one conker hanging in an alienated state - precipitously - at the end of a branch some sixty feet off the ground, then that was the one for me, it was irresistible. In my Cro-Magnon mind it was the largest, roundest, hardest, all-conquering conker of all time and nothing would stop me from making it my own. Nothing that is, excepting that all-pervasive gravity I've been talking about! Are you sitting comfortably? Yes? Then I'll begin. Once upon an autumn in the lyrical land of yore a tiny boy with match-stick legs and the biggest brown boots in Christendom made his yearly pilgrimage to the church of the Holy Cross to honour the Gods of the sacrificial conker. Like Jack of the fabled beanstalk he began his ascent and the land of the golden-egg-on-the-face waited to crack the shell and make the abysmal yoke that would take smirk from the visage of its next addled victim. The fires of acquisition were reflected in the foliage of the tree. Like an amber flame it flickered through the smouldering mists of a soon to be solemn September. Though at the opposite end of the equinoctial spectrum a sacrifice was about to be made that would hold as much significance for the sacrificed as that attributed to the Person of the Paschal-Lamb. It must be said in passing of course, that like the other two wretched criminals to be crucified along-side Him, I was about to suffer for my own sins and not for the sake of humanity in general. Let's not split biblical hairs though! Remember! It's only a story! Having already inextricably tangled the traditions of fable and parable in accordance with the customs of my unconscious artifice I'll stretch the bounds of symbolism a little further. If you think an Ascension in autumn is rather out of place then the descending tongues of Holy Fire in that mellow and fruitful season certainly put the seal on this authorial covenant as far as belief in suspension is concerned. Yes, that's the way it was as the fiery branch I stood on snapped - a touch unbelievably when you consider my diminutive stature - flared out on the feathery air and took the side of science over religion. What did Galileo say about a cannonball and a feather? Fortunately for me he was wrong. He didn't take air-resistance into account, or that of the Pope come to that. Something that I'm still paying a flagellatory penalty for I might add! Anyway, the branch was transformed. It had become 'The Tree'. Cruciform in horizontal the branch and I were in suspended animation. It was the Wilderness and the Garden of Gethsemane all rolled into one. I hadn't had much of a life up to then, but what there was of it flashed immediately in front of my widening eyes. It's funny just how many Hail Mary's one can say in mid-air without the aid of a safety net, or a rosary for that matter. That was probably the closest I've ever come to experiencing a true, blindingly religious conversion. While the cock was crowing in one ear the dove was whispering in the other. Like an angel's holy wings the many-branching faith I clung to floated slowly and fabulously to the ground. Son of Daedalus out Hope was re-united with his glorious father. The horse-riders of the Apocalypse had fallen at the first and like Pegasus unchained I'd mixed every available myth known to the occidental. I breezed across the winning-line ecstatic in the knowledge that inspiration was still safely in the hearts and minds of men - and more to the point boys - and that poetry had lived to write another day. Hippocrates was right; I must stay away from the Hippocrene!

The religious life is okay for some I suppose but having failed in my attempts to have my conversion witnessed by adoring fans of the vestal-virgin variety, the transubstantial significance of it all had made little impression on me. And apart from that - as must be obvious to all students of theology - the direction of my spiritual journey on that particular day was decidedly upless! So in the manner of all fallen souls I converted upless into hopeless and reverted to my evil ways. Sex was becoming obsessive. Not that we were doing any of it you understand, its just that the rumours about were rife both in the world and in our awakening bodies. How images - non-existent 'things' that they are in terms of tangibility rating - passing innocently through the eye could have such an effect on the juvenile metabolism confounds me. But affect me and Charlie and Eddy they undoubtedly did. Every time we saw a sexy lady something incomprehensible happened between eye and brain and hormones. I have been known to quiver on the spot, transfixed by the pert uplifting tilt of a womanly breast. Why I didn't feel the same about pendulous pears, bananas and other fruity facsimile is a matter for the anthropologist alone. Although it has to be said that the sight of a woman unzipping a banana and popping the temptational flesh into her mouth did, and still does, have its attractions. Something the manufacturers of chocolate-bars are happy to exploit. And by the by, it's little wonder that my bathroom scales are beginning to affect something of an overburdened grimace! We weren't exactly at the flashing stage at that time - not in public that is, at least - but we were definitely in danger of being classed as sex-pests or peeping toms. Close to where we lived an unfortunate lady of our acquaintance was to become the major recipient of our lustful droolings. She was probably in her late twenties and built in the substantial manner of all Hollywood sex-goddesses of the day. Pencil-skirts and the upwardly traceable seams of fine denier stockings were all that was needed by way of impetus to activate our licentious imaginations. That her breasts were the biggest things in a hammock before or since Jane

198

Mansfield wasn't of itself an incidental of course. But those legs! Those high-heeled, short-stepping, scissoringly luscious legs! We would follow them anywhere. Indeed, we could be seen regularly following them right up to the round, wobbly, alternating pulse and contraction of her delectable buttocks. She didn't seem to mind our sexual persistence and in no way gave the impression of being somebody ready to rush off to the law at either the drop of a hat, or a panty-girdle! That we popped up then disappeared like ghosts in the shadowy realms of a quantum mechanic's nightmares didn't seem to disturb her in the slightest. Confronted time and time again by the feigned nonchalance of our ogling selves she would shoot a smile straight from the director's couch with all the sensual aplomb reserved for the rhythm-school of method acting. This in essence was *libre échange,* Adam Smith himself would have been proud of us. She had the goods and we the pubescent currency. She was as amply supplied, as we were demanding. As transactions go though I think that she probably got the best of the deal. Here expectations were neither as great nor as poorly understood as ours. At every glance from us her collateral was increased, we continually added to her assets and reserves. She had to do little more than just be herself to have her worth confirmed, whereas with us it was different. At that age we weren't' as yet fully sure of what it was we really wanted. We had a wealth of vast, confused, uncontrollable feelings. We knew that they were somehow displaced. But displaced from what? Aye, there's the rub! The only thing that I can say by way of consolation as far as those budding sexual entrepreneurs were concerned, is that although vague as to the outcome of their dabblings in the market, that didn't inhibit their dealings, nor their eye for the futures, one bit!

Whilst we're being City-minded our sexual stocks and shares can be expressed in the terms of another of our voyeuristic interests. The woman - or truth to tell, girl, inflated to womanhood by the scrip issues of youth - worked in a London office. Her commuterly life-style was - as is usually the case - reliant on the transportational skills of British Railways! This fact not withstanding, time and distance between her house and the station itself, suffered from the same chronic inconsistencies of scheduling. Her temporal loss was our heavenly gain. Female flesh in the static manner of the best - 'the show must go on' tableau of the Windmill Theatre tradition - was exciting enough in its own way, but bodily bits on the move in belated response to alarm clocks and timetables, were far more speculative and promissory. I don't think that we were quite into the age of the mini-skirt, but loose wrap around tartan just above the knee, held precariously in place by one uncertain silver-pin was just as desirable. It was probably at that time that my love of the Scots was formulated. If there was such a clan as the Mac-eyes-out-on-organ-stops, then I was just the laddie for a quick skirl in the rumbustious heather. Every morning, this breathless hind from the braes of my mind's Balmoral, shied past my window and bolted in a cute Caledonian manner down the bridle path of my misspelt Sassenach dreams. My faith in the Gay Gordon's had been restored. I'd have heeled and toed myself all the way to John o Groats and back again just for one valedictory doech an doris from her train-late trembling lips. One morning in late summer Charlie, Eddy and myself were busily doing nothing about our boredom when that doe-eyed monarch of the glands came sleeking past us in the direction of the station. "Caw, jus' look at the jugs on that!" whooped Charlie, coming over all unnecessary. And if that wasn't bad enough loudly repeated the truism for doubly obvious good measure. "Shut yer gob!" insisted Eddy, undoubtedly love struck. "She might 'ear yer." "Don't care if she does," continued Charlie. "If yer've got good tits, yer likes to be told abaht it, don't yer." Well, even I have to admit that that wasn't very bonny of him. The look on Eddy's face had taken on the same changeable nature as the Scottish weather. He wore the sort of rock-hard, shadowy scowl that one usually associates with Glencoe in the teeth of a blustering sou'westerly, if boredom wasn't to turn into blood feud, then something would have to be done, and quickly.

200

"What d'yer fink abaht Flora McDonald," I said, historically. "What the Rob Roy are yer on abaht!" or some such would have been an interesting retort. But being as I was the closest the three of us could muster as far as British history was concerned, all I received in reply was "Hey!" "Who!" That was enough however. They'd been deflected from their mutually murderous intentions. "She's gorn off dahn the alley," I observed. "Let's folla 'er!" Like three highland stalkers we filed singly and stealthily into the bridle path and kept our safe, down-wind distance from the quarry. She was moving so quickly that sometimes in order to keep up with her we would occasionally find ourselves caught out in the open. Once, when we thought that we were stranded in full view, she cast a furtive glance back across her shoulder and then sidled off into the bushes. That's it we supposed. We'd been rumbled. She's run for cover. Just in case we were wrong we hung back for a few minutes and waited to see what would happen. To our surprise she re-emerged from the bushes, adjusted her clothing, and continued on her way. What could she have been up to? Torn between pursuit and curiosity we teetered by the hedgerow. Curiosity won and we entered the musky darkness. As our eyes grew accustomed to the light we became aware of a long strip of cotton wool, smeared with blood. "Oh no! She's been injured," declaimed Eddie, in a lovelorn amateur dramaticky sort of way. "She's bleedin'!" It couldn't be denied. As we picked up and closely examined the offending article, it was obvious to one and all that it was a bandage of some sort, and a recently soiled one at that! Eddy was mortified. What was wrong with the poor girl? Was she going to die? He was inconsolable. "Don't worry," said Charlie, reassuringly. "It can only be a scratch, she wouldn't be able ter walk ovverwise." That was the height and depth of our medical knowledge. Monthly to us meant little more than a pinch and a punch and no returns! The thought that along with fish, frogs and chickens, women could also lay eggs hadn't occurred to us at all. And even it had have done we would have expected them to be laid in nests or stuck up against the stems of water-plants, and not just wrapped up in cotton-wool and thrown carelessly into a hawthorn thicket to incubate on their own! We liked women very much. They were good to look at. They smelled nice. And as I'd already found out to my culinary advantage, they tasted pretty good as well. But they were strange mysterious creatures and getting stranger by the minute. More would have to be learnt about them, and soon. A period - if you'll excuse the pun - of enforced study would have to be embarked upon. I'd done all I could with the practical thus far; the time for theory had arrived.

Apart from magazines concerned with reinforced concrete and sundry knitting patterns, reading material in our house was rather limited. There were some books admittedly, but you had no fear of suffering from literary indigestion no matter how eagerly you devoured them. Most of the intellectual roughage was in the form of non-fiction. There was a set of general knowledge books - musty and mildewed even before I got to them - that dealt with such indispensable day to day subjects as aeronautics, physiography and shorthand-typing. Mind you, because of that series of tomes I now know the difference between Pleistocene and plasticine and can explain it to the uninitiated *à la* Pitman! The only thing those books didn't tell you were what to do with all the useless information once you'd absorbed it. I couldn't see any future as a shorthanded aeronauticalist so I used them as target practice for my Bowie knife instead. Another set of tomes we had was called something like 'Practical Knowledge For All'. Those got closer to the craze for utility at the time. If you desperately wanted to know how to fix a ballcock or to learn the words and music for 'Swing Low Sweet Chariot' then those were the books for you! Personally I wasn't interested one jot in the difference between a cistern and the Sistine Chapel and although joining a gospel choir may have been spiritually uplifting, I couldn't, apart from the most tenuous linkages, see how it would further my developing sexual career. Three other works I remember from the time did seem to be linked to my quest, if in a rather strange,

202

perverse and incongruous manner. The Catholic Dictionary - almost unintelligible to the less than congenitally devout - did at least have one immaculate concept to its credit. I can understand how that particular volume found its way onto the hallowed shelves of Linford Hall, but how 'Freud, his Sex and Dream Theories' got there is something of a mystery! No more mysterious, mind you, than the far from immaculate haul of phallic fish that we are constantly dredging up from the unconscious depths of our primal septic tanks according to Sigmund's tortuous reasoning. As you can imagine the conflicting ideas I became heir to because of my delvings into the extreme and soundless pages of those two classics of human circulatory thinking, have not served me well where questions of logic and concision are concerned. The third book however was a different kettle of conundrums! This was the real - if unpalatable - thing that had found its way surreptitiously into my bedside cabinet. My parents had undoubtedly made a connection between the dilation of my pupils and the breathless shuffling sounds coming more and more frequently from the bathroom, and decided that before I went blind altogether they'd offer me the prospect of some clinical enlightenment. Sadly, the manual they'd chosen for me was obviously designed to turn one off of sex forever! It seemed to me little more than a hymen's guide to do-it-yourself gynaecology! There were hand-painted colour plates in there that would have made a bucket of wattles and tripe look positively decorative in comparison. A penis on its own already has the air of a wrung turkey's neck about it, but why I should have to be subjected to diagrams of one cut painfully into every available section and projection, eludes me to this day. Tubes, veins, glans and foreskins have never been required reading on my part. I put the book back in the cabinet where it belonged and lived with the tacit, all-knowing look of its existence for the rest of my teenage years. It would all have to come down to the Essex County Council I'm afraid. I had my library tickets, just a short cut across the railway-lines to Vange, with a contrived studious look about me, was all that I needed. Vange library couldn't quite have

203

been called an edifice of learning. The only real difference between it and the plotland shacks that lined the encompassing unmade roads was that it was a marginally bigger shack! Inside it was permeated by that same dank, bungaloid smell so redolent of the area in general. The librarian and I had a somewhat one-sided relationship. She knew what I was really up to and no matter how hard I tried to disguise my scurrilous flickerings through the pages of 'her' books, I couldn't hide my stuttering embarrassment in knowing that she knew. " 'A 'a 'ave yer got any books on Africa," I stammered. "What do you want it for," she teased. "Doing another school project are we?" "That's right," I said, walking suspiciously through the green channel. She stamped my passport with a grin and sent me off to the relevant exotic shelves. As one would presume there were some mighty volumes on Africa and without porters I could only manage to ferry them one at a time over to the reading desk. As you've no doubt already gathered it wasn't the text that interested me. It was the photographs that I was rampant for. Not the Sahara, Mount Kilimanjaro, or the Victoria Falls. No my academic research was of a more sociological nature. Village-life, that's what I was after, and preferably female village-life. Dusky nubiles grinding corn, poverty and their hips, were grist to my lusty imperialist mill. If Africa had anything going for it at all, to my puerile and chauvinistic mind, it was that the sun, it seemed, always set on Marks and Spencers. Underwear, let alone clothes, was conspicuously absent. Attitudes of Empire seemed to allow for the exposure of black skin in publications destined for a wide readership, whereas portrayals of blanched nakedness were reserved for students of art and medicine. I made my worldwide erotic journeyings through the pages of those books and knew every sensual shade of brown through chestnut to ebony. Racism was as big a problem then as it is nowadays. If after reading the last paragraph or so, I said to you that it was something that had never really occurred to me, you may well raise a quizzical eyebrow or two. But I can honestly say to you that what ever there was by way of prejudice in my innocent soul resulted from processes of a historical nature and wasn't due to any congenital deficiency on my part. Me and my golliwog read Robinson Crusoe from cover to cover many times without me once sending him out for firewood or provisions or patronizing him in any way whatsoever. There was racial harmony in my nursery. Parents and real bogeymen were the enemy not xenophobia. And what about sexism then, I hear the sisters amongst you asking? Well, I'll tell you what about sexism then. It's not just a black and white bloody issue, is it!

Every good story needs a ghost. Arguably, it could be said that I've failed miserably on the first count and that I've yet to come up with the storyteller's goods, let alone a good story! And secondly it should be said that there are more than enough ghosts in this book already to last a couple of death-times. But I think that the heady mix of S, E and X thus far encountered necessitates this diversionary tactic. The effects on heartbeat and pulse-rate may be the same from the spirit world as it is from that of the sperm but at least you'll stop bumping into walls for a page or two! And even if you do bump into one there's always the chance that you'll be able to sail straight through it. The church of the Holy Cross, in Old Basildon, was supposed to be the haunt of a headless monk. Why they are always headless is one of the great-unsolved spectral mysteries of all time. And even more irresolvable is why do they invariably have to carry their cerebral lost property around with them under their arms? You would think with all the insubstantial fortuities of ghosthood to fall back on, that heads could be easily levitated and placed firmly, if lightly, back on their lonesome shoulders. But no, gore seems to be the order of the day and ghosts with their heads in the right places have never been as popular as the decapitated variety. Religion and bloodshed were no strangers to the area. William the Conqueror's half brother Bishop Odo (the bloody bishop) was granted a manor at Vange and one at Basildon - along with 214 others nationwide - after the conquest. One of his fellow butchers, Ralphson of Turold - like Odo himself, also depicted in the Bayeux Tapestry - became his tenant at

Vange. Suen, the sheriff of Essex, and another post-conquest land-grabber, whose castle was at Rayleigh, was the lord of the manor at Bertelsden or Battleswick as it may have been called. Now non-existent, it is nevertheless thought by local historians to have been on roughly the same site where now stands the church of the Holy Cross. With such bloodthirsty Norman foundations to build upon it's little wonder that we ended up with the ghost of a headless monk of our very own! What started as a by the by, nothing much to report by-line in one of the local rags, was soon picked up by the more sensational sections of the national press. Everyone who wasn't anybody claimed to have seen the apparition in his or her search for fame, and the subsequent influx of hard currency! At first local wags caught up in the spirit of the thing - or no thing, as the case may be - would engage in elaborate hoaxes for the sake of the banks of expectant cameras. Oversized robes and tonsorial footballs would be employed with the hopes of fooling the assembled gallery of press and public. It was not unusual to see two or three ghosts at a time vying for the available limelight. All those otherworldly shenanigans stopped abruptly when a number of local psychopaths seemed to decide simultaneously - and not a mite illogically - that the best way to catch a ghost was to shoot it! This of course had the effect of interesting the gutter press even more and before we knew it both radio and television had swelled the already swollen ranks of the curious and the ice-cream salesmen alike. No self-respecting ghost would be seen dead in such a set-up. Ghost-hunters from all quarters breezed in on the psychic winds. This in turn inspired the police who were thenceforth manifest in ever increasing numbers. I've never seen a ghost before, and I'm sorry to disappoint you, but I didn't see one then and I haven't seen one since. I've been scared by the thoughts of them. Have even felt as though I've detected the waft of their chill and unholy presences. But that sounds more like the lead-in to yet another ghoulish mother-in-law joke than anything else. No, if there was such an entity as the headless monk of Holy Cross, then the chances are that we frightened the poor soul

206

away! Another spooky aspect of the area in question was the seemingly spontaneous combustion of barns, halls, farms and manor houses. Hardly a month went by without one or another of those local landmarks being raised to the ground by fire. What I resented more than anything else was the fact that those conflagrations were invariably blamed on us newcomers. "It's them lads from London," you'd hear insistently. They're a bad lot you know." There are still as many Londoners living in Basildon now as there were then, more probably. I just don't believe that all Londoners are born arsonists. If there were as many fires per/year, per/capita, proportional to the differences in population between then and now, the place would be continuously under the hose-pipe and knee-deep in firemen. Coming from an exploited working-class background I know the meaning of - but not the financial implications of - such words as: Insurance, compulsory-purchase and corporate development, amongst others. But what I do know is that many of those buildings had stood the test of centuries before that rash of burnings laid them to waste. I also know that those dwellings that survived those incendiary attacks are still there and will almost certainly stand for many centuries to come. Very strange! Very spooky indeed! Perhaps the saddest loss of all was that of the thatched thirteenth century barn attached to the church of the Holy Cross. A magnificent medieval structure reduced to the ashes of memory, along with the hapless headless monk, and the vinegar-cured, oven-hardened, leaf-flickering days of conkerdom.

Chapter 13. The Long Short Trouser Caper.

Another winter came and went with hardly a facial or pubic hair to show for its trouble. Full-length mirrors had begun to work overtime. Muscle-less arms were being flexed, blackheads squeezed and pimples endured. Things were changing right at the core of my very being and I was confused and squeaky-voiced on the subject. Some of the magic had already gone out of Christmas; snow was suddenly cold and girls incomprehensibly warmer. But in spite of all this inner sexual activity, as spring approached once more this particular young man's fancy turned unaccountably to thoughts of motor-bikes! Perhaps at a subconscious level I realized their mechanized equivalence to the galloping steeds of yore. Once I'd mastered the stubborn beasts I could kill the dragon of adolescence, rescue all the maidens of my dreams and roar off deep-throatedly into the four-stroked, twin-exhausted sunset. Well, that's the way I like to think of it! In truth, it was a far grubbier business than that. At times Eddy's father's workshop looked more like the pits at Brands-Hatch than anything else. His elder brother and his friends seemed to live in that greasy, spanner-filled environment for most of their lives. It was a veritable production line and the works machines produced there were to my uninitiated eye at least, of a professional standard. Beezers, Nortons and Triumphs appeared to be the favoured mounts. For reasons of esoteric precision certain parts of those machines were interchangeable. This in turn facilitated the interchangeability of their names and glistening roadsters would come out of the factory with such wondrously hand-painted designations as Tribsa and Triton. As far as my proto-engineering memory serves me, much of this two-wheeled reciprocity was to do with the whipless superiority of Norton Featherbed frames. This would eventually have to be put to the test of course. At about that time I met another likely-lad who was destined to become the guiding light that would lead me out of the confining tunnel of my heterosexual darkness. His name was

208

Dave Parks and like myself was one of the baby-faced variety of prepubescents. But where as his lithe, angelic looks seemed to make him irresistible to girls and women of all ages, my cherubic locks and lingering inanities seemed ripe only for reproach and rebuffal. I was obviously missing something very important *à propos* the coupling stakes and hopefully this lad would be able to supply me with the *pass partout* to the liberating world of sexual adventure. But for the moment it was motorbikes. First master the phallic symbolism, depress the clutch, engage gear, twist the wrist and accelerate! In those days such formalities as licences, tax and insurance - let alone crash helmets - were almost unheard of. Being as we apprentices to the high-speed arts of sexual impressiveness were to learn our skills on the unmade roads and alleyways that surrounded us in plenty, the chances of actually impressing anyone were next to zero. That didn't matter one jot! Eddy's elder brother was a born leader. He was strong and aggressive when necessary, but mostly he controlled with kindness. He never tired of our constant demands for his attention. "Give us a ride Reg," begged Eddy, twisting an imaginary handle-grip. "On the Triton mate, it's brilliant." "Sorry," replied Reg, apologetically. "It's to good fer the fields, yer can 'ave a go on the four-square if yer like," he continued. "It's great ova the mud." That multi-cylindered beast was notorious. If the Triton was the thoroughbred of the motorcycle world, the Ariel Square Four was the percheron, and a recalcitrant one at that!" You're not gettin' me on that fing," said Dave, determinedly. "It's friggin useless!" "Me neiver," said Charlie en pillion. "It's a bleedin' deaf-trap!" Well, I may have had only four fingers on each hand, but that was more than enough for even my less than arithmetical self to see that they'd all taken the regulation one step backwards. "No!" I screeched, appealingly. "Not me please, no, not me!" "Reg - very bravely I thought - volunteered to ride on the back and give me instructions *in situ*. Well, I'd never blow raspberries in church again. How the organist ever managed to co-ordinate hands and feet for a bar or two, let alone for the whole of the toccata and fugue in D minor, was astounding.

"Pull the clutch in, kick it inta gear, let the clutch out, accelerate, decelerate, pull the clutch in, kick it inta second, let the clutch out, accelerate, brake! Both brakes! Hand and foot! Caw, what's the friggin' matta with yer, yer stupid prick!" So much for driving lessons, I thought. I bet that many of the ladies amongst us have just shot a withering glance in the general direction of their tutorialistic husbands! Bushes and fields are hard, right enough, but not as hard as your average hard-rutted unmade-road! Brushing myself down whilst expelling the odd contrived ooh and ahh! In the hopes of displacing any further abuse, I turned a downcast, sheepish eye towards Reg, and Grovelled. "I'm eva so sorry Reg, honest I am; let's 'ave anuvver go," I added with all the unction of engine oil. "I promise I'll try 'arder, come on!" Beast, the Square-Four may have been, but I'd felt the liberating effect of the wind through my hair. I'd felt the dull, rhythmic thud of its pulsating pistons and on top of that I'd felt all the latent combustive power responsive to the merest twist of my limp-wristed whims. Charlie, Eddy and Dave came running up to us. ! Is yer bofe alright!" they enquired, with a sort of mass-insincerity. "We faught yers were dead!" What worries me about both my friends and human nature in general is the look of disappointment I seem to detect on the faces of those solicitous about my health when I reply in the physically affirmative! "I wanna go!" "No I'm next!" "What abaht me!" It's funny how attitudes change once the test pilot has proved the viability of a project! All those erstwhile shirkers of responsibility now wanted to share in the glory, seeing as they no longer saw the possibility of personal injury. Well, as Napoleon said to Josephine, *"nicth t' nacth mon cabbage!"* If I'd been thought valorous enough for the inaugural flight, then nobody, but nobody, was going to dislodge my epaulettes. "Right o Merv!" ordered *mon general.* "Let's try agin." I looked back over my racing shoulders and saw the disgruntled footsloggers receding into the blue-aired and expletive distance. Before me was the open road. Well, cinder-path, to be more precise. Bushes, clouds and the scattering wildlife were no more than an exhilarating blur. I toed the gear lever into third, pulled back on the accelerator and sped out - eye-wateringly - towards the checkered-flag of my newly acquired accomplishments.

Just a couple of fields and unmade roads away from where I lived, stood the smallholding belonging to the Patterson's. Now the Pattersons were a motley crew. It was a matriarchal society presided over jointly by a mother and daughter. Seniority was - as could not be otherwise - on the maternal side. But when you consider the fact that she waited expectantly by the letterbox every day for a telegram from Her Majesty herself, you will understand what I mean when I say that seniority in the Patterson household was really just incidental. Her daughter was an octogenarian herself and as a consequence of a long life looking after her forever-aging mother, she was so worn down, that at times she looked the older of the two. The subject of their authoritarian regime was Frank. He was a relative of theirs, but how many times removed, it is impossible for me to say. Rumour has it that he had been removed from his brains at birth! But personally I found him to be more funny than silly. And anyway, anyone who was prepared to give you sweets and money in return for friendship was worthy of the utmost consideration. It's so long ago now that I couldn't tell you exactly how old Frank was, but I would have put him somewhere in his mid-twenties. He was a sinewy, dark, curly-headed man with large protruding eyes, made even more prominent by the enhancing effect of wire-rimmed, pebble-lensed, National Health glasses. Add to this the elephantine proportions of his ever-mobile ears and you'll know why we gave up on Walt Disney and started chicken farming instead! Or was it homestead? Well, you know what I mean, don't you? The family home was more of a nightmare than a dream. It was a carbon copy - or would have been given a lighted match - of many of the shacks scattered across the plotlands. Square, squat, made of wood, tin and asbestos. Stinking of mildew, sun-shot and dust-moted through the rickety rafters. Set in its own squalid acres it grew vegetables - and tumbledown sheds - along with its fruit-trees and poultry-runs. The back end of the 'property' butted onto a hawthorn thicket. Along its frontage ran a rutted unmade road, rock-hard in summer and impassable at most other times of the year. Beyond that the aspect was typical of the area in general. Open fields, smallholdings, thickets, bramble brakes, clumps of tall elms and other sundry trees. In fact it was the paradise I've been trying to convince you of all along. The thing that attracted us to the Patterons more than anything else was Frank's obsession: wheels! If it ran on wheels, then Frank had one, bicycles, mopeds, motorbikes, cars and trucks. Well, we'd had some fun in our little lives, but the transference from wooden-carts and pram-wheels to this, was overwhelming to say the least. Their place wasn't just a smallholding - enough of an attraction in itself - but it doubled up as a breaker's-yard, making it irresistible to the Mecano-minded. Some of the cars were straight out of the gangster movies. I especially remember a great, long, sleek, Vauxhall 16. As black as the thoughts of a speak-easy moll it luxuriated at prohibitive length amongst the seductive grasses. Chromium-spoked, white-wheeled tyres - with one leather-strapped on the back for good measure - highlighted its slick, unpolished elegance. Inside, more chrome, leather and walnut panelling assailed the glittering senses. There it was that my rough uncultured mind was re-upholstered. Though I'd probably never become YOU, I could at least set my sights on the NON YOU world of the *nouveau riche.* If it had been good enough for Al Capone then it would be good enough for Baby-Face Linford! That - at the time in question, and still at the time of writing - I've never managed to raise enough collateral to fly even the smallest of white-flags whilst trembling behind my Chicago typewriter, is beside the point. I could dream couldn't I? Still can for that matter. And still do! It was there that I learnt to drive on four wheels, steer through the open window from the running board, and how to masturbate an adult. Some of these things may appear to be mutually exclusive at first glance, but in Frank's world, if you wanted to drive his cars then you had to be something of a poet. "What rhymes with Frank," he'd enquire, bardically. "Wank!" we'd all reply in lyrical unison, and he'd give us sixpence and his ignition key. Amongst other things! Nowadays the poor soul would probably be locked-up for life in the hot-cocoa wing of the Scrubs for such illicit activities. He'd be branded as the worst sort of paedophile imaginable and subjected to front-page vilification from all sections of Fleet Street. Truth is, he was no more culpable than we were. *En toute complicité* as they say in the land of crime and passion. We didn't just do it for material gain; we enjoyed it. Sweets, money and driving lessons were just the cherries on *les gateaux*, if you see what I mean. I have to admit that I grew quite fond of that purple-headed beast. All you had to do was show it a page from Tit-Bits and it reared up barbarically. I'd never seen anything like it. Compared with our skinny, fangless vipers, that one-eyed hairy snake was positively serpentine. Yea, verily I say unto you all, I was tempted - God forgive me - and I just couldn't resist the temptation. I know that under normal circumstances it's the snake that's supposed to be fascinated by the charmer, but with that pointer to porcelain - like the mirror image of my soon to be sullied soul - all logic had been coiled widdershins. It was thick and hot, and like the gear-stick itself quivered in response to the throb of some hidden engine. "Put it into first," Frank would command, breathlessly. "Second! Ooh! Third! Aah! Fourth, quick, quick, fourth! Ooh! Ooh! Aah! I'm coming! I'm coming! I've come!" And come he did. Great splurping torrents of the sticky, glutinous stuff would ejaculate in all orgasmic directions. So there it was, my response to the problems of population control, another sixpence was popped into the piggy bank, and I had a little hard-on of my own to take away and give a good seeing to. All very innocent really, don't you think? Excuse me a minute; I've just got to pop off to the laboratory. Don't worry; I won't be long. Fingers in your ears if you don't mind!

Apart from sex and jalopies there were other things to interest us at the Pattersons. If you didn't want to be Fangio or to languish in Reading Gaol you could forget the Tosser's Tournament on the Isle of Men proper and do a Geoff Duke up the alley on one of the many mopeds available. Not exactly the twelve-geared, two-stroke speedsters of present day motor sports but quick enough for us in their power-packed or belt-driven sort of way! We would use these rearing machines to mount raids on the back-shop. Like a ravening gang of rubber-hoofed, cranked-up desperados we'd gallop towards the confectionery equivalent of the Wells Fargo office. He'd never make sheriff that man at the general stores. He treated us to the same sort of mistrusting respect as is usually exhibited by the lily-livered when confronted by infamous outlaws. As I got older I knew exactly how he felt, but at the time I couldn't really account for his troubled, flustering nervousness whenever we appeared out of his loan-sharked, debt-infested woodwork. Whenever we bundled into his shop he would hop backwards and forwards from counter to counter, eyeing us suspiciously like a startled jackrabbit. "Do you boys want to buy anything or not?" he would snap, acquisitively. "I can't stand around here all day, I've got better things to do." "What d'yer fink of this Merv?" Charlie would say by way of a diversion. I'd rush over to Charlie, and then Eddy or Dave would pipe up from somewhere else with another summons. He knew our ploys of course but without a horse to call his own he found it difficult to get us all into the same corral at once. Someone would pay for a Jamboree-Bag or some-such thing and while he was at the till the rest of us would stuff our chaps with loot and hightail it back to the hideout. Occasionally we'd attempt the impossible and take the mopeds out after dark with no lights. On one ditch-full thundery night I remember, whilst in the process of blind-boys-motorized-bluff, we came - shudderingly - upon a courting couple on their way home from Pitsea Pictures. It may have been dangerous riding without headlamps, but some of the people you meet down crepuscular alleyways are best not seen at all. And more to the point, if a group of mobile lunatics are about to crash into them, well, it's better they don't see you! As soon as we heard his voice we knew who it was. You've heard of him before under such pseudonyms as: 'local roughneck' and 'nasty-person X'. "What the effing 'ell

214

are you basstards doin'?" he enquired, less than mutedly. Even in the dark I thought that it was pretty obvious, but knowing who it was who was asking, we forewent the facetious answer. The lucky ones veered left and suffered no more than the reciprocal puncturing of a hawthorn hedge. As for sizzling Dave Parks, and me we took the diminishing heat off the courting couple, and had our vicarious ardour dowsed right up to our newt-niffing snouts. When anybody laughs at your misfortunes it hurts, but when a bully - especially one with a tart in tow - guffaws in your drenched direction, it becomes almost embarrassingly unbearable. Still, at least the cock-happy pratt thought that our dunking was sufficient punishment in itself and we would live to ride another day. As a postscript to the crazy mechanical world of Frank Patterson it should be noted - to our eternal shame - that we occasionally stole one of his bikes and sold it to the gypsies. If that weren't enough, by way of adding insult to felonious injury, we would listen sympathetically as he related the miserable details of the theft to us, and would then commiserate profusely at the heartless immensity of the crime. Undoutedly, if I or any of my former cellmates could sneak a look at St Peter's incriminating scroll of plusses and minuses we'd be dumbstruck down to the very bottom of our very mischievous boots! Personally I'd need at least a mile of Indian rubber to erase half of the sins I've committed in the name of fun and friendship. Lock up your daughters. Lock up your orchards. Lock up your bikes. Lock up your locks! Nothing was sacred; all was to be picked, pocketed or profaned.

Thirteen years old and still in short trousers. What chance did I stand in the world of men and 'Spick and Span' super models? I needed more than my angelic blue-eyed looks to get closer to the centre of the relational web. In fact angelic looks were more of a hindrance than anything else. Girls preferred their mates to have a touch of the 7 o/clock, shadowy hairiness about them, and they wouldn't have gleaned much of a harvest from my fine, blond stubble. Well,

215

I couldn't do anything about my looks - that was God's business - but I could do something about my clothes; and that was my parent's business. I plagued them from dawn to dusk, day in and day out, about the need for a teenager to be suitably apparelled. My father wasn't impressed. He told me that he'd left school at fourteen and that he was still wearing short trousers at the time. In fact as he would say gleefully - by way of his carpenter's nail in the coffin of my insistent demands - I wear them even now in the summer months. I tried reasoning with my mother, but as anyone who knew her would instantly tell you, that was something of a neurotic contradiction in terms! I told her that boys of my age were already thinking seriously about marriage and that if she ever wanted any grandchildren then I should have to have my bald, bird-like legs covered up as soon as is conveniently possible. Then she would say something along the lines of: "If my grandchildren are goin' to turn aht anyfing like you, I'd sooner do my baby-sittin' fer an heronshaw." I didn't understand the bird-brained significance of the remark then, and I find the less than subtle linkages somewhat tenuous even now. Her favourite rejoinder though, was: "Yer always scuffin' the bleedin' skin on yer knees, so what's the point of buyin' yer long bleedin' trousers? You'd always be puttin' bleedin' 'oles in 'em, an' we're not made of bleedin' money, are we?" It was bleedin' impossible to get through to my parents on any subject, but if that subject concerned money as well - especially their money - well, blood and stones would be mutually permeable by comparison. If blood from stone couldn't be extracted, then the wearing down potential of water on stone would have to be employed. I kept up a cascading torrent of pleas from the craggy determined edge of my tumbling, word-loosened lips. Nobody, not even my parents, could stand it. Slowly but surely my rock-erosive tantrums wore away at their resolve. A rift had appeared in their defenses and I worked away at it with the alternating ravages of heated argument and frosty silence. They cracked! Promises skittered from their mouths, like scree down a mountainside. At last, I was to be long trousered. The bubbles

216

of ridicule would soon be burst and my spated, inflated ego, would be brim to overflowing. I thought' for one delightful moment that I'd won, but I hadn't reckoned with either their cunning or the variable nature of cloth. When my new trousers arrived - and they were that stiff they could have arrived on their own - their texture was that of a cross between coconut matting and fibreglass. I would have to wear them of course. I'd made so much fuss about them; I couldn't give in now. No sir, my trousers and me were going places! Exactly where or how we'd get there I'd yet to fathom. Monkeys it seems are always scratching themselves or each other and this it appears does nothing to the detriment of their sex-lives. In reality it may even add to their bestial delights. Not so with human beings. To scratch is infra dig. Epithets such as Nitty-Nora are bestowed at the merest hint of a twitchy finger. The anti-scratch lobby was vast and all-powerful. If you partook of that skin-scraping pursuit and escaped the appellation, lousy, then you could rest assured that other some equally repellant nomenclature will be attached to your person. As you can imagine summer and hirsute grey-flannel trousers were not exactly woven for each other! It must be said - somewhat indelicately perhaps - that a sweaty crotch and wool-worsted are not precisely the best of bedfellows. Whenever my hand and scrotum came together in the quest for comfort, there was no dissolving the partnership. My festering gusset and me were infamous. I've always been strong on pheromones but where sexual theorists get the idea that they're attractive to opposites is a whiffless mystery. As soon as I got within scratching distance, girls in tight womanly huddles, would scatter like shrapnel in all directions. Nose-pinched vollies of laughter would follow the detonations of my crotch everywhere. All along the corridors of my lonely and unrequited youth the echoing ring of feminine derision haunted my scurrying footsteps. Personal hygiene was becoming a catch phrase in those days and the cock-eyed, insensitive rendering of 'you're never alone with Lifebuoy' just added to the smokeless fuel of my fiery detractors. Would the Sir Roger de Coverley or the Gay

217

Gordons change my alienated status in anyway? The only thing country-dancing had going for it as far as I could see was that there were invariably an equal number of girls and boys involved in the process and that no matter how shy or tardy you were you would eventually be coupled. If that's not too strong a word for it! Mind you there were some girls in my year that had as much in the way of ugliness about them, as I had had in the stench department. It would be indelicate to name names but there were a couple of girls there that would never want for work in the pantomime season. And I don't mean 'Puss in Boots' either! Not exactly Prince Charming myself I don't suppose I had much to complain about. But complain I did, often, whether loudly or in muffled asides under my putrefying breath. This - as you've already gathered - wasn't glass-slipper country. Wellingtons would have been - and were in the case of those two bucolic agricultural girls - more appropriate! They would have been at home in any barn dance, especially one organized by 'Old Mac Donald'. When the summons was issued, "take your partners, for the Valetta," or some other lightly fantastical measure, the newly assembled pairs would lope out across the dance floor like Noah's unholy charges entering the Ark. First on the floor - as always - were the sleek gazelle-like groupings of prefects and monitors. They were closely followed by a mixed menagerie of giraffes, hippos and water buffalo, and following up at the rear came the gibbons and gorillas. In my case the mutual distance required because of simian stench and welly shuffling female disfigurement probably gave rise to something like the appearance of two sumo-wrestling orangutans. No matter how hard I tried to get in first I always ended up with one of those great razor-stropping wenches from the circus. The beauties would detect my advances with their olfactory radar and sidle off hurriedly into the arms of future commodores and admirals. The monsters of the deep on the other hand just bided their sub aqueous time and flexed their slimy tentacles. No more than I stinkingly deserved you might say, and you might very well be right. My only consolation being that you'd have to say it

218

at a smell-reductive distance. So there!

Another torture endured at the time by those unwanted and
unlovable amongst us, was 'sport'. Like many before and since
I just dreaded 'games'. Forged, hand-written notes and
outlandish excuses just wouldn't wash - something of a
coincidence, don't you think - in our school? If you could
breathe and stand up - even on one leg - then your character
would have to suffer improvement! Gym - whoever he was - I
could just about cope with. Prancing about in pumps and
baggy-shorts was just about tolerable indoors. The horse, the
bars and the vicissitudes of trampolining had something
invigorating about them. Particularly when it was the short-
frocked, navy-knickered, chunky-monkeys' turn on the
apparatus! But the outdoor, totally masculine world of
football, rugby and cricket added exhausting insult to my
enforced celibacy. If my Military Two Step left a lot to be
desired then you should have seen me in the crease or at a
scrum. Not that you'd see me in or out of either very often. On
the sports field I suffered the same fate as the ugly girls at
country dancing. Captains of neither sport nor industry have
ever seen me in terms of team spirit or leadership potential. I
wonder why? If the twelfth man at cricket acts as medic,
refreshments organizer or general porter; then what does the
thirteenth man do for a living? It was no use asking me to
keep score; you wouldn't have needed to be a mathematician
to calculate the odds against my success in that area! My head
rattled like an abacus admittedly but that's about as far as it
went. I never made the first team in any of the aforementioned
activities. I invariably ended up on the sidelines with the rest
of the congenitally uncoordinated and pretended to be
showing an interest in the ongoing proceedings whilst at the
same time kicking great divots of earth from the playing field
when no one was looking. Well, one has to do something to
restore one's existential credibility, doesn't one? Even worse
than sport itself were the showers afterwards. I had enough of
an aversion to water as it was without having to share it with a

load of well-hung sporting types hanging their Olympian bits and pieces for all the world to see. That time of side-glancing measurement was very dispiriting indeed. If you've lived either a faithful or a solitary life and you think that one penis is much the same as another, then you're in for an inside, eye-opening shock. I think that local inbreeding may have had something to do with some of the donkey-like appendages that swung pendulously in my line of envious sight. 'The long and the short and the tall' had everything to do with it. Those that weren't hung like donkeys - myself included - wore their towels on the journey from the changing-room to the showers. Sporty exhibitionists delighted in ripping our modesty blankets from us *en route* and making little jokes about our even smaller ones. Wimps were towel-whipped unmercifully until red welts striped their withdrawing buttocks. The rest of us suffered nothing more serious than a tongue-lashing. Though that itself left scars of its own. Through the partially obscuring steam of the shower-room proper you could take a closer look at the competition. For the sake of the ego, those with more than their age should have allowed, were automatically put down as being nothing more than freaks of nature. The remainder one could compare oneself with to some advantage, roundheads, cavaliers and fifty-fifties jostled in soapsuds and steam to gain the approval of my connoisseurship. As the effects of friction and heat lit fires in our pubescent loins sizes began to equalize. Glans from the inner reaches of foreskins popped out of their pies like plums. Roundheads stood their protestant ground, thickened and empurpled puritanically and the sizzling fifty-fifties stretched in their skins like sausages in a frying pan. From my meticulous mental examination of the penile environment I would say that although sizes vary considerably in the flaccid state, once erect, we're talking about a minimal degree of difference between the procreative organs. There are dwarfs and giants amongst them but that only serves to underline the average. If you think that all this talk has everything to do with male obsessiveness, then I can only say that you didn't have a gym-mistress like ours. She thought nothing of meandering through the boys' changing-rooms whenever the fancy took her. That she always gave us enough time to be fully undressed before she'd come in under the slightest pretext, says something about my conjecture that she was as much involved with phallic comparison as I was. Although she seemed ancient and therefore relatively unimportant to us at the time, in retrospect I think she was probably only a teenager herself and was perhaps engaging in some market research of her own! When women say that size is not important I just don't believe them. I don't mind them massaging my diminutive member but when it comes to my ego they can keep their platitudinous, patronizing insincerities to themselves! If I want to hang lead weights off the end of it then that's my insecure business. My one last and lingering memory of sport at school is the smell of the gym, the changing-rooms and the equipment. They were some of the few of life' s fragrances that came close to being as sexually musky as my own. So if you're looking for a good lay, phone Basildon 69666 anytime after detention. *Bon courage!*

221

Chapter 14. Trappers.

A break from sex - or in my case the almost constant preoccupation with it - was sorely needed. A return to the wildwood and the ongoing development of one's field-craft would surely separate the mind from the genitalia, for a while at any rate. Out across the wilderness from where I lived stood a semi-detached pair of derelict houses. They were not the type of dwellings one normally associated with the plotlands. They were two-storied, brick-built properties with wooden-joists and flooring, sash-windows, slate-roofs and character. Real houses in fact, as opposed to some of the ersatz excuses for living accommodation found elsewhere in the vicinity. They had obviously been purchased in the compulsory manner of the time and their occupants forced out into the - conforming for their own good - modernity of the council estate. We knew those houses - eponymously - as the Harris's. I didn't know the family in question personally but sufficient to say they were extended beyond the familial bounds of understatement! It may well have been the principal of divide and rule and not the need for building land that prompted the Development Corporation to scatter the tribe in all possible directions across the growing New-Town. Apart from the disruption to family ties, the subsequent loss of their rusticated way of life must have been of soul-destroying dimensions. The ubiquitous rows of elms, hawthorn thickets and wide vetch-flowering meadows were what they had to leave behind for the sake of the so-called garden-city philanthropy of the developers. The lyrical uplifting sound of the skylark would from now on be replaced by the echoing reverberations of the gavel and the sonorous minutes of the last extraordinary council meeting. Bucolics would have to be ceded in favour of bureaucracy and town planning and none of our lives would be enriched in triplicate because of the transformation. But for the time being the Harris's, and similar dwellings, islanded as they were in the remaining green, tidal surges of the countryside, were still there for both the young and the nature lover alike. Not forgetting the wildlife of course! Although we didn't agree with the green-belt diminishing policies of the planners we unwittingly assisted them in their task. They had no need of demolition experts. All of the expertise they needed could be safely left - did I say safely - to the shoulderless swing of our never ceasing irresponsibilities. Sledgehammers, scaffold-poles, axes, and anything else with heavy destructive potential, would be lugged across the summer fields with mayhem in the forefront of our malicious minds. The only des res's for miles around were to be near raised to the ground by the tenacity of our deconstructive efforts. On one occasion whilst enjoying a tea-less break from our labours we noticed - through the newly affected holes in the roof - a jackdaw pop down the chimney with a beak-full of wriggling, squiggly unmentionables. This, followed closely by an eruption of muffled high-pitched squawking, alerted us to the possibilities of even greater and more profitable adventures. Surely there was a ready market for fledgling jackdaws? Tea break over we set to work on the chimneybreast. If not exactly steeplejacks our tree-climbing activities had at least made us relatively sure-footed. That particular skill was very much needed seeing as by this time - due to our demolitionary talents - there were no floorboards left in the house and the only way to get to the right place on the chimneybreast was to do a tight-rope act across the open joists. Correct, unseeable distances were ascertained by the agency of string, an improvised plumb bob, and Charlie's rooftop bravery. "Right o, drop it dahn the chimney mate!" I shouted, at the apex of my voice. "But be careful," I added, cautiously. "You don't wanna 'it one of the little bleeders on the 'ead wiv ha'f an 'ouse-brick, does yer?" "D'yer fink I'm a pratt or suffink?" came the indignant reply. "D'you wanna come up 'ere an' do it yerself?" Of course, I didn't. Soothing words would be needed. "I was only sayin' mate," I proceeded. "I didn't mean nuffin' by it, you're doin' a great job, honest!" Stupid pratt, I whispered under my breath. "Who the 'ell does 'e fink 'e is, Sherpa bleedin' Tenzing or summit!" Rather a serendipitous pun don't you think? I climbed down from my unvoiced thoughts and started again, more diplomatically. "Drop the line dahn the outside of the chimney now Charlie, let me know when it's at the right lenff and I'll make a mark on the bricks." Charlie, appeased by my more reasonable approach, did as was requested and the point of forced entry was decided upon. It didn't take us long to scrape away at the decaying mortar and loosen a couple of bricks. Before you could say 'Jack Corvus!' we were peering into the abysmal reaches of the chimney space. As our eyes became accustomed to the darkness the gaping mouths of two demanding chicks screeched at us from an unruly nest of sticks and straw. They were well advanced in age, nearly fully feathered, and, we thought, almost ready to leave the safety of their avian home. And leave that warm familial security they did! Despite the aerial chiding of their distressed parents, Jack and Jill, as they were to become known, were popped down inside our shirts and chicknapped! I loved Jack. I'd had all sorts of pets before - and since - but none of them have had the off-hand irreverent charm of that particular bird. He was cocky, cock-sure, and sadly in the end so cock-happy that he left home because of it. My parents didn't want anything to do with him of course. For some reason they preferred poncey little poodles to the more diabolically inclined members of the crow family. Whether this had anything to do with the acquisition of status of the 'up with the Jones' ' variety I wouldn't like to speculate, but if I wanted to keep him I would have to keep him in the garden-shed and look after him myself. That was no hardship to me. Not only would I have a feathered friend but also it would be one with a similar disposition to my own. All talk of notching the end of his tongue to enable him to speak more easily was immediately silenced. If he didn't want to talk, then why should he? I knew exactly how he felt. Like my recalcitrant self he would be seen and not heard and he was certainly surly enough to carry off his form of dumb insolence with equal aplomb. I had him for a month or two, fed him on mealworms, maggots, bread and seeds, and watched him grow in stature. When he was able to fly I let him out all day and he followed me everywhere. Alighting on my head or shoulder intermittently much to the amusement of my friends and neighbours. If he had stature, then I had status! The birdman of Sandon Road was becoming famous and I revelled in the glory. I'd read about imprinting somewhere along the dusty shelves of Vange Library and felt that this must be the reason why we had become so inseparable. As usual in matters of intellect, I was wrong! It was cupboard love only. As soon as his hormones got the better of him the call of the wild was too strong for him to resist. He came back to visit once or twice, but along the same lines as many of my other friends he was eventually lost forever to the restrictive worlds of sex and mortgages. I don't think I'd ever been as sad as I was then. The sense of loss was total. Whenever I see a flock of rooks in the winter I chack along meaningfully with their diminutive grey-headed companions knowing full well that owing to my earlier associations we have a cross-specific understanding. That I get wry looks from scarecrows and ploughmen doesn't worry me one bit. When you've shared a real and deep secret with nature no amount of barracking - verbal or otherwise - can lessen the resultant esoteric enrichment. A replacement for Jack flew into my life unexpectedly one day, on the wing of a prayer, so to speak. Flo, as she was to be called, was a pigeon. What sort of pigeon I couldn't tell you. Feral, domestic, wild, I just don't know. I know that in an earlier chapter I've been less than kind to such feathery pies on wings, but times change and attitudes mature. Well, there's another *deus ex machina* for you! She had all the qualities of natural diversity, a plump, many-checkered, hybridized perfection of form and temperament. One minute you would be pigeonless, then at the rattle of shingle in a tin, epiphany! That her manifestations had religious significance for me had - it must be added - no reciprocal enlightening spiritual effect on my parents. My mother reserved the same feather-brained disdain for pigeons as she did for moths. They were fluttery incarnatory fears and irritations that had to be shooed away from the neurotic corners of her dust-free, homogenized existence. From my

225

father's horticultural point of view they were no better than cats. They ate or disturbed far more in the garden than they could ever repay by the way of fertilizer and so would be the catapulted targets for the pebbles he kept in a saucer on the upstairs' windowsill. In truth she did eat a lot for her size. Peas were a paternal specialty on the Linford Estate and Flo was undeterable in their glossed and succulent presence. If it had been down to our garden alone I'd have probably been able to sulk my way into the continuity of ownership. But unfortunately Flo would gorge her crop-full, pot-bellied self on the neighbour's fruit and veg as well. That was all the ammunition my father needed. Every new complaint was a pebble in the pouch of his agricultural resolve. Flo would have to go and another fault in the subsoil of my shifting relationships would have to be added to my emotional profile. She may not have been fully wild but she was a game bird nevertheless. A concerted effort was made by both my father and our neighbours to encourage Flo to take up residence elsewhere. The amount of pebbles hurled and catapulted in her direction would have been enough to have denuded Chesil Beach! Not only was she glanced by them on numerous occasions but suffered no few direct hits. Would she go? Would she hell! At times she had the look of one of those model aeroplanes flown by remote control. Her limits were invisibly proscribed. Under a hail of stones she'd lift on her thunder clapping wings up into the imprisoning skies and circle above us as if on the end of imaginary wires. The homing instinct may well have its advantages in the natural world but the stubborn insistency of this lode-stoning primal urge was more than out of place in that stone-loaded, heartless neighbourhood. It may well be just prejudice on my part but pigeons appear to me to be thicker on average than other birds. From personal experiment alone I can vouch for the fact that they're definitely lower down the scales of the intellectual quotient than jackdaws. Even so, the Pavlovian effect of trajectorially polished quartz against the cranium eventually knocked home its message! The invisible circuits were gradually broken. The ever-widening concentric rings of

226

valediction spread out across the blue waves of the air, leaving Flo in the full flight of my childhood fancies to fade out of my effing alliterative life forever. She was free; but I, was desolate.

My experiences with Jack and Flo were beginning to have an effect on my relationships with wildlife in general. That's not to say that I'm prepared to take the moral high ground as far as animal rights are concerned even now, and I certainly wasn't then. If for no other reason than my love of fishing - wavering atheist that I undoubtedly was - I was more than happy to go along with the biblical interpretation of events. Animals were there to be used and by God I was going to use them! As mentioned earlier the headmaster of our school was an avid environmentalist. Nothing unusual nowadays perhaps, but in the fifties he was almost an endangered species himself. He tried his utmost to encourage us of the bombsites and the resultant brain disfunctionality to take a more enlightened approach towards ecology. That we couldn't even spell the word let alone understand any of its symbiotic concepts didn't dissuade him in the least. We would have films and lectures on every green-minded subject imaginable. I think he was convinced that if he bombarded us often enough with the interrelated intricacies of man and his environment, that as dim as we were, we would all in the end realize the conservational necessity of the harmony he preached. Perhaps he even had a point. In my case, although it has taken an inordinately long time, the fruits of his labours are beginning to ripen. Apart from meat eating and the almost idolatrous worship of fish I am very much of New Age potential. Others of my earlier acquaintance were not - and *entre nous* - probably never will be. Bob Cole, now there's a name to strike terror into the peacefully green at heart. Not that he isn't a conservationist, he was then, and he definitely is now. But he's one of the old school of hunting, shooting and fishing conservationists. His theme song is 'you're never alone with a ferret'. I've known him man and boy for forty years or more and I've never seen him without one. His trousers were

227

legendary. People who didn't know him thought that he had some sort of incurable mobile legs syndrome! He would take his ferrets everywhere. He lived, ate, drunk and even slept ferrets. Rabbits weren't his mortal enemy, he loved rabbits, he even kept them as pets. But he knew that they were a pestilence brought over by the Norman nobility and considered it his God given Saxon duty to keep a check on their blue-blooded proliferations. He even thinks 'Watership Down' to be the best book ever written in the English language, albeit a touch too romantic in places. A raging environmental battle went on between him and the headmaster through the whole of his secondary school career. He swears that this has had an educationally prejudicial effect on the rest of his life and that truancy was merely a consequent incidental! Mr. Vivian Robson, animal rights worker, conservationist Vs Bob Cole animal wrongs conservationist was a contest never to be fully resolved. Mr. Robson who sadly died a couple of years ago, ended up as the chairman of The Essex Naturalists Trust, whereas Bob Cole owns his own country-fairground, leases fishing rights on his own lakes and organizes lurcher and terrier races. If Mr. Robson could see the work being done on Bob's land in the name of native species of flora and fauna perhaps he would have seen the need for compromise in matters of natural history. Who knows? WAGBI and the RSPB did in the fifties and their cooperation has been very profitable indeed. But that was a rare instance and sadly the polemic between field-sportsmen and other types of animal lovers is as fiercely contended now as it ever was. Bob Cole practiced his art in an area of Vange known locally as The Sand Pits. An ideal maze of abandoned sand and gravel workings riddled with rabbit warrens and covered in bright, yellow-flowering gorse. Believe it or not, rabbiting has its inherent dangers. On one occasion having broken out in more spots than adolescence could account for, Bob decided to go to the doctors. At first the medic put it down to nothing more sinister that the greasy normalities of trans-pubescent pustularity. But after several visits accompanied by an ever-increasing incidence of pimples, another diagnosis would have to be sought. Those clinical investigations turned out to be something of a warren in themselves. Every time the doctor introduced an intuitive ferret into his medical-lexicon, so to speak, it came up against a cul de sac and would have to be dug out again and tried elsewhere. As is the way with intuition, intangibles come together and possibilities present themselves. "Do you go rabbiting," he enquired, with a twitch of his professional nose. "I might," said Bob, furtively. "What's that gotta do wiv it, or you fer that matter?" "You've got a form of myxomatosis I think," replied the doctor, triumphantly. "Nothing to worry about," he continued, putting the rabbit back into his diagnostic hat for future reference. "It won't do you any harm." But it would if the prognosis was followed to the letter. No ferreting! No way! He'd wear gloves if necessary; he'd even stop eating his viral pies. But to live without catching a rabbit. Impossible! Along with his best friend he decided to make a foray into another area, hopefully free of the dreaded disease. The problem was that this new area was on farmland close to the Halfway House and therefore prohibited to poachers. I say a problem, but that assumes that you're of the same lily-livered persuasion as myself and not imbued with the qualities of back-woodsman-ship so evident in the Bob Coles of this world. By all accounts things were going swimmingly. Ferrets were keen, nets bulging, and rabbits punched by the proliferating dozen. But then the farmer arrived on the scene. "What are you little bastards up to!" was the question he aimed along the admonitory length of two soon to be smoking barrels. "Get off my bloody land," Bob and his friend didn't need to be asked twice. They knew the score and were fifty yards away before the shot struck home. Bob's highly peppered arse singed all the way back to Pitsea. There wasn't much he could do about it, if he told anyone in authority his complaints would obviously backfire on him, and he'd find himself in even greater trouble. But he was in pain. If he couldn't go back to the doctors, what could he do? He would have to do something that's for sure. His partner in crime had bolted and he couldn't reach the excruciating area himself to remove the offending shot. By chance in his hour of need he met another of his venatorial friends, Newmangle. Why anyone should cop for such a peculiar nickname I couldn't tell you, but suffice it to say that the etymology will no doubt turn out to be as weird as the recipient himself. That boy was strange indeed. A skinny gangling little creature, puffed up with festering boils and suffering the indignity of a prematurely receding hairline. There's ugly, and there's UGLY! If you'd have seen that dark, devious little character scurrying hungrily across a spider's web, you wouldn't have given him a second glance, excepting perhaps you happened to be an entomologist and were engaged in some sort of scientific research! If I ever wanted shot dug out of my backside then he'd be the very last person I'd turn to for help. Still, needs must, as they say, and he was all there was available. Local folk-law has it that you could hear the screams all the way from One-Tree-Hill to Hadleigh Downs and back and that Newmangle's fiendish chuckling could be heard even further afield. It seems that even after the shot was removed the depraved Newmangle continued with his subcutaneous delvings unable to tear himself away from the sadomasochistical pleasures of his task. The pair of them are still good friends of mine but at the time of writing I don't suspect I'll ever see them holding hands in public. Certain experiences in youth leave one with ingrained suspicions where other people are concerned. After all, a man and his buttocks are sacrosanct!

In a near impenetrable jungle of sloe and hawthorn at the back of the Patterson's, Charlie, Eddy, Dave parks and myself built a summer camp for our diabolical amusement. The inner reaches of that thorn thicket were as dark as most of our deeds. Except for a clearing where we built our camp, sunlight hardly ever reached the ground. As a consequence of this the whole area was carpeted with a decomposing mulch of springy leaves. In the dry-season it was copper-bronze and crisp to the touch, but after rain the squelching humus became as black and acrid to the nostrils as a Highland peat bog.

Although very few people ever got to the centre of that shadowy thicket, all around its edges there was the accumulated rubbish of plotland throwaways. Broken china, tin cans, bottles and unwanted kitchen utensils were strewn all across the leaf-fallen periphery. It was there that I found my one and only classical robin's nest. A domed structure of grass, dead-leaves and moss, nestling at a jaunty angle in a beat-up, black-leaded kettle. The white eggs - blotched and spotted with reds and browns - were difficult to get to without causing irreparable damage to the nest, but that didn't stop me and the robin's eggs in my collection and the occasional swops all came from that secret and seemingly endless supply. The camp itself was nothing more or less than a miniature copy of the shanties we saw around and about us every day. Wood, tin, and corrugated iron, all jumbled up together and held in situ with nuts, bolts and six-inch rusty nails. For comfort - and hopefully sex - the ground was covered by an 8' x 4' sheet of ply and a mattress. We put up shelves and to make it seem more homely we lined them with coloured-bottles and bits and pieces of broken china that we'd found lying about the place. For both heat and cooking we had an old night watchman's brazier, which we'd stolen from a building-site. That was an essential piece of equipment and well used. Pots, pans and kettles, proliferated in the undergrowth like mushrooms over the marshes in autumn, so we had all the hardware we wanted. All we needed now to make our ravenous lives complete was meat and veg. That too was relatively easy to obtain. Bird-traps were my specialty. A garden sieve propped up with a stick attached to a length of string was all that was necessary. The trap was baited with stale bread and all you had to do was keep out of sight and wait for the hapless bird to hop in under the mesh. Pull the string and *voila!* Lunch. I've tasted starling, sparrow and blackbird and I have to admit that for the life of me I still can't understand the continental predilection for passerines! Wood pigeon, well, that's a different matter altogether. I may have been a mite squeamish about plucking and gutting them, but it has to be said that it was well worth the squeam involved.

231

They were *delicieux*. Fruit and veg of the season was equally available. All we had to do was to creep out through a hole in the hedge into the Pattersons' garden and raid the crops. Better than that even we could get into the back of their chicken-coop through a loose board and steal their eggs without being observed. We had many a mock-serious conversation with Frank about the erratic nature of egg production. "I don't understand why they won't lay regularly," he used to say to us while all the time scratching his addled-pate. "They always used to!" "Rats!" we'd reply in unison, twitching imaginary whiskers. "No," he'd cogitate. "Can't be rats, they'd leave some shells behind." "Grit!" we'd cluck, strutting around him and flapping our elbows. "No, they gets plenty o' grit," he'd say, still scratching his head and frowning. "They gets plenty o' that." It says a lot for the trust and innocence of that man that never once did he suspect us of being the culprits. Friendship meant a lot to Frank and it's a shame that we weren't more amicable ourselves. We used to attract gullible girls into the camp under a culinary pretext. For reasons of propriety and because I can't think of any girl's names beginning with X Y and Z, the three girls we most commonly invited to lunch will henceforth be known as Anne, Babs and Chris. They may have been gullible where sex was involved but they weren't exactly the 'Three Little Maids from School' of the Gilbert and Sullivan variety. They were proto-Essex girls of the first order. Street credibility was second nature to them. Shoot first and ask questions later was their chief maxim! They weren't to be messed with, but we did, and we suffered the inevitable consequences of our actions. The reason we chose them as our dinner guests was because of their variability. Between them they covered most combinations of girlhood. Anne was tall, blond and lithe in an Amazonian sort of way. What she lacked in bulk she more than made up for with her goddess-like mythical lineage and her cool blue stare both chilled and heated us unaccountably. Babs was just about her opposite in every way, dark, dumpy and doey-eyed. She reminded me of nothing less than an African fertility-doll, but unfortunately that's as far as she or

232

the metaphor went in that direction. Chris on the other hand was of Celtic extraction, a green-eyed, ginger-haired, vixen of a girl. Her head tossing, freckled, come and get me if you dare look drove me crazy. I could have easily took the Catholic faith more seriously if she'd have, just once, promised to make a dishonest man of me and lead me from the land of Blarney into the green and paradisal island of her kisses. But alas, the stone of my blarney wasn't to be reciprocated. When we got them into the camp for lunch, or preferably supper, we'd invite them into the makeshift parlour. Proceedings would invariably start with one or the other of them, or all three, casting aspersions in the direction of our decor. "Bleedin' scruffy in 'ere init!" would say Anne, less than classically. "Stinks an' all dunnit," would rally Babs in support. "What's all them bleedin' broken bottles fer," Chris would Celtisize. "Don't make no blimmin' sense does it," Not an auspicious start you may think, but we were well used to such shenanigans. We knew this as a necessary preliminary, a kind of displacement activity that helped to soothe the anticipatory nerves and make room for the inevitable hormonal surges to follow. My problem with the 'fight or flight' theories of adrenaline was that I wasn't interested in either option but still suffered from the uncontrollable, panic-inducing rush of the poisonous stuff. We knew that they weren't interested in starling-pie or nettle-soup. It would be just a matter of time before they came to the boil themselves. Dave was always the first to make a move. "Show us yer tits Babs," a mile or two away from the courtship equivalent of subtlety. "I'll let yer 'old me willy if yer do!" "Yer filthy beast!" she protested, with her fingers already working at the buttons down the front of her blouse. "Only a look mind." "Christ! I'm finding this page difficult to write without dribbling or drooling. She had beautiful breasts. If she could just learn to keep her mouth shut for an aeon or two her demeanour would have become a pearl-rich, far less irritable aphrodisiac. My hands and her breasts were an undoubted match, but true to her word the fit was never tested. Dave being Dave, he didn't just show her his willy, but under an

233

excitable rain of nervous giggles he stripped off completely. This was do or dare time of course and being as none of us wanted to do a forfeit we all followed Dave's lead. My abiding recollection is the hairlessness of the situation. Apart from the tops of our heads, none of us boys, or the girls for that matter, had a hirsute between us, especially between the legs! Mind you I always preferred the bald mount of venus; still do in fact. It seems far less dangerous to me in some strange, unaccountable way. More like going to the vestal temple than the red-light district somehow. We all just sat there touching each other. Or more precisely the girls prodded and poked themselves while we reciprocated man to man! It was sex by proxy almost. Not as good as the real thing but better than nothing. You had to start somewhere, didn't you? Whenever I feel old, unloved and unwanted - which is much of the time sadly - I just think back on those days and remind myself that it's never been any different. I'm still doing it by proxy but at least I don't feel that I have to do as often or for as long. Youth isn't everything! Another year or two and I should be able to get my Papal Edict annulled and be ready to enter the monastery. They were beautiful days though, and beautiful girls. I don't suppose 'look but don't touch' was a bad maxim. It was, after all, the cheapest form of family planning. We had all the excitement of kisses and climaxes; we just had them at different times, and in different places. Ah! Wasn't it ever thus? Once the girls had left we'd get back to the all male world of adolescent debauchery. Dancing naked around the campfire - camp, being the operative word - at dusk on a warm summer's day it was delightful. I can understand the joys of naturism even if I do still suspect naturists of varying degrees of voyeurism and exhibitionism. I think that nudity is probably the reason why God invented the mosquito, but then we can always thank the Devil for smoke! There was a lot of auto erotica in those days. We would stand in a line by the fire and see who could come first. Assuming that you could come at all of course. I used to excuse my impotence by saying something like; I've already done it three times this morning. No one believed me, but they all had their own reputations to protect, and wouldn't challenge me unless they could come up with the goods themselves. Which, as I remember, wasn't that often! Those boy's games were relatively innocent. Bum-buggery had been heard of but wasn't indulged. We all knew of others who had done it and would regale each other with all sorts of crude stories about people pushing shit uphill without a wheelbarrow. But in truth most of our knowledge on the subject had come from the backs of toilet doors and most of that was probably apocryphal anyway. Living in an agricultural area, rumours of bestiality were rife but no doubt equally unfounded. Although, some of the smirks I've detected on the faces of pigs and chickens still makes me wonder! Whether any of Frank's animal charges got sweeties or a ride on the back of a moped only Frank - and perhaps the slaughter man - would be able to tell you. As for me it was still girls that I was interested in and you don't find many of them in the butcher's window, Not in Pitsea at any rate!

I don't know what happened to Frank, or his old aunts come to that, but one day they were all there and the next they were gone. The mystery lay more in the fact, that although nobody was living in the property anymore, no removals had taken place. The curtains were drawn but we could see through the cracks in them that everything inside was still as it always had been. I often felt guilty at the time that the old ladies may have died from shock. We regularly crept up to their windows at night, rattled the panes, pulled contorted faces, and screeched eerily in their direction. At their age such diabolical antics could have been extremely dangerous. But when you're kids you just don't think about such things, unfortunately. Perhaps it would be more honest to say that WE didn't think of such things, and that not all youngsters were - or are - as despicable as we were. I like to think that the vanishing act occurred because of the fact that the old aunts became even more ancient and couldn't manage the smallholding anymore and that the council moved them into a residential home somewhere. Frank couldn't have coped by himself anyway and would have probably been shipped off to another relative.

Who knows? With all this talk of guilt, you might think that we would have left things as they were, and kept away from the place for good. No chance I'm afraid. The temptation was too great. No sooner had we found it empty, than we decided to break in. That shack was another of the many archetypical Aladdin's caves of my youth. A lifetime's worth of accumulated treasure was secreted about its many nooks and crannies. It was the crock at the end of every child's rainbow and there wasn't a leprechaun in the whole of Ireland who could keep us away from its glistening gold. Once inside - full of our criminal selves and brazenly careless of thoughts of detection - we switched on the 'steam-driven' 27-valve radio and set about our ignoble business. In the wake of the radio's warmed-up banshee wailing we peppered the airwaves with emissions of our own. "Look at this!" broadcast Charlie, in his worst BBC accent. From the lucky-dip into one of the draws in the sideboard he'd come up with one of those multi-purpose pen-knives so favoured by the Swiss Army and removers of stones from the hooves of lame horses everywhere. "What abaht these!" countered Dave, trying to out do him. "They're fantastic!" He had a fist-full of sepia-washed and hand-painted postcards depicting the lilac-laned Edwardian world of a long ago lost and leafy England. Vying for attention with the radio and our high-pitched excitable voices, the cranked up, needle-scratching sibilance of a breathlessly wound Mario-Lanzaphone, crackled through the spiralling grooves of our delighted ears. The place out-did our every expectation. Marbles of every diffusing shade and size - both clear and translucent - stared out from their caches with a wanton and misty-eyed magnificence. In the workbox of a treadle-powered Singer Sowing Machine, spools of coloured cotton unwound their feminine threads and embroidered the masculine haberdashery of our minds. Books on animal husbandry and horticulture opened their yellow-faded plates and pages for our bucolic edification. If in the future we ever needed to graft scions onto rootstocks or geld Welsh-Cobs and Shires we would have technological know-how! Eddy called me up into the loft. "Come an' look at this Merv!" he bellowed through the trap door. "I've struck gold!" Gold it wasn't but it was a box-full of money, all sorts of exotic coinage doublooned and ducatted through our seven-sea-ed, square-rigged, imaginations. Great cart wheeled copper pennies and ha'pennies lay like treasure in our groatfull hands and florins and joeys whispered their wishful hints and silvery indiscretions. On opening another small, heavy, cast-iron casket our eyes were assailed by an indecipherable stash of bronzed and hand-wrought currency. Those irregularly punched plugs of ancient metal were inscribed with some sort of cuneiform lettering and may well have been worth a fortune. But to us patriotic imperialists they were merely foreign curiosities and were passed over in favour of the British legal tender. Nevertheless I kept those strange precursors of money as we know it for years, but along the way they were either stolen or swopped or otherwise dematerialized, and so my chances of making a killing at the V and A have been permanently devalued! "Serves you right!" I hear you say, judiciously. The major find we made at the Patterson's has also unaccountably vanished along with my youth, a magic lantern, a real candle-powered projector of antique images. We sat in the attic puffing away at Woodbines and sucking gob-stoppers as everyone from Prince Albert to Mickey-Mouse painted the walls of our flickering Platonic cave. We had racks of slides, an endless supply of candles, and all the time in the world. Ah! Happy days. But as I was so often portentously informed by my all-knowing mother: "God pays debts without money!" In this particular case retribution came in the form of elderberry wine. We found crates of the fermenting, noxious, excuse for burgundy stacked up against the chimneybreast. It may or may not have been a good vintage. Being a bit of a plonker myself I just couldn't tell you! But as far as *dégustation* is concerned neither my compatriots nor I needed an official invitation. Personally I thought that it had a very delicate bouquet and that its fruitiness went well with the Woodbines and gob-stoppers. And anyway, glasses are for wimps aren't they? Well, we'd masturbated together so we saw no good

237

reason why we shouldn't vomit *en masse* either! After all, it was just another form of bodily ejaculation. Emetics; semetics, semantics, what's the difference! It's peculiar how after just a few swigs from the bottle the stills projected onto the wall from the magic lantern became blearily transformed. Mickey-mouse was decidedly more animated. I didn't think that he was any funnier but that didn't stop our inebriated laughter rising to a fever pitch. The slow downward curve on the chart of drunkenness was made more acute with every tilt and swallow. In fact at a certain point in the proceedings the line stopped abruptly and we fell off the bottom of the graph into alcoholic oblivion. In my case it was even more unfortunate than that. Whilst teetering tipsy-toed across the joist in the loft - full of Walt-Disneyed bonhomie and slowly becoming something of a cartoon of my own - I slipped - perhaps staggered would be a better description - and went crashing through the ceiling. The floor beneath and the contents of my queasy stomach were about to make a long-winded acquaintanceship. The three hysterical stooges aloft guffawed inanely through the gaping hole and then threw up in concert adding considerably to my already sickening discomfort. Walking home in dehydrated and unsteady single file we reflected upon the evils of drink and thought seriously about signing the pledge. "Never again," slurred Eddie repeatedly as he kept bumping into himself and tripping over his own feet. "Me neiver," came the double-visioned response in triplicate. I listened to the resolve leaching from their tainted-purple lips and for once in my life both believed and agreed with every sobering word. But this wasn't New-Year and even then resolve was known to weaken. In truth our souls were more tainted than our lips and for the time being at least the Devil had far from finished with our reprehensible education. Despite our wretched physical state crime had paid in full and we had pockets crammed with booty to prove the undeniable fact. Neither drink nor burglary had been erased from our shameful agenda and the Sally Anne Basher would have to wait a very long time for the re-emergence of our once and redemptive innocence.

Chapter 15. Bait and Tackle.

Although we had the blessing of the creeks and marshes, for us anglers of a more refined nature, the nearest freshwater river of any consequence was the River Chelmer. Not wishing to cycle the twenty intervening country miles to pursue our hobby - and not having enough money for the bus-fare - we had to make do with the local lakes and ponds. Perhaps 'make-do' is the wrong phrase. There were in fact some beautiful little fisheries in the area. And some not so little! Stanford Warren for instance, owned by the Shell-Mex Angling Society and opened up as day-ticket water, was a complex of gravel-pits covering several acres. Other waters in the neighbourhood ranged from the large single lakes Like Woodies in Corringham, down to the bomb-cratered, crucian-infested ponds scattered about the surrounding farmland. At that time - as well as this - I was not a very wealthy individual. Most of the tackle I used was begged, borrowed or stolen. I shall have to keep this book well away from my elder brother. If he finds out just how often I raided to holy-of-holies of his bedroom cupboard and snuck off with his prize piscatorial possessions he'd be straight round with the 'priest'. For those of you conversant with the world of angling you'll know that it's not confession I'm talking about! Without doubt my favourite venue at the time was Woodies. It was a fair sized ex-gravel working encompassed by elms and other mixed deciduous trees. One side of it was overlooked by the ancient parish church of Corringham and the equally ancient Bull-inn, and the raucous hubbub from the village rookery added, paradoxically, to the sense of rural tranquility. Its southern flank looked out through the trees and bushes onto the couple of miles of fleet-crazed marshes that lay between it and the Thames Haven Oil Refineries. It was reed-lined, lily-padded and lush. The sense of its otherworldly, float-twitching magic haunts me still. Wheat, hemp, bread and maggots peppered the sun-glazed water like shot from a gun as we sat there mesmerized in the undergrowth feeding our swims and our memories. Tench, crucian, roach and bream were our coveted prizes, but after long, fishless hours spent with flake, crust and hemp, we usually reverted to the despised maggots and settled for a ravenous, suicidal perch or two. Whenever I think of the denigratory nature of jokes about the Irish I'm chastened by my memories of Paddy Cane. Being a member of the same church I knew him and his family very well and when I saw him fishing I would always go over for a chat. Cane by name and cane by temperament where his tackle was concerned. I never once saw him fish with anything more sophisticated than Spanish-reed, a wooden centre-pin reel, loaded with cutty-hunk and size 8 hooks. All of our infinitesimal hemp-orientated intricacies were lost on him. "Big 'ooks and worums, dhats all yer need," he'd say in his best Bernard-o-Venables accent. "You won't be needing all dhat fancy stuff o' yours." We laughed at all this piscatorial naivety of course and would rib him in our dumb Anglo-Saxon way. But we always ended up laughing on the other side of our ground-baited witticisms. He was one of those men who could have caught salmon down a sewer. "Big baits, big fish," he'd crack by way of an Irish truism. "Be Jesus, I'll be having anudder one!" And anudder one he would be having an' all an' all, time after nauseating time again. That man and the 'doctor fish' - tench to the uninitiated amongst you - must have been on the same sub-Hippocratic wavelength. Great olive and bronze slabs of fish would come to his net with dispiriting frequency. The whole worum and nutting but the worum," as he used to say. His best trick - or worst if you felt that your sporting prowess was in question; which in my case usually was - was to name the species of his next catch in advance! "I'll be having a bream dis time," he'd say confidently as he threaded another wriggling victim onto his size 8 hook. "Dhey likes a worum does bream." "Yer gotta be jokin'!" I'd say hopefully, against all the odds of Anglo-Irish protocol. "There's no way yer can keep usin' the same bait an' know what sort o fish you're gonna catch, it's impossible." But alas, the said bream would surface from the unfathomable depths of the lake, simultaneously with the emergent smirk across his sun-worn, peat-brown, radiant face. If the Chinese were inscrutable, then he was one of the Dublin Dynasty! What made things even worse was that his form of inscrutability came under the dissemblance of simplicity. That was his art, the art of all the Irish in fact. Giving the appearance of simplicity on the surface, whilst already having made the connections at depth. He would out-fish the rest of my angling fraternity and me, worum for worum, for the remainder of my childhood and well beyond. St Patrick may have been your man for snakes, but where fish were concerned St Peter and Paddy Cane had us swallow their devilish bait, hook, line and gullible sinker. I'm not so sure about Jesus but if Paddy Cane had told me that he could walk on water, I think that simple faith and a reverent, ritual imitation of his fish-landing omnipotence would have been genuflexion enough!

One of the greatest joys of my young life - apart, that is, from the anticipation of sex - was night fishing. Woodies was a favoured location for that nocturnal activity. There was room in one corner of the lake for the erection - if you'll excuse the obsessive word - of a couple of tents and space enough left over for a few of us to fish side by side through the rat-rustling, owl-hooted, early hours of our dreams of leviathan. It was the sort of adventure that none of us could have coped with in solitude. We loved fishing and caught some of our biggest fish at dusk and dawn and in the bat-haunted darkness itself. But like the shoals we were pursuing we needed the safety of numbers. At around that time there was broadcast one of the most frightening television programmes I can ever remember. 'The Quatermass Experiment'. It was some sort of sci-fi horror thriller in which Professor Quatermass duly saved the world from extinction. Although I can't recall all of the details of the plot - mostly because I either had my hands over my eyes or my fingers in my ears - the series was characterized by compounded build-ups in suspense followed by sudden and gruesome denouements. In one episode a man fell into a large spherical tank, full of some unmentionable liquid, and came up covered from head to foot in flesh-corroded, terrifying disfigurement. Now all of this may seem a million miles away from night-fishing, until that is, I tell you that much of the series itself was filmed at Shell-Haven. Across the marshes from Woodies were the tank farms, the cracker, and the flares. At night they were all lit up and to the fertile mind a distinction between the fiction of the 'The Quatermass Experiment' and the real world of petro-chemicals could not be easily drawn. We fished all night in the flickering glare of that high-tec, alien complex and regaled each other with as many gory details from the series as we could remember. It was a surreal, shivery world, of ghostlike whisperings through the leaves and of star-sunk luminary echoes cast in the narcissistic waters of our ever-increasing self-doubts and diabolical fears. We would dare each other to walk the perimeter hedgerows alone, but rarely would anyone take up the challenge. In the early hours of one moon-gladed summer morning, we of the fearless foursome decided to beat the bounds of our trepidation by doing a circular tour of the lake together. Beside a lake things don't so much bump in the night, but splash, plop and rustle. The moon was tremulous across the water. Fish jumped and radiated their sudden and startling presence. Bats were tangled in the upstanding hair of our bristling imaginations and moths rusted our eyelids through the air-borne lunacies of their corruptive fluctuations. As we walked gingerly along the southern flank, peering through the ghostly gaps in the foliage and out across the mist-enshrouded marshes towards the shimmering luminosity of the refineries beyond, a distorted, scar-crossed, scarecrow of a face, glared back through the hedgerow and started to shout obscenities. "You bloody, fucking, cunts!" it nominated. "Why don't yers all piss off"? As idiots go we were quicker on the uptake that most. That Frankenstinian visage could have been 'The Quatermass Experiment' gone wrong for all we knew, and screams and adrenaline weren't going to hold us back to find out! I'd attempted a few world-records in my time, but I'd never before managed to get ahead of the sound of the starting-gun. The blocks lay smouldering behind us as we cut a terrified swathe through the reeded margins of the lake. When it's as dark as a dungeon and the spirit is tortured where do you go to hide? That was the question we asked of our ever-diminishing tails as we spiralled into the huddled outcome of our involved geometry. There was nowhere to hide. Either your heart exploded or it didn't. Options were to either face it out or to faint. The Tower of Babel was as a post-graduated course in modern languages as compared with the screeched incomprehensible ravings of the damned. We didn't know what to do; so we did nothing. It must have taken an hour at least for our pulse-rates to settle back to something near normal, and even longer for our courage to return. We eventually made our way back to our swims, shut ourselves up in our tents, and turned on our torches. Whoever the apparition was we saw no more of him. He was probably just a gentleman of the road resting his weary bones in one of nature's four-posters. On the other hand, it could have been the spirit of Izaak Walton himself trying to communicate his thoughts about our studious yet incomplete understanding of his magnum opus! But for me it had everything to do with 'The Quatermass Experiment'. Fact and fiction in my mind were never fully discerned. Still aren't! From that moment on any shadows falling eerily across my tent would be instantly zapped by my ray gun.

The best bloke to go fishing with was Dave Parks. I'd been closely studying his technique for a long time. Once when I was at his house he asked his sister June if she would like to varnish his rod. He moved out from behind the kitchen table and his cock stood out as proud and predatory as a jack-pike. She didn't need asking twice and immediately set to work with the Vaseline. I suppose she felt that it could only be classed as incest on a technicality! If she'd thought about such things at all, that is. "It's your turn now Merv," he wheezed. "She just luvs doin' it." Being a Gemini I was naturally in two minds, but seeing as June and birthdays went together in my case, I decided to accept my present graciously. That was the first time in my adolescent memory that my cock had been

244

handled by a member of the opposite sex. I'd already experienced the physical sensation of alien hands on my erectile penis, but nothing could have prepared me for the full psychological shock of the heterosexual wank. No wonder God kicked Adam and Eve out of the garden. Nobody should be allowed to enjoy themselves as much as that. If this was real sin, then I was made for the job. She shuffled me backwards and forwards around the kitchen like a horizontal pogo stick. I was puffing and panting like a steam-train with sticky valves. "Harder! Harder!" I hissed. "No softer! Softer! Quicker! Quicker! No slower! Slower!" I think that that was probably the first headache she'd ever suffered from in her entire life. "I'm not doin' it anymore," she said, in one quick hands off movement. "Yer talk too bleedin' much." Whatever the truth of the statement as a general principle, it certainly didn't apply at that precise moment. I was dumbfounded! Coitus interuptus was one thing, but to stand there rampant knowing that I wasn't going to make the full conjugation was too much Latin to bear. Like so many times since I was left in that interclimatic limbo-land of sexual unfulfilment. My high-pitched pleading went unheeded as she took herself and her prerogative well out of range of my insistent needs. "Don't go!" I begged, pathetically. "I luv yer!" Her power was now absolute. I was beginning to understand some of the historical reasoning behind the exploits of the Witch finder General! The way I felt at that moment couldn't have been entirely of my own doing. Nobody feels that helplessly lustful of his own accord, there must have been some supernatural agency involved. The ducking stool, the scold, the tongue-clamp, even the red-cloak itself seemed eminently suitable to the occasion. The reincarnated wishes of Matthew Hopkins himself followed that heathen sorceress into the realms of broomsticks and familiars whilst taking a box of Swan-Vestas from out of his puritanical pocket.......

At Jackson's pond, still smarting from the rejection, I was just about managing to console myself with some crucian-carp fishing, when Dave's latest girlfriend came to join us. " 'Ello

gorgeous!" he gushed, unctuously. "This is me mate Merv."
Georgina blushed a bit, giggled a bit, and said nothing,
beautifully. She had a dark Polynesian air about her and to my
mind's eye she was sexy and saronged with a yellow water
lily fixed to the black sheen of her oh so strokeable hair. I'm
not the greatest fisherman the world's ever seen at the best of
times, but when your friend's canoodling on the bank with
crumpet, then concentration is near impossible. She may have
been shy but as evidenced from the escapade with June, Dave
had a way with women. I tried to concentrate on the float but
just couldn't. Out of the corner of my eye cotton was being
replaced with skin. Dark, sun-bronzed, nubile skin at that!
Dave was unstoppable where sex was concerned. It didn't
matter to him that he was outside the parish church and could
have been stumbled across any minute by the vicar or his
parishioners. When he got the whiff of sex his tongue would
start to loll and if needs be he'd have stayed out panting all
night. Georgina wasn't so keen. One had the feeling that she
wanted to please right enough, but perhaps not quite so
publicly as Dave was seeming to demand. The verbal
exchanges were becoming just as hot as the sexual ones. "No!
Not here, not now, someone might see," said Georgina in
deshabillé. "Stop it!" "Don't worry, no-one can see us,"
replied the octopus, sub lingerie. "Open yer legs." But
someone could see, and in the case of pubic-hair, could see
for the first time. What the difference is between the hair on
the head and that of the nether regions I've never fully
fathomed. But just the black, swarf-curly, sight of it was
electrifying! I found that my misogyny had dissipated
considerably and that my sexual resolve was beginning to
harden once more. Although, Georgina's resolve was
beginning to make an exhibition of itself. "Stop it! Stop it!
Stop it!" she blubbered, distraughtly. "I don't wanna do it
anymore!" Where had I heard all this before? What was it
about women, I thought. They take you right to the point of
no return, then throw a wobbly, and leave you stranded in
mid-passion. Even as a peeping tom I was about to suffer the
same frustrating fate. "Come on!" urged Dave in the manner

246

of a true fisherman. "Jus an 'andful of sprats, that's all I want." Well, he didn't make his catch. She jumped up, readjusted her clothing, and fled in unaccountable tears. "They're very emotional is women," said Dave, philosophically, and threw some ground bait into the waiting pond. What was the matter with him? How could he treat things so casually? I was hot, hard and frantic, and needed to do something about it urgently. I nipped off behind a tree and proceeded to finish what I'd already started. Guiltily, still worried about the 'never the twain shall meet' lust and love theories of Dave Parks, I climaxed and climaxed and climaxed. This was the world's first never-ending wank, the first - and never to be repeated - tug at the bootstraps of my ejaculatory being. I could have papered the walls of the Sistine Chapel with the tacky effluent of my mortal sins. That anathema was a distinct possibility didn't worry me in the slightest. There was no time for the fears of the bell, book, and candle variety. As a novice in the art of masturbation - with tangible results I might add - my fears were of a more immediate nature. Would I ever stop coming? Why had I never read the volume my mother and father supplied me with? Was this a punishment for my evil ways? Was I going to die of pleasure? As is the case with all good things it did come to an end eventually. The contractions in my loins began to subside, vision returned, and I was overcome by the desolate feelings of post-masturbatory depression. Fishing and girls just didn't go together. Having angled for both I knew which was the easiest to catch and to keep. The primitive instincts of the hunt would have to be kept separate from the primal urges of the flesh. Easier said than done. Who chases and who's caught? Even to this day, angling and erections are a mutually integral part of the same archaic order of things. When I look at a fish in a glass-case I am overwhelmed by the thoughts and desires associated with taxidermy. And I'm still the world's greatest wanker. Always will be I suppose.

Girls were becoming expensive. Not only did you need to pop sweets and ice creams into their ever-open mouths - like

247

some sort of feather-brained feeding ritual - but you also felt obliged to complete the analogy by strutting around like a demented peacock. All that courtship activity required longer arms and shorter pockets than was usual in my tight-fisted case. You don't mind if I use a swearword do you? Good. WORK! Would have to be found. There was nothing else for it. We had more than our fair share of scams to support us fiscally, but none of them could supply the regular, gilt-edged, mind alleviating securities that we needed for woo-manship. I decided to get myself a paper-round. Not being a great lover of yawning *en bicyclette*, I opted for an evening round. Providing I didn't have detention to detain me, I could usually finish my task in an hour or two, and therefore have plenty of time left not to do my homework! It should have been the ideal solution to my pecuniary circumstances, but as it turned out, not only did it fail to ease my financial situation but caused more than enough problems in other areas. Seven shillings and sixpence a week wasn't a lot even then, especially for someone with my expensive tastes. On top of that one was constantly at the beck and call of absent-minded, grey-haired, blue-rinsed old ladies bristling with shopping-lists. One predatory octogenarian in particular caught me nearly every time. I used to creep up the stairs in her block of flats with all the tiptoed deliberation of a ballet dancer - all to no avail. It was uncanny. From within her lair - without the aid of a hairnet or an ear trumpet - she could hear the slightest of vibrations as they stuck the web of her Cooperative Wholesale intrigues. She was a lovely old dear really and always used to give me a little something for doing her errands. But that wasn't the point though. The fact was that she was just one of a summoning tribe of spidery old souls who were waiting for me - or anyone else for the matter - to puck at the threads of their isolate existences. Mostly I think that the shopping-lists were a pretext only. They wanted nothing more than to spin a yarn or two. To wrap you up in the delicate silks of their lavender-scented conversations and to keep you trapped at the edges of their radiating loneliness. Sadly, I wasn't a social worker and even if I'd had the mind or the patience to listen to the gloss of their gossamer lives, spun out and glistening tenuously through the eau de cologne and strands of shimmering nostalgia, I wouldn't have had the time. This was business after all and I'm afraid that sentiment definitely had cramped quarters. Dave Parks and I worked for the same newsagents. If Dave was something of a Casanova on the loving front, then he was without doubt a Fagan in the realms of employment. Under the sharp, accustomed eyes of the shop assistants he could nip in and out behind the counter pretending to count or mark newspapers while all the time filling his bag with cigarettes. I don't know where he got his nerve from, but that boy was destined for the SAS I thought. He tried to train me in the arts of palming but although I managed to prove myself worthy of the tuition on a few occasions, for my part it was more often than not a case of all beer and no bottle. Unless the counter was completely devoid of staff, then I was devoid of courage. Nevertheless, that didn't stop me from taking my share of the ill-gotten gains. I was smoking so many fags at the time that it's surprising that I ever found enough breath to pedal my bike around the estates! Unhealthy as it was having a constant supply of cigarettes from the newsagents, as if that wasn't enough one of my customers used to invite me in to smoke his as well. And that wasn't all he offered either. It started off with tea, cakes, and compliments about my physique, then slowly over the weeks moved on to wrestling matches. He was a very ordinary looking middle-aged man. He had a wife, two sons and two daughters and an air of familial responsibility about him. Looking back I trusted him completely. My gullibility astounds me. "Flex your arms Mervyn," he said callisthenically as he tweaked my biceps. "Ooh! I bet you're a strong boy." "I am," I replied naively. "I'll show yer if yer like." "How are you going to show me," he encouraged. "What can you do?" "I can lift a chair up by one leg," I enthused.” That’s strong, that's really strong. It's not much fun though, is it?" he countered cunningly. "Can you wrestle?" "Yeh I'm a good wrestler," I boasted, somewhat stupidly. "I could beat yer anytime." "Oh, I doubt it," he continued, insidiously. "After all, I'm a grown man." The trap was set and all he had to do was spring it. I can't tell you just how many times I rolled around on the floor with that paedophile, growing in confidence all the while under the weight of his body and compliments. "My, yes, you are strong!" he'd say submissively. "See how long you can hold my shoulders down." "Turn me over, lay on my back." How was I to know that he was getting his rocks off at my expense? To me he was just another form of the ubiquitous scoutmaster, concerned with the physical well being of the young in general. It wasn't until he came down the stairs one day in his pyjamas, with his great dangling penis swinging in the suddenly enlightened air, that I began to realize my mistake. "Would you like to hold this?" he propositioned, with his hand round the neck of the strangulated monster. It's at moments of revelation like that - assuming of course you can effect a means of escape - that invaluable lessons are learnt! "Yer filfy ol' basstard!" I yelled at the pitch of betrayal as I crashed tearfully past him and made my speedy exit out of the front door. "Yer bloody liar, yer bleedin' good fer nuffin' liar!" If my father - and perhaps even the man's own family - had found out about that incident, I dread to think what would have happened to him. My father alone was somewhere to the right of Attila the Hun when it came to matters of masculine honour, but then, perhaps the wrestler himself had suffered from similar paternal influences. What is it they call it, cycles of deprivation? Whatever, what with the shopping lists, the homosexual advances, and the starvation wages, the sheen had been well and truly rubbed off newsprint as a means to instant wealth and happiness. Not to mention the near permanent tarnishing of my own Jack-the-Lad reputation! Earnings would have to be sought elsewhere. And where better than Pitsea Market? I got myself a job with Rella's - a children's clothing stall - at twelve and six for six hours work on a Saturday morning. This was the acme of Micawberisms. Income and expenditure were in the right fiscal balance at last and although the overall hours were similar to the paper-round they were at least contracted into the space of one short morning. I was at home there with the environment, the spiel, and God forgive me, the moneybag! You'd think that good wages and conditions would be enough for me after the experiences with the paper-round. Not a bit of it; whenever Rella went off for coffee and what have you, and left me to look after the stall on my own, I just couldn't resist and illicit dip into the bag. The silver coinage that cascaded through my pilfering fingers was as clear as a mountain stream. Oh, that the same could have been said about my conscience! I just couldn't leave the loot alone. It started 'innocently' enough with just the occasional sixpence. Moved to shillings and florins and became unstoppable with half-a-crowns. She must have known. At times I was trebling my wages. Why she didn't say anything I'll never know. Either there was that much money involved in the market game that she was prepared to cover the losses, which I doubt, or she liked me enough to want to see me get hooked by the money-bug, and take over from her when she retired. Who knows? Stranger things have happened. What I do know is, I was probably richer then than I'd ever been before, or have been since for that matter. I wasn't the only one either; all of my friends it seems had a lucky dip of their own. To the trained, judicial eye, our newfound wealth should have been both obvious and suspicious. But it says something for the times we lived in that nobody seemed to notice. The didactic endings of just about every 'cops and robbers' movie I saw in the fifties, made a heavy point of saying that crime doesn't pay. Experience was proving differently. That was a pivotal time in my life and the fulcrum of events could have seesawed me in any direction. Ultimately I would take the advice of the Church and the moviemakers and suffer from the penurious results of such ill-considered social and spiritual meditations.

At that time though I was still avoiding the Via Dolorosa and decided that if I was going to take the road of evil then I should need to be dressed for the part. There was a clothes shop in Pitsea known as Alf the market man. It was owned by a thin, asthmatic, taciturn man, but mostly run by his two slick and garrulous sons. I thought I had some spiel but it was as nothing when compared with the banter that flowed pre-eminently from the lips of those two old time tuck-up merchants. I don't suppose we ever got any real bargains, but you felt as though you had and that was the main thing. They were like a music-hall turn. They could play us off one against the other and sell us almost anything. "It's 'im init Tony," he'd say with a look impressed by one's sartorial acumen. "I don't know Roy," Tony would say, hesitatingly. "Wiv the right accessories, yeah wiv the right accessories." If necessary they'd even go into a tap-dancing routine! I don't care whether I got a bargain or not, as far as I was concerned I always got a good deal. Perhaps the schmutter wasn't the best quality merchandise. Maybe it was a joke that I could haggle over the price for an hour, until I got it down to twice the price it should have been in the first place. But it was fun. God was it fun. It was an all singing, all dancing, Alhambra of a gentlemen's outfitters. Whether you wanted hound's-tooth check or corduroy, Fred-Perry or a button-down, fly away collar, there you could get it and what's more get it with a smile. It may have been an off the peg establishment but everything about it was bespoken of with style. Cheap and cheerful would be the absolutely perfect epithet! For the budding man *à la mode* Alf's was the place to be seen in. If the scrunched fist of a fitting wasn't good enough then you were sent in the direction of Mrs. Papworthy for alterations. Entering the domain of Mrs. Papworthy's was an H G Wellsian experience. You could see the date flickering backwards on the dial with every step you made towards her copse-centered time capsule. If plotland life was in general primitive, then this was primordial. Not that her shack was that different from others attached to the local smallholdings. It just seemed farther out than most and not just in physical terms. Comforts of the post-war, increasingly mass-produced world had just not reached Mrs. Papworthy. Well-water, pot-black stoves, and oil-lamps were the order of the day. The old timber-framed, asbestos-roofed, porched and pebble-dashed building nestled in its enchanted surroundings. Bird-songed and bee-buzzy, for all the hard work that was needed to keep it going - especially for an old lady living on her own - it was idyllic. Where the woodland trees ended the orchard ones began. Honeysuckle, wisteria, ivy and Virginia creeper climbed and clung everywhere. Trellises were swamped in the stuff, windows encased and verandas invaded. Logs were chopped, blocked and faggoted into moss-green piles. Cottage blooms scented the multicoloured air and plucked butterflies from the resentful blue and cumulous-loaded summer skies. Lilac and laburnum smouldered with smoke and showered with golden sparks in their rightful season and a tide of grasses and wild flowers washed up continuously, only to founder on the evergreen shores of that prelapsarian Eden. The curdled pink suffusing cream of garden roses reverting to type drew you in through the tunnel of their fragrant petals to the door of that mythical seamstress. On entering her abode the allusion to the 'Time Machine' was complete. It was like the womb of all time in there. Dark, dank and silent, save for the labouring heartbeat of a dusty long-case clock. There was a sense of gestation in the atmosphere. The past in the form of sepia prints and photographs was visibly fading and about to be re-absorbed by the present. Cheap, china souvenirs from Clacton and Margate sat side by side with ebony-carved fertility goddesses from darkest Africa. It was as if all time was one time and all places one place. Everything and nothing had happened in that house. History clung to every mildewy corner, yet the mildew itself was timeless, a moist, musky reminder, of nature's infinite regressions and projections. Even in deepest summer it was like being in the underworld. Heavy velvet drapes were drawn against the intrusive sunshine and through the soft chinks in their sumptuous armour gold-shafted swords cut into the moted flesh of daylight. Rippling shadows were folded layer on layer into the cool recesses of that Orphian otherworldliness. To speak at all was like coming up for air. For the third time she asked me what it was that I wanted and half-drowned in the mystery of the place I responded. "I'd like yer t' turn these trousers inta drainpipes," I said as I surfaced into spell-shattering dialogue.

"Can yer do 'em?" Her puffed-up Persian familiar stared from above the willow patterns in a Welsh-dresser, with an inane northwestern grin on its face. "What d'you think Cheddar," she inquired paradoxically. "Can we do 'em?" "Miaow," said the moggy. That I happened to be wearing them at the time was of no consequence to Mrs. P. She was no prude. "Get 'em off lad," she domineered. "I aint got all day." Sitting in the underworld in one's underpants, being looked at quizzically by a Persian familiar, while an enchanted seamstress eases your gusset and cackles a shortsighted thread through a needle's impossible eye, can be rather disconcerting. Do you come here often didn't seem at all appropriate. "Bin busy Mrs. Papworthy," I tendered by way of barelegged embarrassed conversation. "What's it got t' do wiv you!" she snapped, even more disconcertingly. "People wiv legs like that shouldn't ask rude questions." She was well known for her eccentric waggery and one just didn't quite know how to approach her. "Put the kettle on lad," she commanded. " Them legs o' yourn have turned a peculiar shade of blue, don't want yer dyin' on me before I gets me money, do I? " I don't think that I ever had a proper conversation with her. It didn't matter though, I'd learnt a lot about ironic weight and timing and what she couldn't do with a needle and cotton would be enough to stitch the splitting sides of a Harley Street surgeon. And more than that, she was cheap! Mercifully cheap! Mind you, the results of her handiwork were not always appreciated either by my parents or my educators. I remember a distinctive pair of hound's-tooth check trousers that were the cause of much unnecessary trouble. When you consider just how difficult it is to get into drainpipes you wonder why it is that some people seem to spend so much time trying to get you out of them again! Or perhaps that's exactly the point, the perversity of the adult mind and temperament. My teachers just abhorred high fashion. Black and white drainpipes, they said, were not the thing for school, especially when they came combined with eighteen inch winkle-pickers, the compulsory red-fluorescent shirt and a heavily Brylcremed hairstyle complete with duck's arse. I was insistent. If it meant even more time wasted in detention, then so be it. Even the cruelty of remarks along the lines of: girls weren't smiling in my direction admiringly, but were in fact teetering on the edge of uncontrollable derision, couldn't deflect me from my purpose. I knew the truth. I was dapper and eminently desirable. It went without saying, did it not? After a few days of *haute couteur* intransigence on my part the headmaster was summoned. "Linford!" he snapped in an authoritarian manner. "I've had just about enough of your Bow Brummel antics; If you don't go straight home and change into something more decent, you'll be expelled." Well, that sounded like good news to me, but unfortunately I knew that my parents would see things differently. "And get your hair cut while you're at it!" he snipped as a passing shot. There was nothing for it, I had no option, I would have to do as I was told. I thought that in order to save face I would comply with everything but the haircut. Surely, even in a world as uncultured and unsophisticated as that one a duck's arse would be permissible on its own? It was a mistake. My penchant towards recalcitrance was always getting me into deep water and this was to be no different. "Linford!" he screamed, accusingly. "I thought I told you to get your hair cut." "I can't afford it sir," I prevaricated. "I'm skint." "What about your parents," he suggested, "Surely they could give you the money?" "I come from a poor family," I continued, thinking I was on the right tack. "We're ever so 'ard up!" "Right!" he said, decisively. "I'll pay for it myself, come with me." Horror of horrors, I was to be taken by the head by the scruff - if you see what I mean - bodily over to Barnets the hairdressers to have my duck's arse erased in public. This wasn't going to do a lot for my fashionable standing in the community. That the headmaster's cranium was growing up through his own hair like a mushroom out of the cerebral humus may well have had something to do with it! Whatever, I swear I saw something other than a purely educational gleam in his eye when over the creeping hairs on the back of my neck the snippers moved inexorably towards my doomed and double-tailed masterpiece.

255

Chapter 16. Last Flings.

Some people go train spotting for a hobby; others are more interested in bird watching. For myself - individualist that I tried to be - at one end of the summer I observed luggage racks and at the other I collected place-names on the backs of coaches. These two pastimes may seem somewhat eccentric and unconnected, until that is, you realize just how exotic and adventurous my spirit was! The luggage-observation tied in with my family's holiday plans. As soon as I found out where we were going I got out the maps and started to pour over them. That may have been sufficient in spring to keep my appetite whetted but by the time summer came maps were beginning to lose their fascination and I was in dire need of some hands-on experience. Time moves for no Mervyn! As they say. If a holiday's booked for August you just can't - without the aid of Dr Who that is - get it in June. And relativities being inversely proportionate to age, a month or two in adolescence is equivalent to the autobiographical ramblings of Methuselah! All I could do was sit forlornly on Friday nights and Saturday mornings on a bench beside the A13 and study the passing luggage. I can't quite describe to sane individuals the excitement felt at the sight of a rooftop pile of suitcases and flapping plastic sheets. I can only assume that twitchers have something of the same thrill on their first sighting of the lesser-spotted oslem hawk or some such rarity. Kent and Sussex, Somerset and Dorset, were recreated on the racks of those vintage cars, and caravans or trailers conjured up Devon and Cornwall immediately. That they were all probably making their slow way home to the East-End after a wet week on Canvey Island never entered my poor deluded head. The wanderlust was on me and nothing short of Westward-Ho, expandable snake-like straps, and crocodile-clips, would suffice. We did go on holiday - every year in fact - and occasionally got as far as Exmoor or Mevagissy. The places always came up to expectations even if the weather invariably didn't. Fog and rain are much the same anywhere I

257

suppose, but when you've travelled all night and three hundred miles to find them, the effect is all the more dampening. No, the real problem with real holidays, were the real people that you had to go with! No doubt they thought the same about me, but that's their business. And anyway, I've cheated; they can't answer me back. Which is a grand reversal of fortune. No, it has to be said, that my imaginary holidays were by far the best. If nothing else I found my rightful place in the pecking order and could scratch around for all the candyfloss I wanted. I think that both my parents were reincarnations of Cromwell and being as my mother was a Catholic I suppose that's a bit heartless. But enjoyment was an anathema to them. More particularly if the enjoyment in question had anything to do with yours truly. I was usually glad to get back to Pitsea. If I was going to be told-off all of the time I preferred more space to sulk in than that afforded by a mobile home. Fantasy was - and still is - better than the real thing, and at least in Basildon I knew every delightful corner of the dream-inducing territory. At the other end of the summer, in conjunction with the Southend-on-Sea illuminations, the beanos started in earnest. Coaches from all over the South East and beyond would converge upon the local public houses. The Railway Hotel, the Gun Inn and the Pitsea Bull, were the favourite stopping-off points in our area. The Railway Hotel - known locally as the Flying Bottle - was undoubtedly the most frequented and that's where I spent most of my time collecting place-names. I didn't put them in a book or do projects on them or anything sensible like that. I just gazed all misty-eyed at such exotica as Hemel-Hempsted and Wellyn Garden City and imagined - as subsequent travels have proved - the unimaginable. The majority of the charabancs came from the East End so I wasn't just familiar with the names, I knew the places from first hand experience as well. Stepney, Poplar and Canning Town were all places very much of my earliest acquaintance. And the people, their accents, and their drunken antics, were so much a part of my formative education that their staggering bravado and equilbrial ineptitudes were also far from strange or

258

inconsistent with my memories! For the observer of humankind and its follies, that was definitely to place to be. If I'd have had the necessary intellectual wherewithal that would have been the place to formulate one's thesis on inebriation. A dipso-doctorate would almostly certainly have followed. They were pissed when they got to Southend in the early evening, and on the way back from the illuminations - Which must have been something of a psychedelic experience - they were legless for last-orders. Separate men and women's works outings amalgamated under the influence and like the beer trouble was brewing. Fights and fancies went hand in hand, so to speak. Luckily most of them were too drunk to make a job of any particular contretemps. Swings were swung and missed and slurred contenders spiralled helplessly onto the punchless ground. There was always more by the way of abuse than ABH, although, the occasional bottle or broken glass found its target. Black Marias were called and offenders removed to the cells. Much of the real mean-spirited violence came from the locals feeling put out at the beer-spated loss of their riparian rights. As for the day-trippers, they were for the most part out to enjoy themselves, and full of bonhomie. If they had to crawl back to their coaches on hands and knees, covered in their own or other peoples blood and vomit, then so be it, they were having 'a good time'! Their worries would come later in the form of pregnancy, divorce, and blood feuds. For the time being it was Souffend, kiss-me-quick, and to 'ell wiv the consequences!

As much a part of summer in the Basildon area as the stopovers made by beano charabancs *en route* to the illuminations, were the travelling fairs. Three sites come readily to mind. One in a field at the junction of Timberlog and Bull lane in Vange and another and another alongside Honeypot Lane, close to where the Town Centre now stands, were relatively small affairs. A major ride or two and a few attendant stalls and food-outlets were all they had to offer. But they were nonetheless welcome for that. By far the largest fair of the season was to be found at a place known as

Craylands. This also bordered onto Timberlog Lane but was much further inland and out towards Nevendon. Much of 'the fun of the fair' was to be had long before the lights were up and the music blaring. From the moment the first lorries and trailers arrived the local grapevine was activated. Like stevedores at the dock-gates, queues of hopeful youngsters, waited to see what jobs were on offer. I was never lucky enough to be taken on by one of the rides or stalls, but was happy nevertheless, to take part in the setting-up and eventual taking down of the equipment. Those fairs were all the more enjoyable to me towards the end of my schooling, not just because they were excellent places for older boys to do some posing, but because by that time my market thievery was in full lamentable swing, and I could thus, just spend, and spend, and spend! I loved the gaudy, brash atmosphere of the fairground. In some strange way it was both all pretence and yet no pretence at all. It may have pandered to fantasy in every conceivable way possible to extract money from your pockets, but it did it blatantly. You knew that the coconuts were stuck into their stands, the darts blunt, and the sights on the rifles crooked. Who cared? Apart, that is, from the odd soulless miser. It was an escapist wonderland. Galaxies of multicoloured lights brought the outer-reaches of reality down to earth for a few glorious summer evenings. The whiplash spun with its load of screaming girls through the constellated darkness of my lewd and licentious thoughts. Rockers with jobs on the rides, sprang as hardheaded and agile as mountain goats, with tattooed, short-changing arms from car to car. The chair-o-planes found me locked in their giddying orbits out across the candy-striped, planetary roofs, of the circulating tents. Bearded ladies flexed their androgynous muscles next to the punch-drunk booths full of brainless and brawnless local challengers. The scrying, mercurial eyes, of quick-witted Romanies, delivered the far from crystal truth as they silvered the seams of their clammy palms. Hot-dogs, popcorn and burgers sizzled and sweetened the scented air and the galloper's tinny tradition vied with the King out of loud and lyrical blue-suede speakers. It was there that the bobby-

260

socked girls swirled through their hooped-skirts and masses of petticoats to favour the breezes with their sheer fluorescent scarves. There, where I swayed and swaggered like a chimpanzee with haemorrhoids in the hopes of catching a quick- mascara-ed glance. Where music, lights and movement, built from the rocketing rides into crescendos of carefree laughter as the stars of the heavens and the stars of our luminant lives melded their moments and were made eternal. When the fairs left town part of me left with them. Being as I usually helped with their dismantling I felt as though I'd willingly colluded in the banishment of my truer and more vibrant self. There was a sadness to be experienced after the fairs left town that stretches the bounds of language. I can take you no further than to the empty field itself after the council had been and cleared the remaining rubbish. Where the stalls and rides had been and light had not reached the ground, we were left with the faded mirror image of what once was. A pale geometry of sadness made of absence, where sound and light - by memory enshrouded - haunted the sudden silence of the soul. Let's not languish too long in such lugubrious surroundings. Across the road from Crayland's field stood the school of the same name. If Timberlog County Secondary Modern was a breeding ground for crime, then Craylands was a literal penitentiary. It was notorious for the disproportional amount of thugs on its register! They were mean streets indeed, knuckles there were dusted with granite, and Eastern National bus-crews on the 244 route had the highest incidence of nervous breakdowns in the country! The girls were equally as hard as the boys and brazen with rumours of sexual impropriety. Tarts, bikes, slags and scrubbers were some of the less than savoury appellations found on the tips of our chauvinistic tongues and were enough to entice us across the threshold of reputation into the red-light district of the weekly youth-club held within the school's unhallowed precincts. Our problem was always how to attract our fair share of attention from the objects of our desires without riling their Neanderthal companions in anyway whatsoever! Not easy when one considers the intractability of

261

congenital paranoia and psychopathy. Those hulks from the backwoods were terrifying. Just thinking of some of their legendary names sends me rushing to 'The Writer's and Artist's Year Book' to study the fine print in the articles pertinent to libel. You can take it as read that I've invoked the customary fictional waiver and have increased my BUPA premium just in case. The nasty-person X of previous chapters was as a church-mouse in comparison with these rats from the sewers of fifties youth culture. Their precocity came mostly in the form of bodily hair. At a time when I was still rubbing boot-polish into my bum-fluffed, kittenish phisog, those snarling panthers in skull and cross-boned, bootlace ties and black drape jackets, were sprouting fur in virile, bristling fistfuls. The task was hopeless. How could the four romantic musketeers ever translate themselves from the bodice-ripping unrealities of 17th century France and come to terms with the knuckle-headed truths of the contemporary chain gang? 'All for one, one for all' were not phrases my reprobational friends and me were *au fait* with. Faced with rock-breaking convict stares of the Crayland mob, I for one was looking for a job in the prison library. We tried of course. Dave was always good for a chat-up line or two. D'you fuck darlin'" he'd say smoothly with a suave curl on his upper labial. "I might, I might not," would come the response through ruminating, pink-blown, bubble-gummed lips. "Well fuck orf then!" would retort the honey-tongued gallant, dangerously. "I'll tell Godzilla if you're not careful," warned the harlot, and Charlie and eddy and I would leave the penniless boasting Gascon to his fate, almost *accompli*. Craylands wasn't the only youth-club in the area. There was another one held in the community-hall in Luncies road. There we listened to the latest hip, hip, vonda heada, heada, hip, hip, sort of music and met nice girls. Well, you can't have everything can you? Carol was the nicest of nice girls. I can use her name with impunity. Neither she nor I have anything to reproach ourselves about. It was love of the purest kind, you'll not doubt be glad to hear. If I'd have been a girl - and there were some doubts about it at the time - I think I'd have been a carbon copy of Carol, a slim, blond, downy-skinned and blue-eyed beauty. We jived through the backbeat pounding of our rhythmic hearts and were self-absorbed in the burgeoning intimacy of our giddying gyrations. We waltzed into each other's quivering bodies and fused into one all-embracing entity. Our eyes wide open; we gazed deep into the blue respective translucence of our innermost beings and tasted the warm, sweet breath, of our expelling, immaculate spirits. Why do girls have friends? Friends with names like glue? Her friend Sylvia was like a Siamese twin. She was coaxially joined and followed her everywhere, like her alter ego. Whenever I asked such things as "Would yer like t' cum aht wiv me Saterdee night?" The response would almost certainly be, "I dunno, I'll 'ave to ask Silv." Silv, could seemingly, dance on her own, and yet still be within shimmying distance of our every whispered utterance! Silv, went to the loo with her, to the rock-caked and Tizer-fizzy counter with her, and worst of all followed her and yours truly all the love-lingering way home after the dance was over. The three of us were inseparable. "What d'you fink Silv?" she would canvass. "Should WE go out wiv 'im Saterdee?" "But I don't wanna go aht wiv Silv," I would say irritably. "I wanna go aht wiv YOU!" "Oh no! We couldn't leave Silv on 'er own, could we" she'd reason. "It wouldn't be fair, would it?" Wouldn't it, I thought! Given half a chance I'd have left her devoid of breath, great sucking limpet that she was. Even love, even soul enriching, young, never to be experienced again Platonic love, had its limits. I tried for a week or two with the jemmy of my smooth rapscallion tongue to prize the contiguous duo apart, but to no avail. They were one flesh and what is worse they were keeping it to themselves. If I wanted anything more than the failed attempts at interface in that three-way *menage a miserable* I'd have to take the advice of Alexander rollicking Dumas and put it about elsewhere!

Sunday night pictures were as much of an institution when I was a teenager as Saturday mornings were at the selfsame fleapit when I was younger. Differences, of course, were both

263

sexual and sartorial. Posing was the name of the game and this was where the art was perfected. Given, that in my case at least, the words pratt and perfected, have to be seen as synonymous. As was the case with the Saturday morning westerns, so it was with the Sunday night horror movies. Pandemonium reigned. Nothing of the film could be seen or heard through the mass circulatory throng of parading adolescents. Like ruffs at a lek, the boys would be puffing out their chests, and scratching the cock-sure ground of their competitive instincts, in front of any admiring hens. Fags would be dangling from their beaks or smouldering nonchalantly between slick, be-ringed talons. Flocks of eager hens would gather in the stalls and cackle over the pecking order. The transparent Zeppelins of inflated Johnnies floated ghostlike through the projector beams and the frantic manager ran hither and thither exploding their ghastly forms with glowing tip an overworked Woodbine. Flunkies were the masculine equivalent to the sanitary towel. They were our outward sign of inner maturity. To have braved the barbers on a Saturday morning and to have come away with a packet of blushless three was one of the major rites of passage. If girls could whisper in exclusively womanly huddles about the mysteries of menstruation then our prophylactic debates could be just as adult and esoteric. We'd look up at the spectral levitating phalluses, back down at our loins, and then shoot a glance at the giggling maidens. Darkness and confidence were proportionately linked. I thought nothing of making a bold move in the pictures, whereas in the whimpering daylight I was less than useless. I chatted up many a willing girl in the musty velveteen recesses of my back-rowed predatory youth. Arms were sneaked lustfully around shrugged shoulders. Hands wandered in the direction of breasts and stocking-tops, and were received or repelled in about equal measure. Always the biggest worry was the kiss. Wet or dry, closed or open, French or puritanically Anglo-Saxon? Recipients would wipe their lips accusingly or even worse make as to spit. Teeth would clatter together like racks of crockery and gobbets of tobacco and popcorn would mix and mingle with their sweet and sour juicy incompatibilities! The only problem I had with the dark - especially in my summer solstice years - was that seeing some of those young ladies home after the performance could be a horrendously enlightening experience! What had appeared to one as a Hollywood Goddess in the suffused and secluded glow of a pre-nuptial B movie could quickly turn into 'The Creature from the Black Lagoon' on re-entering the all-revealing, bat-hung, twilight world of a late summers evening. On one occasion I emerged with a hook-nosed stick insect of a girl. I'm sorry if all this sounds visualist, she was probably one of the sweetest stick insects in the world, but I just couldn't cope with creepy-crawlies and had to give her the Flit. Another was an absolute beauty in every department but one. As I was walking her home I could hear a soft, nylon scuffed, knocking sound coming from the vicinity of her knees and on looking down realized to my horror that she was pigeon-toed. Well you know how I felt about pigeons! I just couldn't fancy her at all once I'd found out the truth about her columbiformed disability. I wouldn't go as far as to say that she should have been nutted at birth, but as far as I was concerned she'd have definitely been better off if she spent more time perfecting her homing abilities, instead of spreading her wings in my non-fancying loft. There was no way that a man of my cultured and sophisticated calibre could be seen abroad with a cack-footed bird like that, the pairing would have been just too incongruous. My greatest disappointment must surely have been with Miss Simpering Strabismus 1959. Now, squints don't bother me at all these days. In fact I have a lot of respect for the wandering independent eye. But then things were much different. I was very much a poet where girls were concerned. 'The right words in the right order' could have been sententiously re-written to express the way I felt about feminine bodily parts. The correct balance between form and content was a prosodic essential. One eye doing its own thing in the dark didn't affect my stress patterns one bit, but in broad lyrical daylight? I'm afraid I never was a member of the avant guarde, the metrical arrangement of her glances were far too dissonant for me at the time. Of late, with my developed experimental attitudes towards vers libre and even sound and concrete poetry, I'd probably welcome her wry, contemporary gaze with open arms, even if it was intended for someone else standing three catalectic streets away. No, there seems to be only one reason why we never spent the rest of our rapt, rhapsodic lives together, and that had a lot to do with the transforming power of language. One of my jealous, philistinic friends, in a rare moment of inspirational genius, suffixed his felicitations as regards our myopic union with the concise, gnomic gem: 'And may you 'ave many cross-eyed children!" The rest as they say opthalmically is history.

The result of all those disappointments in love was a self-enforced period of celibacy. Not that I really qualified for such sexually abstemious pretensions. I decided that I wasn't only going to stay away from girls forever, but that my foul-mouthed, insensitive friends would also be getting a one-way ticket to Coventry. I started to go to the pictures on my own. Not on Sunday nights when the place was more like a lunatic asylum than a palace of entertainments, but on the quieter evenings during the week. I even started to watch and listen to the films, something unheard of up to then! Such films as 'The Kyber Rifles', Agatha Christy's 'Murder She Wrote', and the Ealing innocence of 'The Titchfield Thunderbolt', a movie about a trial of strength between a steam-train and a traction engine that had me on the edge of my Elstree orientated seat for its entire length. Even more strangely I feel in love with musicals. I sang along with 'Seven Brides for Seven Brothers' with all the gusto normally reserved for Christmas-carols and rugby-songs. I tapped hip, enthusiastic feet, through all the choreographical magnificence of 'Porgy and Bess' and wept at the cinematic insincerities to be found in such sentimentalized masterpieces as 'Carousel' and 'South Pacific'. All this I did on my own and despite, or perhaps because of the vicarious tears, did so happily. I loaded up with tobacco, sweets and drink, and settled back easily into a couple of hours of big-screened escapism. The cinema became a big part of my life. In those days, apart from the one-off showings on Sunday night, and the regular serializations of Saturday morning's children's matinee, the main programmes were changed twice a week. My appetite for celluloid became insatiable. Apart from sickness and holidays I attended every available screening. I even remember sitting through endless hours of Tolstoy's 'War and Peace' spread over a couple of interminably bell-rung, cannonading days. My own company may have not been the most interesting this side of Oxbridge, but at least the critical analysis was favourable! The problems of the wider world reasserted themselves with the advent of films on naturism. Those pseudo, psycho-clinical excuses for pornography, re-awakened my latent and repressed longings. All the talk of liberated, wholesome naturalness coming from Mandy and her health-minded friends was as nothing when compared with the stark, undulatory visions of volleyball in the buff. With my new-found rigidity of purpose held firmly in hand, the fantasy world of my bioscopically inclined former self, would have to be forgone for the sake of the new and naked realism. Cigarettes and whisky and wild, wild, women, were about to find their incontrovertible place in the dissolute regions of my freshly aroused perspectives.

Even at fifteen years of age and before leaving school I had already found my way into the smoky corruptive atmosphere of the local public houses. How I got away with it without the implementation of the licensing laws is difficult to assess. I wasn't particularly old for my years, quite the hairless effeminate in fact. I had managed to cultivate something in the way of side-burns and clusters of blackheads may have given the shaded impression of an unshaven look to my countenance. But even so I wasn't exactly your average *hombre de saloon!* And in retrospect I don't think that it could have been my dress-sense that swung the balance of years in my favour. Unless of course the local landlords had a partiality for the traditions of pantomime and thought that my outlandish harlequinade might have increased their custom and consequent takings. No, I can only put it down to the fact that the local bobbies must have turned a blind and somewhat bleary eye in the fading light of liquid backhanders and felt that I'd probably be far less trouble pissed than I would have been sober. And pissed I was more often than not. Such dehydratory delights as Burton Triple X, India Pale Ale and Scrumpy spring light-headedly to mind. The two most unfortunate corollaries to the intake of alcohol are without doubt vomiting and urination. These frequent and near unstoppable bodily emissions were poorly catered for in the Basildon of my youth. Admittedly one could always relax one's muscles and let go in-situ - so to speak - but that was certain to elicit an unfavourable response from Mine-Host! No, like it or not one - for the sake of delicacy and customer relations - would have to face the noxious inconvenience of the outside toilet. If there had been an Egon Rone guide to *les bogs Englais* then those in my particular neck of the woods would have been hard put to raise a single *étoile* between them! The one that used to be outside The Barge in Vange deserves a special mention. To throw up in its puke-laden confines was like breaking a bottle of the finest vintage champagne over the bows of an antiquated, storm-racked, sewage vessel. If I'd have wanted to become a deep-sea diver then that loo gave me all the training I needed. It was there that I learnt how to hold my breath long enough to fart, vomit, piddle voluminously in a fountain, and to study the latest news from Kilroy, all in one stench-weathering series of movements. The brown, porcelained walls of the urinal were hung with the cloacle equivalent of seaweed, without the sweet, sea-salted invigorating waft of ozone. The trough itself was invariably blocked by a jettisoned mix of spew and dog-ends and an ammonial tide of bodily effluent lapped at the feet of all the inebriate beachcombers. Sandals were not for the faint-hearted and itinerant travellers were in distinct danger of becoming millionaires as pegs became as near as damn it compulsory in those contaminated environs. The council cemetery at Pitsea is chock-a-block with the hapless remains of health inspectors too sober to be able to cope with the toxic effects of their investigations. Now, whenever I use

268

one of those high-tec, cleaned anew before every customer, coin operated, space-age toilets; I sit for a while in silent, respectful contemplation and offer a prayer for the departed souls of those poisoned to death in the selfless, beaurocratic performance of their civic duties. If one hadn't got too drunk too early in the evening, there was always the weekly dance to be enjoyed. The Gun Inn at Pitsea had a dance hall attached, so that you could there partake of the twin vertiginous pleasures of drink and terpsichorean roulette. It was the age of the manikin. Or as others less kindly disposed might have said, the era of the tailor's dummy and the pox doctor's clerk. Most of my clothes and accessories were filched surreptitiously from my brother's wardrobe. Apart from the occasional rift in fraternal relations, things like cuff links, ties and tiepins, caused little difficulty. But owing to our differences in age and size other items were more problematical. His tastefully red-checked, lime-woven, double-breasted jacket, must have looked like a triple on me, and the sight of my wriggling fingers poking their tips out of the ends of voluminous sleeves, like blanched worms evacuating a sodden greensward, would have been hilarious. Still, I thought that I was with-it, and that's the main thing, surely? Trousers were equally difficult; although he was rounder than me, I was taller. Wearing my elegant red braces with luminous socks glowing below the plimsole-line, I probably looked more like an applicant for a job with Bertram Mills, than I did the dashing man about the ballroom. It's little wonder that my diary was empty, though at the time I put my lack of assignatory success down to the shyness so often associated with the gentler sex and not to my unwittingly clown like mien. Nevertheless I made the effort. Purple-zitzed and shorn of bum-fluff, I would swagger around the edges of the dance-floor unaware that the ring-masterly stares I was receiving were other than those of staggering admiration. As young and ludicrous as I was, it was there that I felt the first post-seismic tremors emanating from the after-shock of puberty. I knew instinctively that I was entering the adult world and that all things childish would have to be left in the shadowy attics of my memory, along with the hobbyhorse and the Mecano-set. Friends like Charlie and Eddy and Dave were about to be left behind to find their own way into the lunacies of work and marriage and mortgages. I was asked by my teachers if I wanted to stay on at school and further my education but I threw the GCE application forms down a drain on my anarchic way home one wet and surly evening. As for matriculation, my school-leaving exam results were a delightful disgrace. I failed abysmally in just about everything, excepting maths - unbelievably - rural science and social studies. Apart from French my worst result was in English and that must say something about my subsequent and somewhat belated choice of career! The years between the end of this story and the hopefully anticipated publication of this book have been mercifully free of work, marriage or mortgages; but publishers, literary editors and gold-digging middle-aged groupies may yet put an end to my legendary, malingering, idleness! Who Knows?

End